# Artificial Intelligence of Health-Enabled Spaces

Artificial Intelligence of Health-Enabled Spaces (AIoH) has made a number of revolutionary advances in clinical studies that we are aware of. Among these advances, intelligent and medical services are gaining a great deal of interest. Nowadays, AI-powered technologies are not only used in saving lives, but also in our daily life activities in diagnosing, controlling, and even tracking of COVID-19 patients. These AI-powered solutions are expected to communicate with cellular networks smoothly in the next-generation networks (5G/6G and beyond) for more effective/critical medical applications. This will open the door for other interesting research areas. This book focuses on the development and analysis of artificial intelligence (AI) model applications across multiple disciplines. AI-based deep learning models, fuzzy and hybrid intelligent systems, and intrinsic explainable models are also presented in this book. Some of the fields considered in this smart health-oriented book include AI applications in electrical engineering, biomedical engineering, environmental engineering, computer engineering, education, cyber security, chemistry, pharmacy, molecular biology, and tourism.

This book is dedicated to addressing the major challenges in fighting diseases and psychological issues using AI. These challenges vary from cost and complexity to availability and accuracy. The aim of this book is hence to focus on both the design and implementation aspects of AI-based approaches in the proposed health-related solutions.

Targeted readers are from varying disciplines who are interested in implementing the smart planet/environments vision via intelligent enabling technologies.

# Artificial Intelligence of Health-Enabled Spaces

Edited by
## Fadi Al-Turjman

CRC Press
Taylor & Francis Group
Boca Raton London New York

CRC Press is an imprint of the
Taylor & Francis Group, an **informa** business

First edition published 2023
by CRC Press
6000 Broken Sound Parkway NW, Suite 300, Boca Raton, FL 33487-2742

and by CRC Press
4 Park Square, Milton Park, Abingdon, Oxon, OX14 4RN

ISBN: 978-1-032-34580-2 (hbk)
ISBN: 978-1-032-34581-9 (pbk)
ISBN: 978-1-003-32288-7 (ebk)

DOI: 10.1201/9781003322887

Typeset in Minion
by Newgen Publishing UK

# Contents

About the Editor, vii

List of Contributors, ix

CHAPTER 1 ▪ IoT and Machine Learning-Based Smart
Healthcare System for Monitoring Patients        1

SHARAD CHAUHAN, NEHA ARORA, AND RITIKA ARORA

CHAPTER 2 ▪ Detection and Diagnosis of COVID-19 from
Chest X-Ray Images Using Deep Learning        21

L. GOMATHI AND AMIT KUMAR TYAGI

CHAPTER 3 ▪ Analysing the Stages of Diabetic Retinopathy
Using Deep Learning Techniques        35

M. BOOMIKA, K. PRIYANKA, S. SUSHMITHA, AND HARSHVARDHAN TIWARI

CHAPTER 4 ▪ COVID-19 Detection Based on Deep
Learning Feature Extraction and AdaBoost
Ensemble Classifier        47

AUWALU SALEH MUBARAK, SERTAN SERTE, ZUBAIDA SA'ID AMEEN,
CHADI ALTRJMAN, AND FADI AL-TURJMAN

CHAPTER 5 ▪ Deep Learning and Transfer Learning Models
for Detection of COVID-19        63

ABDULLAHI UMAR IBRAHIM, FADI AL-TURJMAN, MEHMET OZSOZ,
AYSE GUNNAY KIBARER, AND SERIFE KABA

CHAPTER 6 ■ Industry 4.0 Challenges and Applications in the Healthcare Industry with Emerging Technologies    103

MEENU GUPTA, RAKESH KUMAR, AND MADHU BALA

CHAPTER 7 ■ Cyber-Security Countermeasures and Vulnerabilities to Prevent Social-Engineering Attacks    133

RAMIZ SALAMA AND FADI AL-TURJMAN

CHAPTER 8 ■ Development of a COVID-19 Tracking System    145

OLUSEGUN ODEWOLE, FADI AL-TURJMAN, AUWALU SALEH MUBARAK, AND ZUBAIDA SA'ID AMEEN

CHAPTER 9 ■ An Overview of Autonomous Perception for a Robotic Arm    159

AUWALU SALEH MUBARAK, ZUBAIDA SA'ID AMEEN, AND FADI AL-TURJMAN

CHAPTER 10 ■ Artificial Intelligence-Based Methods for SARS-CoV-2 Detection with CRISPR Systems    173

ZUBAIDA SA'ID AMEEN, AUWALU SALEH MUBARAK, FADI AL-TURJMAN, AND SINEM ALTURJMAN

INDEX, 191

# About the Editor

**Fadi Al-Turjman** received his PhD in computer science from Queen's University, Canada, in 2011. He is the associate dean for research and the founding director of the International Research Center for AI and IoT at Near East University, Nicosia, Cyprus. Al-Turjman is the head of the Artificial Intelligence Engineering Department and a leading authority in the areas of smart/intelligent IoT systems, wireless, and mobile network architectures, protocols, deployments, and performance evaluation in the Artificial Intelligence of Things (AIoT). His publication history spans over 400 SCI/E publications, in addition to numerous keynotes and plenary talks at flagship venues. He has authored and edited more than 40 books about cognition, security, and wireless sensor network deployments in smart IoT environments, which have been published by well-reputed publishers such as Taylor and Francis, Elsevier, IET, and Springer. He has received several recognitions and best paper awards at top international conferences. He also received the prestigious Best Research Paper Award from *Elsevier Computer Communications Journal* for the period 2015–2018, in addition to the Top Researcher Award for 2018 at Antalya Bilim University, Turkey. Al-Turjman has led a number of international symposia and workshops in flagship communication society conferences. Currently, he serves as a book series editor and the lead guest/associate editor for several top-tier journals, including *IEEE Communications Surveys and Tutorials* (IF 23.9) and *Elsevier Sustainable Cities and Society* (IF 7.58), in addition to organizing international conferences and symposiums on the most up-to-date research topics in AI and the IoT.

# Contributors

**Chadi Altrjman**
Research Center for AI and IoT
University of Kyrenia
Kyrenia, Turkey

**Sinem Alturjman**
AI and Robotics Institute
Near East University
Nicosia, Turkey

**Zubaida Sa'id Ameen**
AI and Robotics Institute
Near East University
Nicosia, Turkey

**Neha Arora**
McKinsey & Company
Gurgoan, Haranya, India

**Ritika Arora**
University Institute of Engineering
    and Technology
Panjab University Swami Saravand
    Giri Regional Centre
Hoshiarpur Punjab, India

**Madhu Bala**
Chandigarh University
Mohali, Punjab, India

**M. Boomika**
Jyothy Institute of Technology
Bangalore, Karnataka, India

**Sharad Chauhan**
Chitkara University
Rajpura, Punjab, India

**L. Gomathi**
Vellore Institute of Technology
Chennai, Tamilnadu, India

**Meenu Gupta**
Chandigarh University
Mohali, Punjab, India

**Abdullahi Umar Ibrahim**
Near East University
Nicosia, Turkey

**Serife Kaba**
Near East University
Nicosia, Turkey

**Ayse Gunnay Kibarer**
Near East University
Nicosia, Turkey

**Rakesh Kumar**
Chandigarh University
Mohali, Punjab, India

**Auwalu Saleh Mubarak**
AI and Robotics Institute
Near East University
Nicosia, Turkey

**Olusegun Odewole**
AI and Robotics Institute
Near East University
Nicosia, Turkey

**Mehmet Ozsoz**
Near East University
Nicosia, Turkey

**K. Priyanka**
Jyothy Institute of Technology
Bangalore, Karnataka, India

**Ramiz Salama**
AI and Robotics Institute
Near East University
Nicosia, Turkey

**Sertan Serte**
Near East University
Nicosia, Turkey

**S. Sushmitha**
Jyothy Institute of Technology
Bangalore, Karnataka, India

**Harshvardhan Tiwari**
Jyothy Institute of Technology
Bangalore, Karnataka, India

**Amit Kumar Tyagi**
Vellore Institute of Technology
Chennai, Tamilnadu, India

# IoT and Machine Learning-Based Smart Healthcare System for Monitoring Patients

Sharad Chauhan,[1] Neha Arora,[2] and Ritika Arora[3]

[1] Chitkara University, Rajpura, Punjab, India

[2] McKinsey & Company, Gurgoan, Haranya, India

[3] University Institute of Engineering and Technology, Panjab University Swami Saravand Giri Regional Centre, Hoshiarpur Punjab, India

## CONTENTS

1.1 Introduction 2
1.2 Literature Survey 3
1.3 IoT Implementation Model 5
    1.3.1 Communication Protocol for a Smart Healthcare System 6
1.4 Machine Learning-Based Application for Different Medical Fields 7
    1.4.1 Identifying Diseases and Diagnoses 7
    1.4.2 Drug Manufacture and Identification 7
    1.4.3 Computer Vision-Based Identification of Medical Imaging 8
    1.4.4 Personalized Medicine 8
    1.4.5 Machine Learning-Based Behavioural Modification 8

DOI: 10.1201/9781003322887-1

|  | 1.4.6 | Maintaining Health Records Intelligently | 9 |
|  | 1.4.7 | Research Work and Clinical Trials | 9 |
|  | 1.4.8 | Data Collection | 10 |
|  | 1.4.9 | Advancements in Radiotherapy | 10 |
|  | 1.4.10 | Making Predictions | 10 |
| 1.5 | Challenges Faced by 5G with IoT and Machine Learning Techniques | | 11 |
| 1.6 | Future Possibilities for Smart Healthcare Using the IoT and Machine Learning | | 12 |
|  | 1.6.1 | Recovery at Home | 13 |
|  | 1.6.2 | Peace of Mind | 14 |
|  | 1.6.3 | Independent Fitness Monitoring | 14 |
|  | 1.6.4 | Medicines at the Right Time | 15 |
| 1.7 | Conclusions and Future Scope | | 15 |
| References | | | 15 |

## 1.1 INTRODUCTION

Due to the inventions from innovative ideas and the latest technology, many of the daily aspects of everyday existence have been digitized [1]. Smart healthcare has emerged as a new technology of this era as it involves all all-encompassing, multi-stage area. The changes are personified in various fields such as scientific model adjustments (informatization creation adjustments from scientific informatization to nearby medical informatization), modifications in medical control and modifications which are need for the prevention and treatment of illnesses (from specializing in ailment remedies to specializing in preventive healthcare). These changes enhance the efficiency and reliability of hospital treatment, which enhances the scientific and health service experience, and represents the future development course of current treatment. Technology by no means replaces people, because the final decision-making authority usually lies with the individual, however, with the course of time, the person may opt for technological solutions that simplify their work and bring about efficiency in the system.

The three words that define the entirety of the Internet of Things (IoT) are convenience, efficiency and automation [2]. The IoT is a game-changer technology that has been creating quite a buzz in almost every industry; however, it has found its greatest reputation in healthcare. Technologies that might be connected to the cloud are certain to make an impact in healthcare. The IoT's modest beginnings in healthcare may be traced to using remote tracking, smart sensors and clinical tool integration in addition to tracking of activity, with various wearable biomedical sensors, smart gadgets for monitoring sugar levels and smart beds [3].

While analysing this, it should be noted that the future of healthcare can be based on the IoT-enabled smart gadgets. For instance, an affected person whose visit is changed is notified about his visit to his medical doctor, whilst simultaneously informing his physician at the same time because their calendars are linked via the Internet. As this affected person is on their way, they encounters a number of visitors and their mobile sends a text to the doctor notifying them that the affected person has various ailments [4]. In the recent past there has been a lot of developments made in healthcare sectors based on machine learning and IoT techniques, so it has become important that a proper clinical facility is provided to patients in emergency situations that provide safety and privateness for patients.

## 1.2 LITERATURE SURVEY

Mahmoud et al. [5] proposed the idea of smart system technology implemented in a smart home. This is like an automation system through which individual users can monitor the condition of their home from any location. Monitoring these conditions requires some smart gadgets based on the latest technologies.. The authors have used Bluetooth-based technology that requires low power and is present in many modern gadgets. While designing it, some extra features were added to improve the security of system. They designed a secure lock system that is used in doors to open and close them. This system can be applied to the latest techniques to improve the system [6].

Javaid et al. [7] have shown how the IoT has been used in different sectors including healthcare, smart cities and industry automation. They discussed visual-IoT in which different visual devices like cameras are used and, with the help of these smart visual devices, data from industry, vehicles and healthcare are collected and used for analysis purposes. For example, in the healthcare sector, images of various body parts of patients are taken which can be very helpful in monitoring the health of patients. These authors also suggested an approach known as secure visual-IoT that can manage security and privacy issue in healthcare systems. This approach is very useful in healthcare systems for monitoring health issues of patients [8].

Sowjanya et al. [9] designed and implemented access entry to manipulate and protect machines by using the Internet of Things. There is always a need for such security systems that help users to provide security in their homes. In this research work, the authors provided a security mechanism with the help of an IoT server to protect door access from unauthorized users. They used some innovative mechanisms and techniques such as various types of scanner, protecting the system by secure passwords and security questions with the help of the IoT and this smart indication can also be used remotely [9].

Aman and Anitha proposed a motion sensing model with pictures based on a smart door device on the android system [10]. In this approach they incorporated the security in the door itself, instead of the lock. Through this idea, the security mechanism has been improved with the idea of merging an android system with the IoT being an innovative one that is helpful in future research also. When the door detects an unusual event it capture and send an image to the owners. Therefore, any unusual event can be monitored. This method basically consists of two main ideas, one is motion sensing and capturing and the second is sending information to the owner's mobile with the help of IoT.

Singh et al. [11] proposed a smart home automation system that would helpful in various applications. This system could change the lives of users by providing smart solutions with the help of home appliances. This would be helpful in operating smart home devices with the help of IoT techniques. This solution also monitors for the presence of any unusual activity inside the home which could prevent significant harm. It can also include monitoring for gas leaks, energy consumed by the home and other security precautions [11].

Chandra et al. [12] presented a system for home automation protection. This includes monitoring the environmental conditions and controlling them with the help of home appliances. The organized framework takes a photograph of any unauthorized persons entering the premises and stealing. This security system takes a photograph and sends it through email. By this mechanism, the security system can be improved in an innovative way with the help of IoT techniques. The IoT server can therefore play an important role in this security mechanism of a home automation system [12].

Sabarinath et al. [13] suggested some security methods in smart home appliances. These methods are based on a facial recognition system that can detect any unusual events that happen in the premises and with the help of IoT techniques the owner of the home can be informed. This smart and innovative method sends notifications to the owner of the smart home and based on this owner can take action. These authors used an Arduino-based microcontroller for providing the interface between components and various sensors for motion detection [13].

## 1.3 IOT IMPLEMENTATION MODEL

This version describes a smart doorbell so that the user can perceive the person that activates it and then notify them through their cell phone [14]. The following five-tier model describes the working of this gadget (Figure 1.1):

Stage 1: This contains the action when someone authorizes or unauthorizes a person to enter the residence and presses the door open button or knocks at the door.

Stage 2: This stage captures a photo of the authorized or unauthorized person with the help of a web camera and sends that image to the database server which is placed at some centralized location.

Stage 3: This involves processing of the image that was captured at stage 2. This unit processes the captured image and sends it to the server which discovers whether that person is authorized or unauthorized.

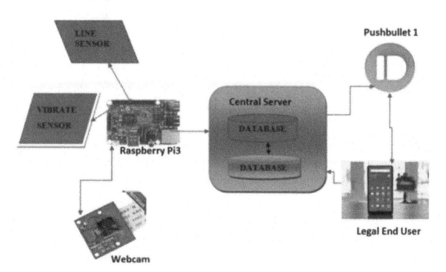

FIGURE 1.1    Description of the model with a database server

Stage 4: After identifying the person, this stage takes the necessary action. If the person is authorized a notification is sent to welcome them and if they are unauthorized then their picture along with a video is sent to the owner by passing a "snap" command.

Stage 5: This is the final response stage that is based upon the notification received by owner. With this information, the owner of the premises decides whether to send a command to open door for an authorized person or not to do so, and this process is carried out automatically.

## 1.3.1 Communication Protocol for a Smart Healthcare System

Already there are number of IoT-based protocols like ZigBee, Bluetooth, etc. for healthcare systems [15]. These are used to monitor the workflow. These are used to monitor the workflow of the information gathered. Device-to-device communication capabilities are permitted on healthcare gadgets that provide the latest methods for diagnosis and treatment. These latest technologies will provide all the information with the help of smart gadgets at any time and avoid delays, which improves the efficiency of healthcare systems [16]. An IoT-enabled healthcare system will mainly focus on the problems faced by patients in daily life and how these issues are resolved by daily monitoring of health status with the help of IoT-enabled gadgets. These smart gadgets are capable of managing patient's records on a daily basis, which is very helpful in clinical diagnosis by providing proper treatment to patients [17]. Raspberry pi-based sensors are used in these smart gadgets for collecting data from the patient's body [18].

Sensors are associated with cutting-edge clinical hardware. These sensors are used for connecting smart gadgets with patients, and with the help of these sensors, the gadgets can collect clinical data from patients which will be helpful in monitoring diseases by doctors. This clinical data can also be uploaded to the cloud through the Internet, which is helpful in resolving the problems of patients by physicians at remote locations [19].

Figure 1.2 illustrates the ideal plan for IoT-based medical care. In accordance with the patient's requirements, sensor hubs are used to display their condition. These sensors record information and send it to the health worker. At that point the health worker gathers the displayed statistics and delivers them to diverse customers such as the cloud, specialists, attendants, and health facilities, which can be improved by specialists properly managing these statistical data [20]. We have found that several researchers have focused on planning and actualizing unique IoT-based medical care

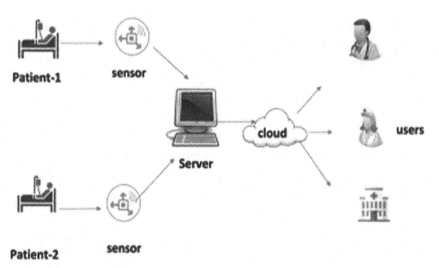

FIGURE 1.2    IoT-based healthcare

management that defines how the medical facilities are properly managed by IoT-enabled devices in healthcare [21]. The IoT cloud-based framework deals with the relevant information regarding hospital treatment and uses the IoT for any avenues which are unexplored.

## 1.4 MACHINE LEARNING-BASED APPLICATION FOR DIFFERENT MEDICAL FIELDS

### 1.4.1 Identifying Diseases and Diagnoses

Machine learning-based approaches are very useful in medical fields for identifying different kinds of illnesses and other medical problems that are difficult to diagnose [22]. It includes cancers which can be difficult to identify at early stages, and also certain genetic factors. There are various examples such as IBM Watson Genomics which uses various methods based on cognitive computing using the genome, which is primarily based on gene sequencing, allowing a fast analysis. Berg, the biopharma company, uses an artificial intelligence approach for oncology treatment. This predictive response-based treatment will be helpful in efficiently diagnosing some recurring medical problems [23].

### 1.4.2 Drug Manufacture and Identification

In the initial stages, some medical trials have been carried out based on machine learning which are helpful in drug identification systems. This can also be used in additional research and development techniques with next-generation technology in the field of drugs for locating opportunities that are helpful in treatment of numerous illnesses [24]. In smart gadgets, several machine learning approaches are used which are helpful in the healthcare sector. One approach is unsupervised learning which is based on finding out common patterns, which is helpful in making predictions in a number of diseases. Machine learning-based technology along with AI-based innovative techniques are very helpful in detecting different types of cancers and also are helpful in recommending drugs for the treatment of these different types of cancers.

### 1.4.3 Computer Vision-Based Identification of Medical Imaging

Computer vision is a technique based on machine learning and deep learning that is useful in diagnosing diseases using medical imaging. Computer vision is helpful in segmenting and classifying medical images. Medical images are analysed accurately with the help of computer vision. As machine learning techniques are growing, IoT-enabled gadgets are being used for diagnosing medical issues through proper analysis of these medical images [25].

### 1.4.4 Personalized Medicine

Personalized remedies can be extremely useful by applying predictive analysis on an individual's health and take precautionary actions and useful decisions for providing better medical facility to patients. Currently, physicians are confined to making diagnoses and prognoses of patients based solely on their calculated analysis and their genetic records. Machine learning plays an important role in assisting scientists to make decisions related to medical drugs which are very effective in the treatment of various diseases. Nowadays, more and more sensor-enabled smart gadgets are being developed in the healthcare sector that are helpful in managing different medical data and allowing daily monitoring of patients by using these technologies [24].

### 1.4.5 Machine Learning-Based Behavioural Modification

In the recent past, machine learning has supported behavioural change or digital interventions which are helpful in patient diagnosis and treatment. Through this revolutionary technique, people can improve their healthcare-related behaviour which can result in improved outcomes in the healthcare sector. These behavioural changes can play an important role in reducing the need for medicines, and machine learning-based gadgets can be helpful in detecting and preventing several kinds of diseases. Somatix, an artificial intelligence (AI)-based software company, has developed a machine learning app that provides remote patient monitoring solutions. It uses patented gesture detection technology for understanding the daily gestures of patients and analyses their subconscious behaviour, which is helpful in understanding the kinds of problems a patient may have. [26].

### 1.4.6 Maintaining Health Records Intelligently

IoT and machine learning approaches are very helpful in managing the fitness and health records of patients. There are IoT-based smart gadgets available that monitor patients' health issues and smartly manage data related to the user's health. With the help of the Internet these healthcare data are uploaded to the cloud, where different scientists can make decisions based on these data which can be helpful in improving the performance of the healthcare field. These latest innovative technologies are capturing the healthcare market with their capability for handling the medical records of patients [27]. One of these is Google's Cloud Vision API, which has provided a dramatic transition in the healthcare industry by managing large amounts of clinical data. They are increasing the power of the patient engagement by providing access to medical data and test records at any place and time[28]. Medical imaging technology (MIT) is an innovative and growing technology for monitoring health statistics with the help of machine learning techniques which are helpful in assisting medical and scientific treatment in the healthcare sector [29].

### 1.4.7 Research Work and Clinical Trials

As the demands of the pharmaceutical industry are growing day by day, research scientific trials are very important. However, these trials require money and time. Machine learning-based scientific programs are very popular because their predictive analysis can be very helpful to researchers and students. The information gathered can include visits of health practitioners, social media and many more. Machine learning can manage real-time data tracking. Information collection based on this real-time data collection can be helpful in clinical trials. It can also be used for digital records that can minimize fact-based mistakes [30].

### 1.4.8 Data Collection

With the growing demand for machine learning over the last decade, for the collection of data crowd sourcing can be used. This allows researchers and practitioners to obtain information uploaded by individuals that is based on their personal consent. This information gathered from different patients is helpful for researchers and practitioners for clinical and laboratory trails. Research Kit developed by Apple enables an iOS app to become a powerful tool in healthcare. This app is helpful in collecting data based on facial recognition and helpful for researchers and practitioners for dealing with different diseases. These innovative methods developed in the healthcare sector are helpful in diagnosing some medical cases that are not easy to diagnose with traditional approaches [31].

### 1.4.9 Advancements in Radiotherapy

Due to the development of machine learning-based techniques in the field of healthcare, one of the main areas to benefit will be the discipline of radiotherapy. When working with medical images analysis, different discrete variables can arise. There are various areas such as cancer foci that describe cancer cells that cannot be seen without a microscope. Here medical image analysis is very helpful for managing and diagnosing these cells. However, with the development of machine learning algorithms, it is very easy to diagnose the problem and identify the variables as these samples can be taken care of on a priority basis. These devices obtain knowledge from clinical image analysis by using different gadgets which are helpful in clinical and medical trials conducted by researchers and practitioners. University College London Hospitals NHS Foundation Trust (UCLH) developed a machine learning algorithm that can easily differentiate between healthy and cancerous tissue and improve the radiotherapy methods to treat the disease [32].

### 1.4.10 Making Predictions

Nowadays, for tracking and making predictions, artificial intelligence-based techniques are used. As in real life, scientists are developing different statistics from satellites, real-time social media updates, Internet site facts and similar types of predictions, and for managing these predictions and statistics artificial neural networks are used which is helpful in various diseases such as malaria outbreaks and excessive chronic infectious illnesses. These kinds of outbreak predictions are very useful in medical sciences and educational structures. There are various Internet-based reporting platforms which are helpful in managing diseases [33].

## 1.5 CHALLENGES FACED BY 5G WITH IOT AND MACHINE LEARNING TECHNIQUES

The main challenge we are facing today is how we can inculcate 5G technological competencies in our systems. The latest trend is "service requirements for the 5G gadget", which is analysed with the aid of 3GPP [34]. This formulates 32 exceptional simple skills, and specifies the overall execution necessities and various safety protocols. The overall performance and reliability of IoT-based systems depends upon different skill sets used by the smart techniques. Those skills which could be related to the IoT are as follows [6]:

- Less network requirement
- Managing resources efficiency (control for IoT, bulk operations for IoT)
- Green computing
- Quality of service, priorities, and policy management
- Capability of the network
- Power performance
- Monitoring quality of service
- Private networks
- Cyber physical control programs in different domains.

It has been observed that the overall performance depends upon various parameters including traffic rate, latency, density, greater reliability and accuracy, and web page traffic. One other parameter based on 5G technology-based systems is key performance indicators (KPIs). For managing and achieving 5G service goals the coordination and exact values of these parameters are required. This also requires different designs that use a radio spectrum and network having different configurations.

These 5G-enabled services have high reliability, which addresses all the issues related to bandwidth and density.. A geographically distributed system requires high reliability for 5G [35]. It has been observed that networks deployed over large areas create issues and this will affect the overall performance of the applications. For managing these issues, a reduced migration time is used for better results. Fog computing can also be helpful in managing IoT services which face the possibility of useful resource failures. Virtual disasters in 5G are present for a shorter time and can be recovered easily.

The use of 5G technology provides skills that current businesses want to include in their infrastructure. Ultra-Reliable Low Latency Communications (URLLC), a subset of the 5G network architecture, ensures more efficient scheduling of data transfers, achieving shorter transmissions through a larger subcarrier, and even scheduling overlapping transmissions. For improving the performance of the healthcare sector, 5G technologies are very helpful in managing complex medical conditions.

## 1.6 FUTURE POSSIBILITIES FOR SMART HEALTHCARE USING THE IOT AND MACHINE LEARNING

As a future possibility in the field of healthcare, fog computing architectures provide the layout for solutions to monitoring healthcare through the use of wearable gadgets and location sensor networks and capable of managing and protecting healthcare data, as these data are accessed remotely by doctors which increases the capabilities of the smart healthcare system. This type of architecture provides solutions that include fog nodes appearing as neighbourhood servers that help in collecting healthcare data and includes all the carrier requirements. The clinical community has been working for more than a decade on monitoring patients' health-related data using remotely supplied reviews to clinicians.

However, we require a multilevel structure that provides solutions and that can be proven as a complete and simplified solution, as shown in Figure 1.3, that will have:

- Edge degree, in which various smart devices including smart watches, smart mobiles, compact structures and gateways carry out collection and processing of statistics data in wireless body sensor networks (WBSNs) [36].

- Fog level that has different machines, servers and gateways that process information from challenge smart networks including location devices that are used to perform neighbourhood data processing and finally provide storage for these data [6].

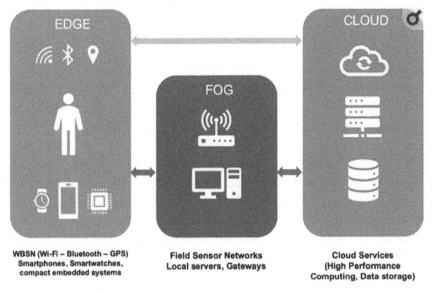

**WBSN (Wi-Fi – Bluetooth – GPS)**
**Smartphones, Smartwatches,**
**compact embedded systems**

**Field Sensor Networks**
**Local servers, Gateways**

**Cloud Services**
**(High Performance**
**Computing, Data storage)**

FIGURE 1.3    Fog/edge computing

- Cloud level that uses cloud services to obtain high-performance computing.

These three levels need to be all carried out for every process, for example, the difficulties generated through static tracking and managing health records of patients. If static monitoring is used for monitoring patient health and updating records on the cloud with the help of a fog level then it will be done after a fixed interval of time. However, dynamic tracking provides real-time monitoring of data and sensors interact with cloud services directly without fog level devices and all data are tracked and uploaded on the cloud in real time [37].

### 1.6.1 Recovery at Home

Tracking patients is limited by the care provided by their own family or domestic nurses when the affected individual is recovering at home.

However, everyday tracking of an affected person is not feasible for this kind of facility; this would be a challenging task for managing and tracking without smart gadgets and technology.

However, with the development of IoT health monitoring tools, the option for the affected person to recover at home will become possible, with the integration of real-time monitoring and other aids [38].

As forecast by Grand View Research, the worldwide IoT fitness tracking market was predicted to reach more than $300 billion by 2022.

These kinds of IoT-based health-monitoring tools are growing and showing increased capabilities daily, ensuring a bright future for the healthcare industry. These tools are reducing the time to consult doctors and health personnel as the live fitness tracking of patients is already available for healthcare workers doctors through the Internet [39].

### 1.6.2 Peace of Mind

A patient at home with no person to take a care of them can be a risky business. This scenario becomes even worse when the patient is stricken by dementia. Thankfully, this situation is alleviated with the use of IoT home health tracking. The addition of wearable gadgets makes it even more helpful. These wearable gadgets track the affected person's data and send this information to their carer. These data can be sent through text or e-mail, while also alerting doctors if required [40].

### 1.6.3 Independent Fitness Monitoring

In medical emergencies, people of any age may require instantaneous assistance. For providing immediate support for patients and the elderly, first a proper tracking system is needed that sends alerts to doctors or physicians in emergency situations. For supporting such situations, IoT-based health-monitoring devices have been increasingly used in the recent past as these properly track patients based on real-time monitoring of fitness and they can send alerts to doctors in emergency situations [41].

In addition, this tool is a boon for everyone; these IoT tracking devices can also provide a sensor network. These networks will display all related issues of patient with the sensor sending an alarm in an emergency [42].

These sensors can be placed in fridges, cabinets, bathroom doors or any other part of the house.

Let's take scenario of Simply Home, one of the pioneers in domestic IoT practices. This device permits tracking of daily activities and sending reports and alerts [43].

Another example is GTX Corp which has tracking devices for people at distant locations. Their gadgets also assist in monitoring sufferers outside the home. Another example is GPS Smart Sole for use by individuals with dementia [44].

### 1.6.4 Medicines at the Right Time

This problem has been reduced with the use of an IoT monitoring device that keeps track of an affected individual's prescribed medicine routine. This can be a great help for those with dementia, for example. Let's take the scenario of an IoT-enabled medical signal which gives signals to patients to take their medicines. [45]. A particular method uses a pill case that lights up when it is time for medication to be taken [46].

Another approach develops smart programs wherein these programs in turn routinely send signals and then the data are saved in a database for later use [47].

## 1.7 CONCLUSIONS AND FUTURE SCOPE

In our proposed work it has been concluded that machine learning innovative techniques and IoT-enabled devices are growing rapidly in managing and monitoring health records in the healthcare sector. Smart gadgets will interact with patients and track their health issues on a daily basis and upload them to the cloud platform through the Internet. Researchers and practitioners use these records for their research work and clinical trials. Doctors can also track their patients with the help of these innovative techniques and smart gadgets. This can save time by not requiring visits to the clinic physically, and so enhancing the capabilities of medical services in the healthcare sector. The future work depends on how we want to shape it with the use of cutting-edge technology in healthcare using the IoT and machine learning. Improvements in the robotization field and android technologies can also be helpful in reducing the effort required, and this minimal effort framework can also improve the day-to-day life of users.

## REFERENCES

[1] S. Li, L. Da Xu, and S. Zhao, 5G Internet of Things: A survey, J. Ind. Inf. Integr., vol. 10, pp. 1–9, 2018, doi: 10.1016/j.jii.2018.01.005.

[2] ITU-R IMT, Vision—Framework and Overall Objectives of the Future Development of IMT for 2020 and Beyond, Itu-R M.2083-0, www.itu.int/dms_pubrec/itu-r/rec/m/R-REC-M, 2015.

[3] S. Chauhan, R. Arora, and N. Arora, Researcher Issues and Future Directions in Healthcare Using IoT and Machine Learning, in Smart Healthcare Monitoring Using IoT with 5G, Ist., G. C. Meenu Gupta and V. H. C. de Albuquerque, Eds. CRC Press, Taylor and Francis Group, Boca Raton, London, New York, 2021, pp. 177–196.

[4] L. Catarinucci, D. De Donno, L. Mainetti, L. Patrono, M. L. Stefanizzi, and L. Tarricone, An IoT-Aware architecture to improve safety in sports environments, J. Commun. Softw. Syst., vol. 13, no. 2, pp. 44–52, 2017, doi: 10.24138/jcomss.v13i2.372.

[5] N. A. Ahmad Mahmud, N. N. Mohamad Yusof, I. Abd Wahab, and N. Amalina Hanapi, The Application of Smart Home Concept into Existing Typical Malaysian Single-storey Terrace Houses: Device Installation, IOP Conf. Ser. Earth Environ. Sci., vol. 498, no. 1, 2020, doi: 10.1088/1755-1315/498/1/012081.

[6] M. S. Hadis, E. Palantei, A. A. Ilham, and A. Hendra, Design of smart lock system for doors with special features using bluetooth technology, 2018 Int. Conf. Inf. Commun. Technol. ICOIACT 2018, vol. 2018-Janua, pp. 396–400, 2018, doi: 10.1109/ICOIACT.2018.8350767.

[7] M. Javaid and I. H. Khan, Internet of Things (IoT) enabled healthcare helps to take the challenges of COVID-19 Pandemic, J. Oral Biol. Craniofacial Res., vol. 11, no. 2, pp. 209–214, 2021, doi: 10.1016/j.jobcr.2021.01.015.

[8] J. A. Kaw, S. Gull, and S. A. Parah, SVIoT: A Secure Visual-IoT Framework for Smart Healthcare, Sensors, vol. 22, no. 5, 2022, doi: 10.3390/s22051773.

[9] S. N. G.Sowjanya M.Tech, Design and implementation of door access control and security system based on IoT, M.Tech, Embed. Syst. Vignan's L. Inst. Technol. Sci. Guntur, A.P, India, pp. 1–4, 2016.

[10] F. Aman and C. Anitha, Motion sensing and image capturing based smart door system on android platform, 2017 Int. Conf. Energy, Commun. Data Anal. Soft Comput. ICECDS 2017, vol. 4, no. 7, pp. 2346–2350, 2018, doi: 10.1109/ICECDS.2017.8389871.

[11] H. Singh, V. Pallagani, V. Khandelwal, and U. Venkanna, IoT based smart home automation system using sensor node, Proc. 4th IEEE Int. Conf. Recent Adv. Inf. Technol. RAIT 2018, pp. 1–5, 2018, doi: 10.1109/RAIT.2018.8389037.

[12] M. L. R. Chandra, B. V. Kumar, and B. Sureshbabu, IoT enabled home with smart security, 2017 Int. Conf. Energy, Commun. Data Anal. Soft Comput. ICECDS 2017, pp. 1193–1197, 2018, doi: 10.1109/ICECDS.2017.8389630.

[13] R. K. Sabarinath, C. Sathyamurthy, V. S. S, and W. R. M, Safety and Security Aspects of Smart Home Applications using Face Recognition, Int. Res. J. Eng. Technol., vol. 7 (2), pp. 261–266, 2020.

[14] S. Abdelwahab, B. Hamdaoui, M. Guizani, and A. Rayes, Enabling smart cloud services through remote sensing: An internet of everything enabler, IEEE Internet Things J., vol. 1, no. 3, pp. 276–288, 2014, doi: 10.1109/JIOT.2014.2325071.

[15] Sharad, S. S. Kang, and Deepshikha, Cluster based techniques leach and modified LEACH using optimized technique EHO in WSN, Int. J. Innov. Technol. Explor. Eng., vol. 8, no. 9 Special Issue, pp. 363–372, 2019, doi: 10.35940/ijitee.I1058.0789S19.

[16] G. Ahmed, D. Mahmood, and S. Islam, Thermal and energy aware routing in wireless body area networks, Int. J. Distrib. Sens. Networks, vol. 15, no. 6, 2019, doi: 10.1177/1550147719854974.

[17] Chandni Sharad Chauhan, Routing Protocol in MANET-A Survey, IJJRA, vol. 1, no. 2, pp. 48–52, 2014.

[18] Z. A. Khan and U. Abbasi, Evolution of wireless sensor networks toward Internet of Things, Emerg. Commun. Technol. Based Wirel. Sens. Networks Curr. Res. Futur. Appl., pp. 179–199, 2016, doi: 10.1201/b20085-16.

[19] U. Varshney, Pervasive healthcare and wireless health monitoring, Mob. Networks Appl., vol. 12, no. 2–3, pp. 113–127, 2007, doi: 10.1007/s11036-007-0017-1.

[20] Sharad, E. N. Kaur, and I. K. Aulakh, Evaluation and implementation of cluster head selection in WSN using Contiki/Cooja simulator, J. Stat. Manag. Syst., vol. 23, no. 2, pp. 407–418, 2020, doi: 10.1080/09720510.2020.1736324.

[21] S. Sneha and U. Varshney, Enabling ubiquitous patient monitoring: Model, decision protocols, opportunities and challenges, Decis. Support Syst., vol. 46, no. 3, pp. 606–619, 2009, doi: 10.1016/j.dss.2008.11.014.

[22] K. Jaiswal, S. Sobhanayak, B. K. Mohanta, and D. Jena, IoT-cloud based framework for patient's data collection in smart healthcare system using raspberry-pi, 2017 Int. Conf. Electr. Comput. Technol. Appl. ICECTA 2017, vol. 2018-Janua, pp. 1–4, 2017, doi: 10.1109/ICECTA.2017.8251967.

[23] D. Tantrigoda, et al. 2016, An approach for visualizing error and obtaining a measure of central tendency regarding a set of time series using discrete haar wavelet, Ripublication. Com, vol. 10, no. 1, pp. 1–18, 2016, www.ripublication.com/jwta16/jwtav10n1_01.pdf.

[24] C. J. Deepu, C. H. Heng, and Y. Lian, A Hybrid Data Compression Scheme for Power Reduction in Wireless Sensors for IoT, IEEE Trans. Biomed. Circuits Syst., vol. 11, no. 2, pp. 245–254, 2017, doi: 10.1109/TBCAS.2016.2591923.

[25] C. O. Rolim, F. L. Koch, C. B. Westphall, J. Werner, A. Fracalossi, and G. S. Salvador, A cloud computing solution for patient's data collection in health care institutions, 2nd Int. Conf. eHealth, Telemedicine, Soc. Med. eTELEMED 2010, Incl. MLMB 2010; BUSMMed 2010, no. i, pp. 95–99, 2010, doi: 10.1109/eTELEMED.2010.19.

[26] C. Krishna, Real-Time Systems. 1999.

[27] Q. Zhang, L. Cheng, and R. Boutaba, Cloud computing: State-of-the-art and research challenges, J. Internet Serv. Appl., vol. 1, no. 1, pp. 7–18, 2010, doi: 10.1007/s13174-010-0007-6.

[28] K. Gulati, K. K. Sharma, S. Chouhan, M. Tech, and E. Institutions, Cloud Computing & Its Deployment Models, pp. 38–40, 2015.

[29] M. Hassanalieragh et al., Health Monitoring and Management Using Internet-of-Things (IoT) Sensing with Cloud-Based Processing: Opportunities and Challenges, Proc. – 2015 IEEE Int. Conf. Serv. Comput. SCC 2015, pp. 285–292, 2015, doi: 10.1109/SCC.2015.47.

[30] V. M. Rohokale, N. R. Prasad, and R. Prasad, A cooperative Internet of Things (IoT) for rural healthcare monitoring and control, 2011 2nd Int. Conf. Wirel. Commun. Veh. Technol. Inf. Theory Aerosp. Electron. Syst. Technol. Wirel. VITAE 2011, 2011, doi: 10.1109/WIRELESSVITAE.2011.5940920.

[31] H. Gupta, A. Vahid Dastjerdi, S. K. Ghosh, and R. Buyya, iFogSim: A toolkit for modeling and simulation of resource management techniques in the Internet of Things, Edge and Fog computing environments, Softw. – Pract. Exp., vol. 47, no. 9, pp. 1275–1296, 2017, doi: 10.1002/spe.2509.

[32] A. Upadhyaya, C. Mistry, D. Kedia, D. Pal, and R. De, A pplications and Accomplishments in Internet of Things as the Cutting-edge Technology: An overview Abstract: Introduction, vol. 3, no. March, pp. 1–11, 2022.

[33] Z. Yang, Q. Zhou, L. Lei, K. Zheng, and W. Xiang, An IoT-cloud Based Wearable ECG Monitoring System for Smart Healthcare, J. Med. Syst., vol. 40, no. 12, 2016, doi: 10.1007/s10916-016-0644-9.

[34] M. Dadkhah, M. Mehraeen, F. Rahimnia, and K. Kimiafar, Use of internet of things for chronic disease management: An overview, J. Med. Signals Sens., vol. 11, no. 2, pp. 138–157, 2021, doi: 10.4103/jmss.JMSS_13_20.

[35] S. Madakam, R. Ramaswamy, and S. Tripathi, Internet of Things (IoT): A Literature Review, J. Comput. Commun., vol. 3, no. 5, pp. 164–173, 2015, doi: 10.4236/jcc.2015.35021.

[36] J. B. A. Maintz and M. a Viergever, An Overview of Medical Image Registration Methods (Cited by: 2654), Nature, vol. 12, no. 6, pp. 1–22, 1996, http://citeseerx.ist.psu.edu/viewdoc/summary?doi=10.1.1.39.4417.

[37] D. A. Ferrucci, Introduction to 'This is Watson,' IBM J. Res. Dev., vol. 56, no. 3, pp. 1–15, 2012.

[38] J. Fan, A. Kalyanpur, D. C. Gondek, and D. A. Ferrucci, Automatic knowledge extraction from documents, IBM J. Res. Dev., vol. 56, no. 3–4, pp. 1–10, 2012, doi: 10.1147/JRD.2012.2186519.

[39] D. Wen, Y. Yuan, and X. R. Li, Artificial societies, computational experiments, and parallel systems: An investigation on a computational theory for complex socioeconomic systems, IEEE Trans. Serv. Comput., vol. 6, no. 2, pp. 177–185, 2013, doi: 10.1109/TSC.2012.24.

[40] Y. Zhuo, L. Yan, W. Zheng, Y. Zhang, and C. Gou, A Novel Vehicle Detection Framework Based on Parallel Vision, Wirel. Commun. Mob. Comput., vol. 2022, 2022, doi: 10.1155/2022/9667506.

[41] D. Xiao, S. Yu, J. Vignarajan, D. An, M. L. Tay-Kearney, and Y. Kanagasingam, Retinal hemorrhage detection by rule-based and machine learning approach, Proc. Annu. Int. Conf. IEEE Eng. Med. Biol. Soc. EMBS, pp. 660–663, 2017, doi: 10.1109/EMBC.2017.8036911.

[42] A. Chandy, A Review on Iot Based Medical Imaging Technology for Healthcare Applications, J. Innov. Image Process., vol. 1, no. 1, pp. 51–60, 2019, doi: 10.36548/jiip.2019.1.006.

[43] F. Ahamed and F. Farid, Applying internet of things and machine-learning for personalized healthcare: Issues and challenges, Proc. – Int. Conf. Mach. Learn. Data Eng. iCMLDE 2018, pp. 22–29, 2019, doi: 10.1109/ iCMLDE.2018.00014.

[44] A. Cahyadi, A. Razak, H. Abdillah, F. Junaedi, and S. Y. Taligansing, Machine learning based behavioral modification, Int. J. Eng. Adv. Technol., vol. 8, no. 6 Special Issue 2, pp. 1134–1138, 2019, doi: 10.35940/ ijeat.F1299.0886S219.

[45] A. Albu and L. Stanciu, Benefits of using artificial intelligence in medical predictions, 2015 E-Health Bioeng. Conf. EHB 2015, pp. 1–4, 2016, doi: 10.1109/EHB.2015.7391610.

[46] P. Verma and S. K. Sood, Fog assisted-IoT enabled patient health monitoring in smart homes, IEEE Internet Things J., vol. 5, no. 3, pp. 1789–1796, 2018, doi: 10.1109/JIOT.2018.2803201.

[47] Michael Hay, David W. Thomas, John L. Craighead, Clinical development success rates for investigational drugs, Nat. Biotechnol., vol. volume 32, no. 1, pp. 20–28, 2014.

# CHAPTER 2

# Detection and Diagnosis of COVID-19 from Chest X-Ray Images Using Deep Learning

L. Gomathi and Amit Kumar Tyagi

*Vellore Institute of Technology, Chennai, Tamilnadu, India*

## CONTENTS

| | | |
|---|---|---:|
| 2.1 | Introduction | 21 |
| 2.2 | Related Studies | 25 |
| 2.3 | Method | 27 |
| | 2.3.1 Dataset | 27 |
| | 2.3.2 CNNs for Transfer Learning | 27 |
| | 2.3.2.1 Approach 1: Pre-Trained Model | 28 |
| | 2.3.2.2 Approach 2: Development of a Model | 28 |
| | 2.3.3 Performance Metrics | 30 |
| 2.4 | Results | 31 |
| 2.5 | Conclusion | 32 |
| References | | 33 |

## 2.1 INTRODUCTION

Coronavirus (COVID-19) is an infectious illness caused by the SARS-CoV-2 virus. The vast majority of COVID-19 patients will have mild to moderate symptoms and will also be able to recover without treatment.

DOI: 10.1201/9781003322887-2

On the other hand, some people will become quite sick and require medical attention. The two most frequent techniques for detecting COVID-19 are RT-PCR and RAT. The Rapid Antigen Test establishes whether or not such a person is infectious, whereas the RT-PCR reveals whether or not the individual is infected with the dead virus. In certain cases, negative RAT findings on later testing have led to a positive RT-PCR. Regardless of the fact that it could report a recovered individual as positive, the RT-PCR was considered to be the most reliable test during the first wave of the pandemic. However, a high-resolution CT scan of the lungs reveals severe lung damage. Patients in the second wave have reported receiving negative results on their initial test, then positive results on their second or third test, or unreported results. This has created a concerning issue because COVID-19 is now misleading in regard to these RT-PCR testing. The failure of these tests is due to a significant change in the virus's appearance and behaviour since the previous year. There have been mutations in the virus's spike protein, which the RT-PCR checks for. Despite the fact that CT scans have been shown to be more effective, an increasing majority of patients and the associated rise in radiological tests make it difficult to trust chest CT scans for every individual from diagnosis to discharge. Additionally, a large reliance on CT scans would put pressure on radiography departments, with chest X-rays (CXRs) being a much more realistic option for COVID-19 diagnosis [1]. Chest X-rays are beneficial in tracing the evolution of lung abnormalities while being less sensitive in recognizing the start of respiratory involvement of COVID-19 [2].

Machine learning offers a lot of help in recognizing the disease through image analysis. Novel coronavirus infections can be classified using machine learning. For the identification or prediction of virus, machine learning requires a large amount of data for analysis. Supervised machine learning algorithms require annotated data to categorize the image into several classes. Over the last decade, great progress has been achieved in this area, with specific investigations being attempted. The pandemic has drawn researchers from all around the world to work in this field. Several researchers have constructed machine learning models that have classified X-ray images as COVID-19 or not using data generated in the form of X-ray images.

Using chest X-ray images, many researchers used deep machine learning systems to determine the presence of COVID-19. However, the majority of these studies [5–8] used a small dataset and only a few COVID-19 samples. As a result, applying the results from these studies is tricky, and there's no guarantee that the reported results will be replicated when these models are tested on a larger dataset. To evaluate the transfer learning technique for identifying COVID-19 X-ray images, a large database must be employed. The development of a deep learning algorithm that can reliably detect COVID-19 illness in an individual based on symptoms is urgently needed.

Process in a Traditional Machine Learning Model

A. Data are loaded by the pandas package, which returns a data frame object with data, in the traditional machine learning model.

B. Remove the primary keys and distinct values columns, as well as any other columns with unique values.

C. To make it easier to model for data training, null values must be substituted with mode values.

D. Label encoding is the process of replacing categorical and text labels with normalized values.

E. Create a machine learning model and test it.

Deep learning, which is effectively a three-layer neural network, is a subset of machine learning. By allowing it to "learn" from enormous volumes of data, these neural networks try to mimic human brain activity, however they stop short of it. While a layer is made a neural network can approximate something, increasing hidden layers can help improve and optimise accuracy. Using deep learning, a program model learns to do categorization tasks directly from images, text, or speech. Deep learning [9] algorithms can reach extraordinary accuracy, beating humans in some cases. To train models, multilayer neural network nodes and a massive number of annotated data are utilized. In traditional machine learning techniques, the majority of the necessary features must be set by a specific domain in order to reduce the size of the dataset and make trends more visible for training methods to work. Deep learning algorithms' most noticeable value is that they seek to learn high-level characteristics from data in a consistent manner. As a consequence, class and the separation of hard-core characteristics are no longer required.

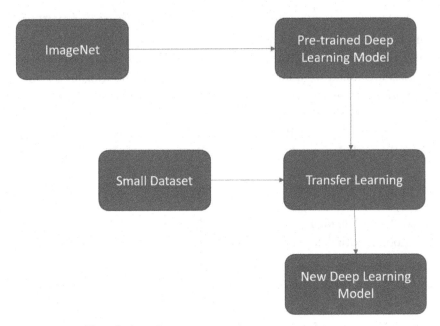

FIGURE 2.1    Transfer learning

A machine learning strategy is one in which a model created for one job is utilized as the framework for a model for another activity. Well before frameworks are a useful tactic in deep learning for vision-based applications processing applications, considering the massive computing and time assets required to create neural network models for some of these functions, and also the extremely large leaps in skill that they provide on related problems. Transfer learning (Figure 2.1) is a method of having taken a framework that's been a formally defined dataset and implementing it to a dataset consisting of fewer values. We suspend the earliest convolution layers of neurons for image recognition but only training the last several levels that generate a prediction. The theory is that the convolution layer extracts broad, low-level features like boundaries, patterns, and gradients that apply across images, while the subsequent layers recognize particular parts of an image.

To summarize, numerous recent studies utilizing a transfer learning strategy to predict COVID-19 X-ray images from labelled data have yielded promising results, but these must be confirmed on a larger dataset. The goal of this study is to see how accurate sophisticated detection of COVID-19 from thorax X-rays is before and after the convolutional neural networks. A total of 1427 thorax X-ray images are processed and used to train the classifier CNNs in addition to do this. Due to the limited size of the samples attached to COVID-19, transfer learning is the preferable approach for training deep CNNs. This is due to the fact that cutting-edge CNNs are sophisticated models that require massive datasets in order to achieve effective feature extraction and classification.

## 2.2 RELATED STUDIES

It is important to understand that a two-class classification means COVID-19 vs Normal, a three-class classification means COVID-19 vs Normal vs Pneumonia, and a four-class classification means COVID-19 vs Pneumonia Bacterial vs Pneumonia Viral vs Normal.

Utilizing 224 COVID-19 images, Apostolopoulos and Mpesiana created a deep learning model with levels of performance of 98.75% and 93.48%, respectively, utilizing two and three classes [10]. The COVID-19 disease was detected automatically using a dataset of X-ray images from patients with common bacterial pneumonia, verified COVID-19 disease, and normal occurrences. They compared the performance of the popular CNN designs for medical image categorization that have been proposed in recent years. The process known as transfer learning was used in this study. A total of two datasets were used. One is a dataset consisting of 1427 X-ray scans, with 224 images showing verified COVID-19 disease, 700 images showing verified common bacterial pneumonia, and 504 images showing normal conditions. The second is a collection of 224 images of COVID-19 illness, 714 images of bacterial and viral pneumonia, and 504 images of normal conditions. The information was gathered from publicly available X-ray scans in medical repositories. The findings reveal that using deep learning and X-ray imaging to derive important indicators connected to the COVID-19 disease is possible, with the best accuracy, sensitivity, and specificity being 96.78%, 98.66%, and 96.46%, respectively.

Wang et al. suggested a deep COVID-19 detection model (COVID-Net) that classified three categories with 93.3% accuracy (healthy, non-COVID-19 pneumonia, and COVID-19) [11]. This study introduces the use of COVID-Net, an open source and freely available deep CNN architecture tailored for the identification of COVID-19 cases from chest X-ray images. COVID-Net was one of the first open source network design features for automatically detecting COVID-19 from chest X-ray images when it was first released. It also presents COVIDx, an open access standard dataset composed of 13,975 chest X-ray images from 13,870 patient cases. Besides that, it explores how COVID-Net makes predictions using a modelling and analysis method in an effort not only to gain additional understanding into significant elements associated with COVID cases, which can assist healthcare professionals in enhanced testing, but also to review COVID-Net in a transparent and accountable manner to verify that it is making predictions based on chest X-ray images.

On a dataset of 310 COVID-19, 657 pneumonia, and 284 healthy chest X-ray images, Khan et al. developed a CoroNet model to classify chest X-ray images that achieved accuracies of 99% and 95% for two-class and three-class classification tasks, respectively [12]. CoroNet, a deep CNN model, was proposed in this research to detect COVID-19 infection from chest X-ray images automatically. It is built on the Xception architecture, which was pre-trained on the ImageNet dataset and then trained end-to-end on a dataset made up of COVID-19 and additional chest pneumonia X-ray images from two public repositories. CoroNet was trained and tested on the prepared dataset, and the evaluation demonstrated that the proposed method attained an accuracy rate of 89.6%, with precision and recall rates for COVID-19 cases of 93% and 98.2% for four-class cases and 95% for three-class classification (COVID vs pneumonia vs normal).

DarkNet, a CNN model that was proposed, has a performance rate of 98.08% for two classes and 87.02% for three classes. [13]. This research provided a new model for automatically detecting COVID-19 utilizing raw chest X-ray images, resulting in accurate diagnoses for binary and multi-class classification. When the study's classification accuracy was tested, it came in at 98.08% for binary classes and 87.02% for multi-class situations. The DarkNet model was employed as a classifier for the YOLO (you only look once) real-time object identification system. They used 17 convolutional layers and applied various filters to each one.

Toraman et al. created a convolutional CapsNet based on chest X-rays and capsule networks for detecting COVID-19, with binary classification efficiencies of 97.24% and 84.22%, respectively [14]. Using chest X-ray images and capsule networks, this study proposes a unique artificial neural network, convolutional CapsNet, for the automatic identification of COVID-19 disease. The suggested method combines binary classification and multi-class classification to deliver timely and effective testing methods for COVID-19 disease. For binary class and multi-class, the suggested method obtained accuracies of 97.24% and 84.22%, respectively.

Chowdhury et al. [15] used pre-trained CNN networks and image augmentation to develop a reliable method for detecting COVID-19 pneumonia from chest X-ray images based on transfer learning. The networks were trained to perform binary and multiclass classification. This model had a 99.7% accuracy.

Using raw chest X-ray and CT scan images from one of the largest COVID-19 datasets, this study [16] used a CNN model named CoroDet for automatic COVID-19 detection. CoroDet, consisting of a new 22-layer CNN model, was created to be an accurate diagnostic tool for two-class classification, three-class classification, and four-class classification. Accuracy, precision, recall, F1 score, specificity, sensitivity, and confusion matrix were compared in the performance of the proposed model to 10 current COVID detection algorithms to see how accurate it was. Their proposed model showed a classification accuracy of 99.1% for two-class classification, 94.2% for three-class classification, and 91.2% for four-class classification.

## 2.3 METHOD

### 2.3.1 Dataset

Our dataset has been constructed with chest X-ray images from publicly available repositories – Kaggle [17,18] and GitHub [18].

### 2.3.2 CNNs for Transfer Learning

CNN is used to analyse a fresh dataset of images for a significant difference and extract features using feature extraction information learned during initial training (Figure 2.2).

CNNs are made up of layers that turn an image into something that the learning model can understand. The convolutional layer produces a feature map by scanning the image many pixels at a time using a filter. The pooling layer reduces the amount of data created by the convolutional layer so that it may be stored more efficiently. The fully connected input layer flattens the outputs into a single vector. Weights are applied to the inputs provided

FIGURE 2.2    CNN architecture

by the feature analysis in a fully connected layer. The fully linked output layer determines the image class by generating final probability.

There are two common ways to make use of a pre-trained CNN's capabilities. The first approach, based on feature extraction via transfer learning, is a technique that keeps a pre-trained model's basic architecture as well as all learnt weights. As a result, the model is only developed to extract characteristics, which are then placed in a new classification network. The second way is a more involved procedure that involves making exact changes to the form before the model in order to achieve the optimum results. Modifications to the design and parameter optimization might be included in these updates. Only particular data from the previous job are saved in this way, while fresh trainable parameters are added to the network. The new parameters must be educated on a large quantity of data in order to be useful.

### 2.3.2.1 Approach 1: Pre-Trained Model

From the available models, a pre-trained source model is selected. Many institutions introduce open source models based on vast and difficult datasets, which can be added to the list of available models. The model can then be utilized as the basis for a model on the next task. Depending on the modelling method, this could include using all or some sections of the model. The model may need to be tweaked or fine-tuned based on the input–output pair data available for the task at hand.

### 2.3.2.2 Approach 2: Development of a Model

You must select a relevant predictive analysis problem involving a large amount of data in which the input data, output data, and/or knowledge gained during the transfer from input to output data are all linked in some way. The next stage is to develop a competent model for the problem analysis. When compared to a simple existing model, the model must perform better with higher accuracy to indicate that some feature learning has occurred. The model fit on the analysis problem can then be applied to the second task of interest to create a model. This may include employing all or parts of the model, depending on the modelling method adopted. The model should be adjusted. It is possible that the model will need to be tweaked on the input–output pair of the next task.

We are going ahead with Approach 1: Pre-trained model. ImageNet is a database of over 15 million high-resolution images that have been categorized into over 22,000 classes. ILSVRC (Large Scale Visual

Recognition Challenge) works with a subset of ImageNet that includes roughly 1000 images in each of 1000 categories. A total of 1.3 million training images, 50,000 validation images, and 100,000 testing images are available. ILSVRC CNNs were used to test approaches for large-scale object recognition and image categorization.

We have adopted VGG19, Inception, Xception, Inception ResNetV2, and MobileNetV2. The parameters – layer cut-off and neural network – were identified as important after referring to a previous study, but there are a plethora of other options that might be studied in future studies to see if they contribute to performance improvement. The layer cut-off parameter, which starts at the bottom of a CNN, corresponds to the number of badly trained layers. The remainder of the levels that are nearer to the extracted feature are made trainable to enable further extracting of information from the final convolution layer. The variable neural network refers to the classifier that is inserted at the bottom of the CNN and is used to classify the retrieved data. It is defined by the entire number of hidden nodes and the entire number of nodes. All CNNs have some hyper-parameters in common.

VGG19 – The VGG19 model is a variation of the VGG model that has 19 layers in total (16 convolution layers, three fully connected layers, five MaxPool layers, and one SoftMax layer). Other VGG variations include VGG11, VGG16, and more.

18 – Layer cut-off
1024 nodes – Neural network

Inception – When broken down into its constituent parts, the Inception module is simple to deconstruct and interpret. It can achieve high-performance gains on convolutional neural networks, effectively utilize computing resources with less of an increase in computation load for the higher yield of an Inception network, and obtain features of the input data at different scales utilizing different convolutional filter sizes.

249 – Layer cut-off
1000 – Neural network

Xception – Xception is a 71-layer deep CNN design.

120 – Layer cut-off
1000, 750 nodes – Neural network

Inception ResNet v2

730 – Layer cut-off
No – Neural network

MobileNetV2 – MobileNetV2 is a CNN design that aims to be mobile-friendly. It is built on an inverted residual structure, with residual connections between bottleneck levels. As a source of non-linearity, the intermediate expansion layer filters feature with lightweight depthwise convolutions. Overall, MobileNetV2's architecture includes a fully convolutional layer with 32 filters and 19 residual bottleneck layers.

10 – Layer cut-off
1000, 750 nodes – Neural network

To prevent overfitting, a drop-outs layer is applied to neural network models with two hidden layers. An optimization strategy was used to create the CNNs. The training lasted 10 epochs and was divided into 64 batches.

### 2.3.3 Performance Metrics

We are utilizing the confusion matrix to evaluate our approach.

In the field of machine learning, the confusion matrix is a tool that can be used to perform predictive analysis. The confusion matrix is mostly used to evaluate the performance of a classification-based machine learning model. Parameters used in our testing approach are as follows:

a. True positives (TP)
b. False negatives (FN)
c. True negatives (TN)
d. False positives (FP).

Instances that were correctly identified as COVID-19 positive are denoted by TP, whereas cases that were incorrectly labelled as COVID-19 positive are denoted by FP. TN denotes instances that were correctly identified as COVID-19 negative, whereas FN denotes cases that were wrongly classified as COVID-19 negative. The accuracy, sensitivities, and precision of the model are calculated using these parameters.

- (TP+TN)/(TP+TN+FP+FN) gives accuracy
- TP/(TP+FN) gives sensitivity
- TN/(TN+FP) gives specificity.

Because of the data imbalance, deciding whether the classifier is superior at diagnosing COVID-19 illness is difficult. Misdiagnosis, especially in the instance of COVID-19, has the opportunity to have devastating consequences. As a result, the COVID-19 class parameters must be determined.

## 2.4 RESULTS

COVID-19 samples from a large chest X-ray dataset were input into five well-known pre-trained CNN models: VGG19, MobileNetV2, Inception, Xception, and Inception ResNet v2. It was found that the VGG19 and MobileNetV2 CNNs tend to have the best classification accuracy when compared to the other CNNs. All of the CNNs appear to perform well in terms of accuracy and specificity, despite the dataset's imbalance. However, because these measures are highly dependent on the quantity of samples used to represent each class, a single evaluation will produce erroneous results. As a result, selecting the optimum model requires balancing accuracy, sensitivity, and specificity. Despite the fact that VGG19 has a higher accuracy, MobileNetV2 has a greater specificity than VGG19, depending on the original dataset findings, this is the most accurate mechanism for the specified classification task and data sample. True positives (TP), false positives (FP), true negatives (TN), and false negatives (FN) related to the COVID-19 class for the highest performing CNNs are presented in Table 2.1.

VGG19:
Sensitivity – 94.17%
Specificity – 98.92%
Accuracy – 98.18%

TABLE 2.1   Study of True Positives (TP), False Positives (FP), True Negatives (TN), and False Negatives (FN) Rate – Binary Classification (COVID-19 versus Normal)

| CNN | TP | FP | TN | FN |
|-----|-----|-----|------|-----|
| VGG 19 | 210 | 13 | 1192 | 13 |
| MobileNet V2 | 222 | 35 | 1170 | 1 |

MobileNetV2:
Sensitivity – 86.38%
Specificity – 97.10%
Accuracy – 95.21%

MobileNetV2 provides fewer false negatives than VGG19, despite the fact that VGG19 achieves a higher accuracy rate. False negatives can be extremely harmful because they mean patients are not treated for infections in a timely manner, so MobileNetV2 may be the best choice.

## 2.5 CONCLUSION

A deep CNN-based domain adaptation strategy for effectively identifying COVID-19 pneumonia is presented in this chapter. Five major, efficient CNN-based learning algorithms for recognizing normal and sick individuals using chest X-ray images were developed, tested, and reviewed. MobileNet v2 was found to outperform other deep CNN networks. The findings suggest that deep learning using CNNs can significantly improve the automatic identification and extraction of crucial information from X-ray images, which is important for COVID-19 diagnosis. Using existing CNNs that have been trained on massive datasets, we can develop accurate deep models on small datasets to improve the accuracy of COVID-19 detection. In this way, rather than developing our model from scratch, we can use pre-trained models with generalizable low-level features to train it. However, there are several limitations to this experiment. A more in-depth analysis, in particular, necessitates a greater quantity of patient data, notably COVID-19 data. After all, powerful deep learning models are typically trained on millions of images, which is difficult in the medical field. Furthermore, overfitting may occur when deep neural networks are trained on a small dataset, restricting generalization. Depending on the potential deep learning models employed to recognize COVID-19 from chest X-ray images, deep learning can still be enhanced and then become a viable option in the battle against the pandemic. Increasing the number of images and employing preprocessing techniques will surely aid in the resolution of the problem. Overall, the proposed model vastly improves upon existing methods, and it may prove to be a low-cost, quick, and useful tool for medical workers to help in the detection and diagnosis of COVID-19 patients while reducing virus infection during the COVID-19 pandemic.

## REFERENCES

1. P. Sun, X. Lu, C. Xu, W. Sun, and B. Pan, Understanding of COVID-19 based on current evidence, Journal of Medical Virology, vol. 92, no. 6, pp. 548–551, 2020.

2. A. Borghesi and R. Maroldi, COVID-19 outbreak in Italy: experimental chest X-ray scoring system for quantifying and monitoring disease progression, La Radiologia Medica, vol. 125, no. 5, pp. 509–513, 2020.

3. A. Narin, C. Kaya, and Z. Pamuk, Automatic detection of coronavirus disease (COVID-19) using X-ray images and deep convolutional neural networks, 2020.

4. P. K. Sethy and S. K. Behera, Detection of coronavirus disease (COVID-19) based on deep features, Preprint, 2020.

5. S. Wang et al., A deep learning algorithm using CT images to screen for corona virus disease (COVID-19), medRxiv, vol. 24, pp. 2020.02, Apr. 2020.

6. A. Abbas, M. M. Abdelsamea and M. M. Gaber, Classification of COVID-19 in chest X-ray images using DeTraC deep convolutional neural network, arXiv:2003.13815, 2020.

7. J. Zhang, Y. Xie, Z. Liao, G. Pang, J. Verjans, W. Li, et al., Viral pneumonia screening on chest X-ray images using confidence-aware anomaly detection, arXiv:2003.12338, 2020.

8. P. Afshar, S. Heidarian, F. Naderkhani, A. Oikonomou, K. N. Plataniotis and A. Mohammadi, COVID-CAPS: A capsule network-based framework for identification of COVID-19 cases from X-ray images, arXiv:2004.02696, 2020.

9. What Is Deep Learning? How It Works, Techniques & Applications – MATLAB & Simulink (mathworks.com)

10. I. D. Apostolopoulos and T. A. Mpesiana, COVID-19: automatic detection from X-ray images utilizing transfer learning with convolutional neural networks, Physical and Engineering Sciences in Medicine, vol. 43, no. 2, pp. 635–640, 2020.

11. L. Wang, Z. Q. Lin, and A. Wong, COVID-net: a tailored deep convolutional neural network design for detection of COVID-19 cases from chest X-ray images, Scientific Reports, vol. 10, no. 1, pp. 1–12, 2020.

12. A. I. Khan, J. L. Shah, and M. M. Bhat, CoroNet: a deep neural network for detection and diagnosis of COVID-19 from chest x-ray images, Computer Methods and Programs in Biomedicine, vol. 196, p. 105581, 2020.

13. T. Ozturk, M. Talo, E. A. Yildirim, U. B. Baloglu, O. Yildirim, and U. Rajendra Acharya, Automated detection of COVID-19 cases using deep neural networks with X-ray images, Computers in Biology and Medicine, vol. 121, p. 103792, 2020.

14. S. Toraman, T. B. Alakus, and I. Turkoglu, Convolutional CapsNet: a novel artificial neural network approach to detect COVID-19 disease from X-ray images using capsule networks, Chaos, Solitons & Fractals, vol. 140, article 110122, 2020.

15. M. E. H. Chowdhury, T. Rahman, A. Khandakar et al., Can AI help in screening viral and COVID-19 pneumonia? vol. 8, pp. 132665–132676, 2020.

16. Hussain, Emtiaz, et al. Corodet: A Deep Learning Based Classification for COVID-19 Detection Using Chest X-Ray Images. Chaos, Solitons, and Fractals, Elsevier Ltd., Jan. 2021,

17. Kaggle.com. 2022. COVID-19 Radiography Database, www.kaggle.com/ tawsifurrahman/covid19-radiography-database.

18. GitHub. 2022. GitHub – ieee8023/covid-chestxray-dataset: We are building an open database of COVID-19 cases with chest X-ray or CT images, https://github.com/ieee8023/COVID-chestxray-dataset.

19. Mooney P (2018) Chest x-ray images (pneumonia), www.kaggle.com/ paultimothymooney/chest-xray-pneumonia.

# CHAPTER 3

# Analysing the Stages of Diabetic Retinopathy Using Deep Learning Techniques

M. Boomika, K. Priyanka, S. Sushmitha, and Harshvardhan Tiwari

*Jyothy Institute of Technology, Bangalore, Karnataka, India*

## CONTENTS

3.1   Introduction                                                        36
3.2   Methodology                                                         36
3.3   Modelling and Analysis                                              38
      3.3.1   Network Architecture and Implementation                     38
      3.3.2   Training Method for the model                               39
3.4   Results                                                             39
      3.4.1   Dataset                                                     39
      3.4.2   Classification Report for the Model                         41
      3.4.3   Confusion Matrix                                            42
3.5   Discussion                                                          42
3.6   Conclusions                                                         45
3.7   Future Scope                                                        45
References                                                                45

DOI: 10.1201/9781003322887-3

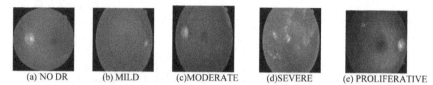

(a) NO DR      (b) MILD      (c)MODERATE      (d)SEVERE      (e) PROLIFERATIVE

FIGURE 3.1   The five stages of retinopathy: (a) no DR; (b) mild; (c) moderate; (d) severe; and (e) proliferative

## 3.1  INTRODUCTION

Diabetes affects the retina of the eye, causing diabetic retinopathy which eventually leads to blindness. Diabetic retinopathy can be classified into five stages, namely no DR, mild, moderate, severe, and proliferative. Research carried out on diabetic retinopathy patients suggest that 90% of cases can have their impact reduced if timely detection and proper treatment are given to patients. For providing proper treatment and avoiding vision loss, the DR stage classification based on severity is extremely important [11] (Figure 3.1).

Statistics predict that by the end of 2030, around 360 million people will have been affected by DR. Currently, in India, 65 million people are affected. During the COVID-19 pandemic, the manual detection of retinopathy was challenging because by the time doctors submitted their reports it would lead to delayed results, miscommunication, and delayed treatment. As a result, patients would have been progressed to the next stage of DR. In order to avoid it, the detection of DR using deep neural networks makes the job easier and can provide the results within a few minutes. Figure 3.2 illustrates the eye conditions of a person with no DR and another with DR.

The purpose of this chapter is to propose a model for diabetic retinopathy detection which automatically learns important features for diagnosing the stages using feature extraction techniques. Automatic DR detection systems are more economical, productive, and systematic as compared to manual diagnostics. Manual diagnosis can lead to misinterpretation and requires more labour than automated systems [14].

## 3.2  METHODOLOGY

- Utilizing Python libraries to import, pre-process, and visualize the images.
- Performing data augmentation to generalize the model.

**(a) Normal view** **(b) View Observed due to DR**

FIGURE 3.2 An example of the patient's eye condition. Here, we can observe (a) how a non-diabetic patient will view the world and (b) how a DR patient will visualize the world

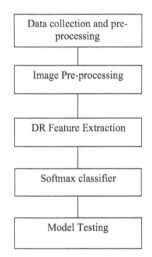

FIGURE 3.3 The work flow of the model

- Building a deep learning neural network model based on CNN and residual blocks (Resnet-50) using Keras, Tensorflow as a backend tool.
- Compile and fit a deep learning model to train the data.
- Evaluate the performance of the trained model and make certain about its generalization using various KPIs, namely accuracy, precision, recall, and F1 values. Figure 3.3 shows the work flow diagram of the model.

## 3.3 MODELLING AND ANALYSIS

### 3.3.1 Network Architecture and Implementation

Here, we train the model using ResNet50 architecture, which is a 50-layer CNN. The images after pre-processing are fed into the layer which applies filters and prepares the feature maps which sum up the presence of the detected features within the input. We used rectified linear unit (RelU), an activation function, because of its computational simplicity and linear behaviour [13].

The pooling layers then help in compiling the features, into average and max pooling layers. The end result obtained from the pooling layers is fed to the fully connected layer which will flatten the image and turn it into a single vector and integrate the information obtained from the patient's eye image. The final layer of the ResNet50 model has been modified accordingly to reduce some convolutions, that go into the softmax layer, which will classify the images accordingly and finally the predictions are made. Additionally, to verify to which stage the images belong to, a binocular network is applied [7]. Figure 3.4 shows the proposed architecture using ResNet-50 with a softmax classifier.

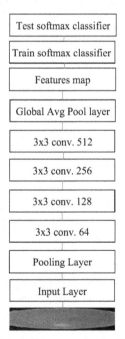

FIGURE 3.4 The Res-Net 50 architecture with 50-layer convolutional neural network

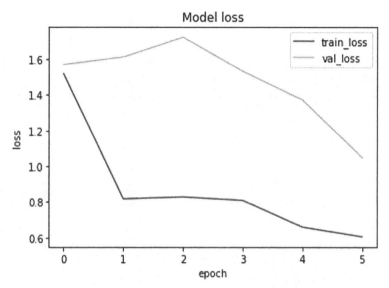

FIGURE 3.5 The graph of the model trained with six epochs

### 3.3.2 Training Method for the model

The transfer learning method is widely used for training the deep neural network model and we have adopted this method to make our model train more efficiently [11]. As CNN grows deeper, a vanishing gradient tends to occur which can impact the network performance negatively. This occurs when the gradient is back-propagated to previous layers, which results in the occurrence of a small gradient. The residual neural network enables training of the layers without having vanishing gradient issues using a skip connection feature [5]. Here, we have trained the model using Resnet-50 architecture. After training the model with six epochs the necessary features are extracted from the global pooling layer and these extracted features are detailed and unique, which helps in classifying the image more accurately. The Resnet-50 model enhances the accuracy of the model. Figure 3.5 shows the graph of the model with six epochs.

## 3.4 RESULTS

### 3.4.1 Dataset

The image dataset is taken from the Kaggle diabetic retinopathy competition. This dataset contains 3611 images which are of high resolution taken using fundus cameras. These photographs have been categorized with a scale of 0–4 based on the intensity of DR [2]. Figure 3.6 shows the visualization of five fundus images based on severity of DR.

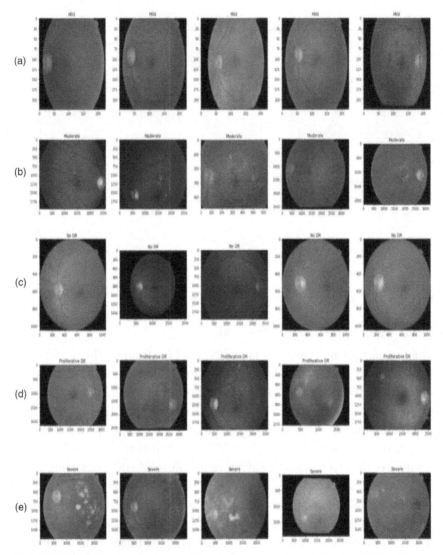

FIGURE 3.6 The visualization of five images per class: (a) mild; (b) moderate; (c) no DR; (d) proliferative; (e) severe

Figure 3.7 contains the bar graph showing the number of images present in each category. Here, no DR has the maximum number of images and severe has the least number of images.

An example is provided of how the model predicts the images based on the pre-trained model.

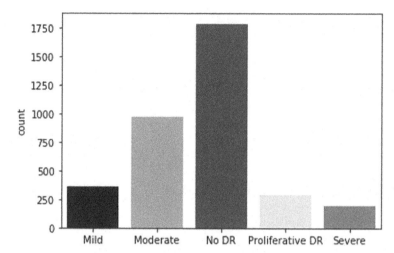

FIGURE 3.7   The count plot for all classes using Seaborn

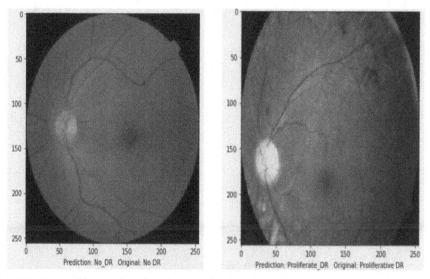

FIGURE 3.8   The predicted and original values from the model

Figure 3.8 shows the actual value vs the predicted image and how the model outputs it. This also illustrates to which class the eye image belongs.

## 3.4.2  Classification Report for the Model

As shown in Figure 3.9, the classification report tells that our model achieved an accuracy of 84%.

|  | precision | recall | f1-score | support |
|---|---|---|---|---|
| Mild | 0.81 | 0.61 | 0.69 | 71 |
| Moderate | 0.74 | 0.84 | 0.79 | 191 |
| No_DR | 0.94 | 0.99 | 0.96 | 374 |
| Proliferate_DR | 0.57 | 0.58 | 0.57 | 52 |
| Severe | 0.82 | 0.31 | 0.45 | 45 |
|  |  |  |  |  |
| accuracy |  |  | 0.84 | 733 |
| macro avg | 0.78 | 0.66 | 0.69 | 733 |
| weighted avg | 0.84 | 0.84 | 0.83 | 733 |

FIGURE 3.9    Classification report of the model

| Original | Predicted | | | | |
|---|---|---|---|---|---|
| **0** | 35 | 21 | 5 | 3 | 1 |
| **1** | 7 | 1.6e+02 | 11 | 13 | 2 |
| **2** | 2 | 8 | 3.7e+02 | 0 | 0 |
| **3** | 3 | 22 | 3 | 30 | 0 |
| **4** | 0 | 18 | 0 | 6 | 14 |
|  | 0 | 1 | 2 | 3 | 4 |

FIGURE 3.10    Confusion matrix for the model

### 3.4.3 Confusion Matrix

The confusion matrix is presented in Figure 3.10.

## 3.5 DISCUSSION

Over a period of time, there have been many projects that have been developed for detecting diabetic retinopathy using machine learning which reduces the time in detecting the diseases (Table 3.1). Since DR affects the blood veins and capillaries of the eye, most research has been done on automatic detection of blood clots, hard exudates, microaneurysms, and haemorrhages, using fundus images.

The paper "DRISTI", by Gaurav Kumar, Shraban Chatterjee, Chiranjoy Chattopadhyay in 2021, used a combination of capsule networks and VGG16, to classify diabetic retinopathy from retinal and fundus images. DRISTI provides a testimonial accuracy of 82.06% and test accuracy of 75.81% for classifying the images based on five stages. The paper also shows that their model can help opticians in diagnosing stages of DR accurately with rapid results and can improve the patient screening rate. In the implementation of capsule neural network (CapsNet), neurons can detect the information and provide feasibility in detecting an object which is present inside the retina. This property of capsule networks makes it simple and effortless, and supports the analysis of medical images. This is the main reason for utilizing capsule networks for training retinal images [15].

The paper named "Detection of Diabetic Retinopathy Using CNN", which was published in June 2021 in the *International Journal of Critical Reviews*, and authored by Abinay Kumar, Shivani Jaya Shyam, Dr. N. Poornima, Professor of Software Engineering Dept., at SRM Institute of Science and Technology, Tamilnadu, proposed a model that achieves an accuracy of 75.2% with Resnet implementation, and the model was trained with ResNet 50 block of layer. Implementation of ResNet50, which is a 50-layer convolutional neural network, applies the filter and prepares feature maps that detect the presence of defective features in the input. It also uses rectified linear unit as its computational simplicity and linear behaviour. However, the model had issues in training because of less availability of fundus images. There were further considerable changes for the proposed model to gather more data [13].

Nikhil M.N., Angel Rose A., a PG student, and Professor at the Department of Computer Application, College of Engineering, Trivandrum, Kerala, India, published "Diabetic Retinopathy Stage Classification using CNN" in the *International Research Journal of Engineering and Technology*. In this article, they used three CNN architectures, VGG16, AlexNet, and InceptionNet V3, to correctly classify the stage of DR. AlexNet contains three fully connected layers in five convolutional layers. VGG16 has three fully connected layers. The width of the network starts with a value of 64 and increases the value by 2 after each pooling layer. To successfully form

TABLE 3.1 Comparative Study on Different Views and Models of DR

| Author | Objective of the Work | Method Used | Result |
|---|---|---|---|
| Gaurav Kumar Sharban Chatterjee (2021) | Detection of diabetic retinopathy | Hybrid deep neural network | Accuracy:82% |
| Abhinay Kumar, Shivani Jaya Shyam, Dr. N. Poornima | Detection of DR based on Binocular Siamese-like CNN | Convolution neural network, Resnet50 Using deep learning | Accuracy: 75.2% |
| Darshit doshi Aniket Shenoy, Dr. Prachi Gharupre | Detection of diabetic retinopathy | CNN Architectures of deep network | Best score: 0.3996 |
| Wejdan L. Alyoubi, Maysoon F. Abulkhair, Wfaa M. Shalash, | Detection of lesion in retina of eye | Multi-level, binary classification, CNN resnetV2 and 50 | Accuracy: 96.5% Sensitivity: 85.57% Specificity: 98.41% |
| Harry Partt, Frans Coenen, Deborah M. Broadbent, Yalin Zheng | Detect stages of DR | SVM classification techniques CNN methods | Accuracy: 75% Sensitivity: 32% Specificity: 95% |
| Nikhil M.N., Angel Rose A. | Early stopping, the model is developed to automatically detect DR | CNN,ANN, ResNet50 | Accuracy: 80.2% |
| Asif Uz Zaman, Shadaab Kawnain Bashir | Auto detection of ophthalmologists | CNN deep learning | Accuracy: 67.96% Sensitivity: 90.8% Specificity: 85.2% |
| Dilip Singh Sisodia, Shruti Nair, Pooja Khobragade | Detection of diabetic retinopathy followed by blood vessels and other features | SVM with linear kernel | Accuracy: 77.56% Sensitivity: 94.2% Specificity: 95.7% |

three CNN networks, we use fine-tuning against ImageNet's pre-trained model. The refinement process was based on the transformation learning concept.

Subsequently, building three separate networks and features of these networks is coupled in order to get greater accuracy and better performance. The system is tested using individual images. These trained network models produced an accuracy rate of 80.1% after combining the features [16].

## 3.6 CONCLUSIONS

Diabetic retinopathy (DR) can cause blindness and visual disability. Awareness about DR must be enhanced in order to prevent blindness among people across the world. In this chapter, our model is developed based on deep learning methods such as CNN, residual blocks, and activation function such as ReLu and softmax classifiers. The model achieved an accuracy of 84%. Thus the model can help ophthalmologists to diagnose DR more efficiently.

## 3.7 FUTURE SCOPE

The accuracy of this model can be improved by using higher resolution images of the retina; to train such a model, a highly compute-intensive CPU and GPU would be required. With the constant improvements in image processing algorithms and techniques, it will soon be possible to have better extraction of images. This model could be used for automatic detection of other diseases such as cataracts, haemorrhages, and other blood vessel problems. The proposed model could be improved if more data are gathered in the future.

## REFERENCES

[1] Pratt, H., Coenen, F., Broadbent, D., Harding, S. P., Zheng, Y. Convolutional neural networks for diabetic retinopathy. Procedia Computer Science 90, 200–205 (2016)

[2] Kaggle dataset: https://kaggle.com/c/diabetic-retinopathy-detection.

[3] Wang H. et al. Hard exudate detection based on deep model learned information and multi-feature joint representation for diabetic retinopathy screening. Comput Methods Progr Biomed 2020;191:105398.

[4] Mobeen-Ur-Rehman, Khan S. H., Abbas, Z, Danish Rizvi, S. M. Classification of diabetic retinopathy images based on customized CNN architecture. In: Proceedings – 2019 Amity International Conference on Artificial Intelligence, AICAI 2019; p. 244–8.

[5] Dutta, S., Manideep, B. C., Basha, S. M., Caytiles, R. D., Iyengar NCSN. Classification of diabetic retinopathy images by using deep learning models. Int J Grid Distr Comput 2018;11(1):99–106.

[6] EyePACs (2015). Diabetic retinopathy detection.

[7] Conde, P., de la Calleja, J., Medina, M., and Benitez Ruiz, A. B. (2012). Application of machine learning to classify diabetic retinopathy.

[8] Pratt, H. and Coenen, F. (2016). Convolutional neural networks for diabetic retinopathy.

[9]  Abrmoff, M. D., Reinhardt, J. M. and Quellec, G. (2010). Automated early detection of diabetic retinopathy.

[10] Silberman, N., Ahlrich, R. F. and Subramanian, L. (2010). Case for automated detection of diabetic retinopathy.

[11] Hagos, M. T. and Kant, S. (2019). Transfer learning based detection of diabetic retinopathy from small dataset. CoRR, abs/1905.07203.

[12] Adarsh, P. and Jeyakumari, D. Multiclass svm-based automated diagnosis of diabetic retinopathy. In: Communications and Signal Processing (ICCSP), 2013 International Conference on. IEEE; 2013, p. 206–210.

[13] Kumar, A., Shyam, S. J. and Poornima, N. Detection of Diabetic Retinopathy Using CNN. In: International Journal of Critical Reviews 2021.

[14] Wejdan, L., Alyoubi, W., Shalash, M. and Abdulkhair, M. F. Diabetic Retinopathy detection through deep learning techniques: Informatics in Medicine Unlocked 2020.

[15] Gaurav Kumar, S. and Chatterjee, C. C. A Hybrid neural network for diabetic retinopathy diagnosis. In: Signal,Image and Video Processing, 2021.

[16] Nikhil M. N. and Angel R. A, Diabetic retinopathy stage classification using CNN 2021.

# CHAPTER 4

# COVID-19 Detection Based on Deep Learning Feature Extraction and AdaBoost Ensemble Classifier

Auwalu Saleh Mubarak,[1] Sertan Serte,[2]
Zubaida Sa'id Ameen,[2] Chadi Altrjman,[1]
and Fadi Al-Turjman[2]

[1] *Research Center for AI and IoT, University of Kyrenia, Kyrenia, Turkey*
[2] *AI and Robotics Institute, Near East University, Nicosia, Turkey*

## CONTENTS

| | | |
|---|---|---|
| 4.1 | Introduction | 48 |
| | 4.1.1 Related Works | 49 |
| | 4.1.2 Contributions | 50 |
| 4.2 | COVID-19 Detection | 50 |
| | 4.2.1 Dataset | 50 |
| | 4.2.2 Transfer Learning | 51 |
| | 4.2.3 ResNet | 52 |
| | 4.2.4 VGG16 | 52 |
| | 4.2.5 AdaBoost Ensemble Classifier | 52 |

DOI: 10.1201/9781003322887-4

4.3    Preprocessing and Training                                    52
    4.3.1    Preprocessing                                       52
    4.3.2    Training                                            52
4.4    Results and Discussion                                       53
4.5    Conclusions                                                  56
Acknowledgements                                                   57
References                                                         58

## 4.1 INTRODUCTION

The COVID-19 deadly disease was first discovered in China, where it allegedly started in a seafood market in Wuhan. The virus spread across other continents within days [1]. By the 16th of March 2020, the number of active and lethal cases reported in the world was 168,826 and 6,503 [2], respectively, and by the 27th of August 2020 the confirmed cases reached 24,514,320 and total deaths was 832,660, the rate of infection increasing exponentially. Fever, dry cough, fatigue, and acute respiratory distress are the most common symptoms of the disease. A very rapid and efficient method for detecting COVID-19 is required to slow the virus's spread as it affects the entire world [3–5].

Due to the widespread global presence of COVID-19, its fast and early detection and a low-cost test are very important, with many people having to be isolated because they show mild symptoms and the virus has an incubation period of 14 days [6]. The benchmark test result for COVID-19 today is the RT-PCR test for the detection of the nucleic acid forms that stem from COVID-19 [7]. The test is performed by collecting respiratory specimens such as oropharyngeal swabs, however human error can occur during collection of the specimen [8]. The PCR test is time-consuming and costly, patients awaiting results must be isolated which will increase cost either to the government or patient, and also the chances of getting the correct result are 30–50% [9]. An alternative to PCR is medical imaging, whereby computed tomography (CT) scan images can be applied, especially in the case of pregnant women and small children [10,11]. Although CT is associated with a high dosage and is also costly[12], it was used for COVID-19 evaluation and profiling in two studies [10,12]. Strunk et al. and Chen et al. [10,13] recommended X-ray rather than CT scans but did not consider pregnant women and children.

### 4.1.1 Related Works

Due to the spread of the deadly COVID-19 virus, several approaches were taken to mitigate the effects of the virus on economic growth, and several hybrid models and hybrid feature extraction techniques were employed to classify COVID-19, common pneumonia, and healthy patient CT scan images in Refs. [3,5]. It was observed and proposed by Al-Turjman and B. Deebak [14] to have an efficient system for patient data privacy, power consumption efficiency, and transmission. To reduce the economic impact caused by COVID-19, Rahman [15] proposed a data-driven AI model to predict lock-down and non-lock-down area boundaries, with many countries using a total lock-down method, which was harmful for the economy, using the proposed model. A near-real-time prediction of areas with high active cases has been predicted and can serve as an avenue for smart cities [16]. An IoT-based system was proposed to identify COVID-19 by gathering information from patients, such as X-ray images, temperature, breathing ventilation, sweat transition, and heart signals. The system classifies X-ray images and predicts the condition of patients using three deep learning models, namely ResNet50, InceptionV3, and InceptionResNetV2. This study will help health workers to manage and detect COVID-19 patients.

Artificial intelligence as an efficient technique has been applied in many medical fields as a fast predictive and efficient way of profiling many medical conditions related to brain surgery, pulmonary diseases, gene editing, and cardiology [17–24]. Different AI models have been employed to classify COVID-19 and non-COVID-19 X-rays and CT scans in which 81.5–95.2% and 95.4–100% accuracies were achieved, respectively [25]. CovXNet was employed to classify X-ray images of normal, COVID, viral, and bacterial types of pneumonia, and the classification of the four classes achieved the highest accuracy of 90% [26]. Farooq and Hafeez [27] employed transfer learning through the Resnet50 pre-trained model, in retraining 41 epochs, which was adopted with an accuracy of 96.3% being achieved for all classes. RT PCR results were compared with CT scan images in COVID-19 detection, with the earlier RT PCR showing negative results while the CT scan results were positive, which illustrates the efficiency of adopting medical imaging in profiling COVID-19 as it can detect the virus at an early stage [28]. Grey Level Size Zone Matrix (GLSZM) coupled with SVM was employed to classify COVID-19 and non-COVID-19 CT scan images, which based on tuning hyperparameter validation of 2-, 5-, and 10-fold achieved the highest accuracy of 99.68% [29]. The classification of pneumonia, COVID-19, and non-relevant to pneumonia or COVID-19 was performed on CT scan images, with the motivation for their work being to find an alternative to RT-PCR, and the highest accuracy score was 86.7% [30]. Loey et al. [31] compared two deep learning models, ResNet50 and Generative Adversarial Network (GAN), and the training was performed on Yang et al.'s [32] dataset; the performance of the model was compared based on a training set with augmentation and without augmentation, and the best performing model was ResNet50 with an accuracy of 92.9%, specificity of 0.871, and sensitivity of 0.778.

### 4.1.2 Contributions

The motivation for this study is to find a way to reduce the spread of the deadly COVID-19 virus and to detect COVID-19 at an early stage, with the presently adopted benchmark COVID-19 testing method by WHO being RT-PCR. However, RT PCR is costly with many people around the world not having easy access to the test as most countries find it unaffordable, especially developing countries. Proposing an accessible method of detecting COVID-19 is very important, which is why we have looked at the best options used for screening COVID-19-positive patients. CT images can serve as a fast and efficient method compared to RT-PCR, and with inadequate numbers of radiologists in the world, the best alternative is to employ efficient artificial intelligence models. Our contributions in this work are:

1. Three pre-trained deep learning models, ResNet-50, ResNet-101, and VGG16, were proposed to classify COVID-19 and non-COVID-19 CT scan images.
2. AdaBoost Ensemble Classifier was introduced as a classifier to the pre-trained models which serves as a feature extractor.
3. The performances of the models based on the two classifiers, Softmax and AdaBoost Ensemble Classifier, were compared.
4. The best performing model outperformed the state-of-the-art models employed on the same dataset.

## 4.2 COVID-19 DETECTION

This section explains the features of the dataset used and the proposed pre-trained deep learning models for the identification of COVID-19.

### 4.2.1 Dataset

In this study, the dataset from Yang et al. [32] contains 349 COVID-19-positive images, and 397 non-COVID-19 images were used for the training

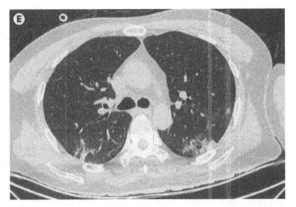

FIGURE 4.1    COVID-19 CT image

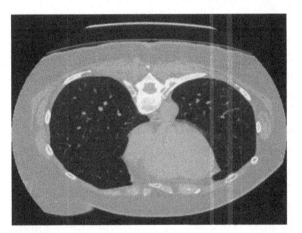

FIGURE 4.2    Non-COVID-19 CT image

of different deep learning networks, 80% of the data were used for training, and 20% of the data were used for testing. Samples of COVID-19 and non-COVID-19 CT scan images are presented in Figures 4.1 and 4.2, respectively.

### 4.2.2 Transfer Learning

Transfer learning is a research problem in machine learning that aims to preserve the knowledge learned while solving a problem and applying it to another, but related, problem. Transfer learning can be achieved by retraining the fully connected layers of pre-trained models and freezing the extraction features such as filters and other parameters [20,26,33–35].

### 4.2.3 ResNet

ResNet-50 contains 50 layers and ResNet-101 contains 101 layers. The key concept behind ResNet is to deal with disappearing gradients. These gradients are caused by piling up a convolution layer over a pooling layer in deep network architecture. ResNet contains shortcuts for the residual block that include identity.

### 4.2.4 VGG16

VGG16 is a deep learning model that contains 16 layers, of these 16 layers, five are convolutional layers, three are trainable layers, and the remaining layers are max-pooling layers. This architecture was the first runner up in the Visual Recognition Challenge of 2014, i.e. *ILSVRC-2014*.

### 4.2.5 AdaBoost Ensemble Classifier

AdaBoost is an ensemble strategy that trains and sequentially adopts trees. Classification precision improves with the inclusion of weaker classifiers in the model. AdaBoost is suited for imbalanced datasets but does not perform well in the presence of noise. The AdaBoost hyperparameter optimization is much more complex than the RF classifier.

## 4.3 PREPROCESSING AND TRAINING

### 4.3.1 Preprocessing

Data preprocessing in deep learning is the process of perfecting data in such a way that it can fit the input of a network and increase the number of datasets for robust and better training. There are several types of data preprocessing such as resizing, augmentation, and smoothing in training medical images. In this study, to improve the robustness of the deep-learning network training and increase the number of training data, data augmentation was performed on the training set data, these augmentation methods are random reflection, random translation along the x-axis, random translation along the y-axis, random rotation, and flip [23,31].

### 4.3.2 Training

In this study, three pre-trained deep learning models were employed, namely ResNet-50, ResNet-101 [36], and VGG16 [37]. Two types of training were performed to determine the models with the best performance.

1 Employing transfer learning using the pre-trained networks for feature extraction and classification

2 Employing transfer learning using the pre-trained networks for feature extraction and AdaBoost Ensemble Classifier for classification.

In the first set of training, two CT scan images of COVID-19 and non-COVID-19 classes were classified by fine-tuning the pre-trained networks hyperparameters Epoch = 20, validation fold = 3, Mini batch size = 20, and learning rate = 0.0001. The whole network structure was used. The batch size determines the stability of training, to reduce error generalization small batch sizes are adopted in most training as although they are noisy, they offer regularization and also make it easier to fit one batch size on GPU [38]. Meanwhile, in the second training, features were extracted using the pre-trained models' layers from the input layer up to the last pooling layer, the fully connected layers and the softmax classifier are replaced by the AdaBoost Ensemble classifier.

## 4.4 RESULTS AND DISCUSSION

In this study, we improved the state-of-the-art models employed on the dataset [32] by employing transfer learning, data augmentation, and changing the architecture of the pre-trained models by applying AdaBoost Ensemble Classifier, the three different pre-trained network ResNet50, ResNet101, and VGG16 models were trained and compared with the state-of-the-art model.

In Table 4.1, based on the three models, ResNet50, ResNet101, and VGG16, ResNet50 achieved validation accuracy = 87.5%, sensitivity = 0.83, specificity = 0.82, precision = 0.99, F1-score = 0.95, Yonden index = 0.78, and AUC = 0.92. ResNet101 achieved validation accuracy = 85.71, sensitivity = 0.83, specificity = 0.87. F1-score = 0.91, precision=0.99, Yonden index = 0.91, and AUC = 0.81. For the VGG16, accuracy = 74.9, sensitivity = 0.89, specificity = 0.63. F1-score = 0.94, precision = 0.88, Yonden index = 0.52, and AUC = 0.76 were achieved. ResNet-50 with AdaBoost Ensemble classifier achieves accuracy = 97.33, sensitivity = 0.92, specificity = 0.95, F1-score = 0.94, precision = 0.935, Yonden index = 0.94, and AUC = 0.989. The ResNet-101 with AdaBoost Ensemble classifier achieved accuracy = 85.3, sensitivity = 0.857, specificity = 0.850, F1-score = 0.845, precision = 0.833, Yonden index = 0.707, and AUC = 0.854, while the third models, VGG16 with AdaBoost Ensemble classifier, achieved accuracy = 78.7, sensitivity = 0.80, specificity = 0.775, F1-score = 0.778, precision = 0.757, Yonden index = 0.575, and AUC = 0.788.

While comparing the performance of the proposed models, it was observed in Figures 4.3 and 4.4 that the model which achieves the highest

TABLE 4.1   Comparison of the Model's Performance with State-of-the-Art Models

| Ref. | Models | ACC (%) | SN | SP | F1-Score | PR | YI | AUC |
|------|--------|---------|-----|-----|----------|-----|-----|-----|
| [31] | ResNet-50 | 76.3 | 0.659 | 0.763 | | | | |
| | ResNet-50+ augmentation | 82.1 | 0.776 | 0.876 | | | | |
| | GAN | 73.3 | 0.8 | 0.943 | | | | |
| | GAN+augmentation | 81.4 | 0.617 | 0.819 | | | | |
| [39] | VGG16 | 76 | | | 0.76 | | | 0.82 |
| | ResNet18 | 74 | | | 0.73 | | | 0.82 |
| | ResNet-50 | 80 | | | 0.81 | | | 0.88 |
| | DensNet121 | 79 | | | 0.79 | | | 0.88 |
| | DensNet169 | 83 | | | 0.81 | | | 0.87 |
| | EfficientNet-b0 | 77 | | | 0.78 | | | 0.89 |
| | EfficientNet-b1 | 70 | | | 0.79 | | | 0.84 |
| **Ours** | ResNet50 | 87.5 | 0.83 | 0.82 | 0.99 | 0.95 | 0.78 | 0.92 |
| | ResNet101 | 85.71 | 0.83 | 0.87 | 0.99 | 0.91 | 0.91 | 0.81 |
| | VGG16 | 74.9 | 0.89 | 0.63 | 0.88 | 0.94 | 0.52 | 0.76 |
| | ResNet50+AdaBoost | 97.33 | 0.928 | 0.950 | 0.94 | 0.935 | 0.94 | 0.989 |
| | ResNet101+ AdaBoost | 85.3 | 0.857 | 0.850 | 0.845 | 0.833 | 0.707 | 0.854 |
| | VGG16+ AdaBoost | 78.7 | 0.800 | 0.775 | 0.778 | 0.757 | 0.575 | 0.788 |

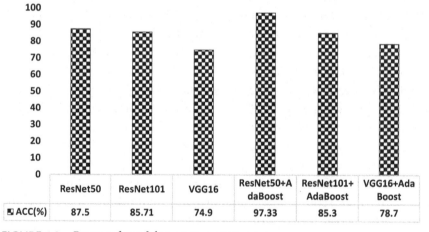

FIGURE 4.3   Proposed models accuracy comparison

accuracy and specificity was ResNet-50 with AdaBoost ensemble classifier. As presented in Figures 4.5 and 4.6, this shows that the combination of the pre-trained deep learning model as feature extractor and AdaBoost ensemble classifier can improve the detection of COVID-19. This combination also outperformed the state-of-the-art models used in classifying

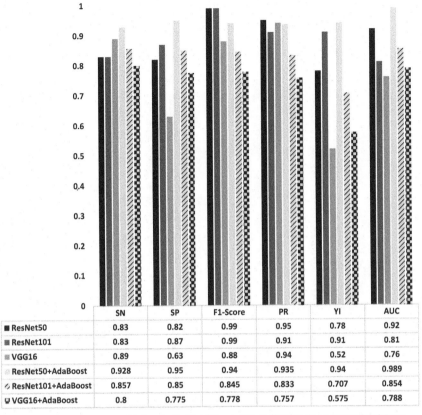

| | SN | SP | F1-Score | PR | YI | AUC |
|---|---|---|---|---|---|---|
| ■ ResNet50 | 0.83 | 0.82 | 0.99 | 0.95 | 0.78 | 0.92 |
| ■ ResNet101 | 0.83 | 0.87 | 0.99 | 0.91 | 0.91 | 0.81 |
| ▩ VGG16 | 0.89 | 0.63 | 0.88 | 0.94 | 0.52 | 0.76 |
| ResNet50+AdaBoost | 0.928 | 0.95 | 0.94 | 0.935 | 0.94 | 0.989 |
| ⁄ ResNet101+AdaBoost | 0.857 | 0.85 | 0.845 | 0.833 | 0.707 | 0.854 |
| ⧉ VGG16+AdaBoost | 0.8 | 0.775 | 0.778 | 0.757 | 0.575 | 0.788 |

■ ResNet50  ■ ResNet101  ▩ VGG16   ResNet50+AdaBoost  ⁄ ResNet101+AdaBoost  ⧉ VGG16+AdaBoost

FIGURE 4.4    Proposed models performance comparison

COVID-19 and non-COVID-19 CT scan images of the same dataset used in this study. Finding a very efficient and cost-effective way of detecting COVID-19 is very important, and an alternative to RT-PCR is looking towards medical imaging, especially for pregnant women and children who are not supposed to be exposed to radiation [10,11]. Studies [10,12] have shown the capability of medical imaging, in this work, we compare the performance of trained models on CT images and achieve very efficient models that can detect COVID-19. As the deadly COVID-19 has been declared a world pandemic, low cost and accessible methods of detecting the virus at an early stage are very important, especially for countries with inadequate health facilities and poor economy. Although CT scans can be somewhat expensive, the performance on this model shows a promising solution.

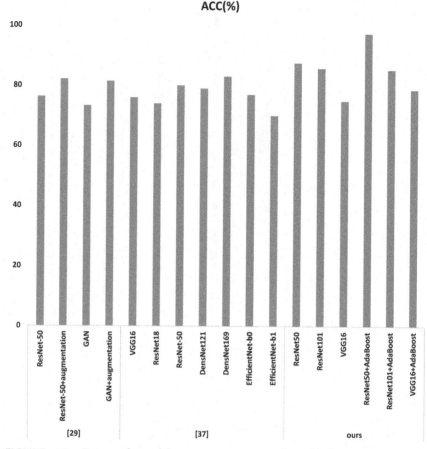

FIGURE 4.5 Proposed models accuracy compared with the state-of-the-art models accuracy

## 4.5 CONCLUSIONS

In this study, we have achieved the classification of CT scan images by employing transfer learning with different classifiers using ResNet50, ResNet101, and VGG16 pre-trained networks. The performance achieved based on the performance criteria validation accuracy, sensitivity, specificity, precision, F1-score, AUC, and Yonden index shows how well the deep learning models can perform in COVID-19 detection using CT scan images. Base on the results on the best performing model ResNet50 with AdaBoost Ensemble Classifier, it shows that we achieved higher accuracy, sensitivity, specificity, precision, F1-score, Yonden index, and AUC compared to the state-of-the-art models employed on the dataset. By adopting deep learning for COVID-19 detection using CT scan images, the method will help in revealing the patient's status

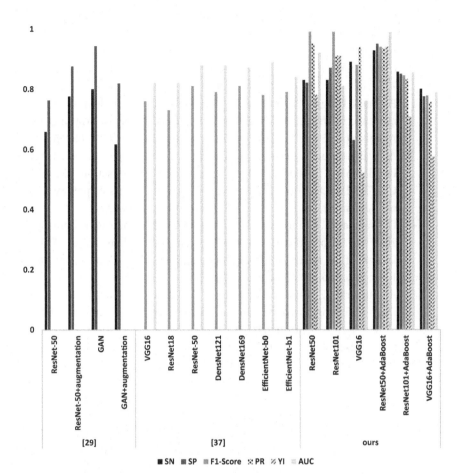

FIGURE 4.6   Proposed models performance compared with the state-of-the-art models performance

very quickly and efficiently. To reduce the spread of the virus, as the virus incubation period is 14 days, though most patients show mild symptoms, before confirming their status they need to be isolated, which comes with cost penalty to the patient or government. However, with early detection patients can be put on medication at an early stage and recover quickly, and for pregnant women and children the CT scan will be the best alternative.

## ACKNOWLEDGEMENTS

This research focuses on those affected by the COVID-19 pandemic and those who are helping to fight this war in whatever way they can. We would also like to thank the doctors, nurses, and all healthcare providers who are putting their lives at risk in the fight against the coronavirus outbreak.

## REFERENCES

[1] N. Zhu et al., A novel coronavirus from patients with pneumonia in China, 2019, New England Journal of Medicine, vol. 382, no. 8, pp. 727–733, 2020, doi: 10.1056/NEJMoa2001017.

[2] P. Zhai, Y. Ding, X. Wu, J. Long, Y. Zhong, and Y. Li, The epidemiology, diagnosis and treatment of COVID-19, International Journal of Antimicrobial Agents, vol. 55, no. 5, 2020, doi: 10.1016/j.ijantimicag.2020.105955.

[3] A. S. Mubarak, S. Serte, F. Al-Turjman, Z. S. Ameen, and M. Ozsoz, Local binary pattern and deep learning feature extraction fusion for COVID-19 detection on computed tomography images, Expert Systems, no. September, pp. 1–13, Sep. 2021, doi: 10.1111/exsy.12842.

[4] D. Wang et al., Clinical Characteristics of 138 Hospitalized Patients with 2019 Novel Coronavirus-Infected Pneumonia in Wuhan, China, JAMA – Journal of the American Medical Association, vol. 323, no. 11, pp. 1061–1069, 2020, doi: 10.1001/jama.2020.1585.

[5] A. Mubarak, Z. Said, R. Aliyu, F. Al Turjman, S. Serte, and M. Ozsoz, Deep learning-based feature extraction coupled with multi-class SVM for COVID-19 detection in the IoT era, International Journal of Nanotechnology, vol. 1, no. 1, p. 1, 2021, doi: 10.1504/IJNT.2021.10040115.

[6] M. Xie and Q. Chen, Insight into 2019 novel coronavirus — An updated interim review and lessons from SARS-CoV and MERS-CoV, International Journal of Infectious Diseases, vol. 94, pp. 119–124, 2020, doi: 10.1016/j.ijid.2020.03.071.

[7] M. J. Awan, M. H. Bilal, A. Yasin, H. Nobanee, N. S. Khan, and A. M. Zain, Detection of COVID-19 in chest x-ray images: A big data enabled deep learning approach, International Journal of Environmental Research and Public Health, vol. 18, no. 19, 2021, doi: 10.3390/ijerph181910147.

[8] R. Liu et al., Positive rate of RT-PCR detection of SARS-CoV-2 infection in 4880 cases from one hospital in Wuhan, China, from Jan to Feb 2020, Clinica Chimica Acta, vol. 505, no. March, pp. 172–175, 2020, doi: 10.1016/j.cca.2020.03.009.

[9] D. K. W. Chu et al., Molecular Diagnosis of a Novel Coronavirus (2019-nCoV) Causing an Outbreak of Pneumonia, Clinical Chemistry, vol. 555, pp. 549–555, 2020, doi: 10.1093/clinchem/hvaa029.

[10] J. L. Strunk, H. Temesgen, H. Andersen, and P. Packalen, Imaging Profile of the COVID-19 Infection: Radiologic Findings and Literature Review, vol. 80, no. 2, pp. 1–8, 2014, doi: 10.14358/PERS.80.2.000.

[11] H. Liu, F. Liu, J. Li, T. Zhang, D. Wang, and W. Lan, Clinical and CT imaging features of the COVID-19 pneumonia: Focus on pregnant women and children, Journal of Infection, vol. 80, no. 5, pp. e7–e13, 2020, doi: 10.1016/j.jinf.2020.03.007.

[12] L. J. M. Kroft, L. Van Der Velden, I. H. Girón, J. J. H. Roelofs, A. De Roos, and J. Geleijns, Added value of ultra-low-dose computed tomography, dose equivalent to chest x-ray radiography, for diagnosing chest pathology, Journal of Thoracic Imaging, vol. 34, no. 3, pp. 179–186, 2019, doi: 10.1097/RTI.0000000000000404.

[13] N. Chen et al., Epidemiological and clinical characteristics of 99 cases of 2019 novel coronavirus pneumonia in Wuhan, China: a descriptive study, The Lancet, vol. 395, no. 10223, pp. 507–513, 2020, doi: 10.1016/S0140-6736(20)30211-7.

[14] F. Al-Turjman and B. Deebak, Privacy-Aware Energy-Efficient Framework Using the Internet of Medical Things for COVID-19, IEEE Internet of Things Magazine, vol. 3, no. 3, pp. 64–68, Sep. 2020, doi: 10.1109/iotm.0001.2000123.

[15] A. Rahman, Data-Driven Dynamic Clustering Framework for Mitigating the Adverse Economic Impact of COVID-19 Lockdown Practices, Sustainable Cities and Society, p. 102372, 2020, doi: 10.1016/j.scs.2020.102372.

[16] S. Pillai, IoT Based Humanoid Software for Identification and Diagnosis of COVID-19 Suspects, vol. XX, no. Xx, 2020, doi: 10.1109/JSEN.2020.3030905.

[17] Z. S. Ameen, M. Ozsoz, A. S. Mubarak, F. Al Turjman, and S. Serte, C-SVR Crispr: Prediction of CRISPR/Cas12 guideRNA activity using deep learning models, Alexandria Engineering Journal, vol. 60, no. 4, pp. 3501–3508, Aug. 2021, doi: 10.1016/j.aej.2021.02.007.

[18] S. Z. Amee, A. S. Mubarak, A. Süleyman, and O. Mehmet, Development of CNN Model for Prediction of CRISPR/Cas12 Guide RNA Activity, 2020, pp. 697–703.

[19] M. E. Karar, S. H. El-Khafif, and M. A. El-Brawany, Automated Diagnosis of Heart Sounds Using Rule-Based Classification Tree, Journal of Medical Systems, vol. 41, no. 4, 2017, doi: 10.1007/s10916-017-0704-9.

[20] S. Hussein, P. Kandel, C. W. Bolan, M. B. Wallace, and U. Bagci, Lung and Pancreatic Tumor Characterization in the Deep Learning Era: Novel Supervised and Unsupervised Learning Approaches, IEEE Transactions on Medical Imaging, vol. 38, no. 8, pp. 1777–1787, 2019, doi: 10.1109/TMI.2019.2894349.

[21] C. H. Liang, Y. C. Liu, M. T. Wu, F. Garcia-Castro, A. Alberich-Bayarri, and F. Z. Wu, Identifying pulmonary nodules or masses on chest radiography using deep learning: external validation and strategies to improve clinical practice, Clinical Radiology, vol. 75, no. 1, pp. 38–45, 2020, doi: 10.1016/j.crad.2019.08.005.

[22] H. Rathore, A. K. Al-Ali, A. Mohamed, X. Du, and M. Guizani, A Novel Deep Learning Strategy for Classifying Different Attack Patterns for Deep

Brain Implants, IEEE Access, vol. 7, pp. 24154–24164, 2019, doi: 10.1109/ACCESS.2019.2899558.

[23] N. Ghassemi, A. Shoeibi, and M. Rouhani, Deep neural network with generative adversarial networks pre-training for brain tumor classification based on MR images, Biomedical Signal Processing and Control, vol. 57, p. 101678, 2020, doi: 10.1016/j.bspc.2019.101678.

[24] M. E. Karar, D. R. Merk, C. Chalopin, T. Walther, V. Falk, and O. Burgert, Aortic valve prosthesis tracking for transapical aortic valve implantation, International Journal of Computer Assisted Radiology and Surgery, vol. 6, no. 5, pp. 583–590, 2011, doi: 10.1007/s11548-010-0533-5.

[25] M. M. Ahsan, K. D. Gupta, M. M. Islam, S. Sen, M. L. Rahman, and M. S. Hossain, Study of Different Deep Learning Approach with Explainable AI for Screening Patients with COVID-19 Symptoms: Using CT Scan and Chest X-ray Image Dataset, 2020, http://arxiv.org/abs/2007.12525.

[26] T. Mahmud, M. A. Rahman, and S. A. Fattah, CovXNet: A multi-dilation convolutional neural network for automatic COVID-19 and other pneumonia detection from chest X-ray images with transferable multi-receptive feature optimization, Computers in Biology and Medicine, vol. 122, no. May, p. 103869, 2020, doi: 10.1016/j.compbiomed.2020.103869.

[27] M. Farooq and A. Hafeez, COVID-ResNet: A Deep Learning Framework for Screening of COVID19 from Radiographs, 2020, http://arxiv.org/abs/2003.14395.

[28] X. Xie, Chest CT for Typical COVID-19 pneumonia, Radiology, 2020, doi: 10.14358/PERS.81.12.21.

[29] M. Barstugan, U. Ozkaya, and S. Ozturk, Coronavirus (COVID-19) Classification using CT Images by Machine Learning Methods, no. 5, pp. 1–10, 2020, http://arxiv.org/abs/2003.09424.

[30] C. Butt, J. Gill, D. Chun, and B. A. Babu, Deep learning system to screen coronavirus disease 2019 pneumonia, Applied Intelligence, pp. 1–29, 2020, doi: 10.1007/s10489-020-01714-3.

[31] M. Loey, F. Smarandache, and N. E. M. Khalifa, A Deep Transfer Learning Model with Classical Data Augmentation and CGAN to Detect COVID-19 from Chest CT Radiography Digital Images, no. April, pp. 1–17, 2020, doi: 10.20944/preprints202004.0252.v1.

[32] X. Yang, X. He, J. Zhao, Y. Zhang, S. Zhang, and P. Xie, COVID-CT-Dataset: A CT Image Dataset about COVID-19, pp. 1–14.

[33] A. B. Haque and M. Rahman, Augmented COVID-19 X-ray Images Dataset (Mendely) Analysis using Convolutional Neural Network and Transfer Learning, vol. 19, no. April, 2020, doi: 10.13140/RG.2.2.20474.24003.

[34] I. D. Apostolopoulos and T. A. Mpesiana, COVID-19: automatic detection from X-ray images utilizing transfer learning with convolutional

neural networks, Physical and Engineering Sciences in Medicine, vol. 43, no. 2, pp. 635–640, 2020, doi: 10.1007/s13246-020-00865-4.

[35] M. Loey, F. Smarandache, and N. E. M. Khalifa, Within the Lack of Chest COVID-19 X-ray Dataset: A Novel Detection Model Based on GAN and Deep Transfer Learning, Symmetry, vol. 12, no. 4, p. 651, Apr. 2020, doi: 10.3390/sym12040651.

[36] K. He and J. Sun, Deep Residual Learning for Image Recognition, 2016, doi: 10.1109/CVPR.2016.90.

[37] S. A. Zisserman Karen, Very deep convolutional networks for large-scale image recognition, pp. 1–14, 2015.

[38] Y. Bengio, Practical recommendations for gradient-based training of deep architectures, Lecture Notes in Computer Science (including subseries Lecture Notes in Artificial Intelligence and Lecture Notes in Bioinformatics), vol. 7700 LECTU, pp. 437–478, 2012, doi: 10.1007/ 978-3-642-35289-8-26.

[39] X. He, X. Yang, S. Zhang, J. Zhao, Y. Zhang, and E. Xing, Sample-Efficient Deep Learning for COVID-19 Diagnosis Based on CT Scans, 2020.

# CHAPTER 5

# Deep Learning and Transfer Learning Models for Detection of COVID-19

Abdullahi Umar Ibrahim, Fadi Al-Turjman,
Mehmet Ozsoz, Ayse Gunnay Kibarer,
and Serife Kaba

*Near East University, Nicosia, Turkey*

## CONTENTS

| | | | |
|---|---|---|---|
| 5.1 | Introduction | | 64 |
| | 5.1.1 | Literature Search | 66 |
| 5.2 | Deep Learning (DL) | | 67 |
| | 5.2.1 | Transfer Learning (TL) | 68 |
| | | 5.2.1.1 AlexNet | 69 |
| | | 5.2.1.2 VGGNet | 69 |
| | | 5.2.1.3 GoogleNet (Inception and EfficientNet) | 70 |
| | | 5.2.1.4 ResNet | 70 |
| | 5.2.2 | Performance Evaluation | 71 |
| | | 5.2.2.1 Accuracy | 71 |
| | | 5.2.2.2 Sensitivity | 71 |
| | | 5.2.2.3 Specificity | 72 |
| | | 5.2.2.4 Receiver Operating Characteristics (ROC) | 72 |
| | | 5.2.2.5 Area under the Curve (AUC) | 73 |
| | | 5.2.2.6 F1-Score or F Measure | 73 |

DOI: 10.1201/9781003322887-5

5.3   COVID-19 and Pneumonia                                                73
    5.3.1   Pandemics and Epidemics of the Coronaviridae
        Family                                                              74
        5.3.1.1   SARS-COV-2 Pandemic                              74
        5.3.1.2   MERS-CoV Epidemic                               75
        5.3.1.3   SARS-COV-1 Epidemic                             75
    5.3.2   Molecular Diagnosis of Coronavirus                    75
5.4   Radiology                                                             76
    5.4.1   X-Ray                                                         76
    5.4.2   CT scans                                                      77
    5.4.3   Lung Ultrasound                                               77
    5.4.4   Radiological Datasets                                         79
        5.4.4.1   COVID-19 X-Ray Images Uploaded
            by J Paul Cohen                                 79
        5.4.4.2   COVID-19 Radiography Dataset                    79
        5.4.4.3   COVIDx Dataset                                  79
        5.4.4.4   HCV-UFPR COVID-19 Dataset                       80
        5.4.4.5   COVIDx-US                                       80
        5.4.4.6   SARS-CoV-2 CT Scan Dataset                      80
        5.4.4.7   Radiological Society of North America
            (RSNA) Dataset                                  80
        5.4.4.8   Chest X-Ray Kermany et al. [50]                 81
        5.4.4.9   ChestX-Ray8 Uploaded by Wang et al. [51]        81
5.5   Application of Deep Learning Models for the
    Detection of COVID-19                                             81
    5.5.1   Binary Classification                                         83
    5.5.2   Ternary Classification                                        87
5.6   Concluding Remarks                                                    94
    5.6.1   Conclusions                                                   94
    5.6.2   Open Research Issues                                          95
References                                                                  95

## 5.1 INTRODUCTION

The emergence of Coronavirus Disease 2019 (COVID-19) caused by Severe Acute Respiratory Syndrome Coronavirus-2 (SARS-CoV-2) in late 2019 has raise global health and socioeconomic challenges [1]. As a result of the wide spread of the disease globally, the WHO declared it a pandemic on 11th March, 2020. The disease had affected over 544,324,069 (confirmed cases of COVID-19), including 6,332,963 deaths, as of 26th June, 2022 [2].

In order to diagnose the disease, healthcare professionals have relied on a laboratory bench assay known as reverse transcription-polymerase chain reaction (RT-PCR) based on RNA or DNA hybridization. This technique utilizes nasal samples collected from the patient which are amplified using a PCR machine. To detect the virus, a probe designed with marker labels hybridizes with the target nucleic acid which leads to the release fluorescent dye which can be measured by the device with the outcome presented on a screen [3]. Other approaches explored by scientists for screening of the virus include computed tomography (CT) scans or chest X-ray (CXR) scans. The use of CXR and CT scans are the two basic approaches employed by radiologists to discriminate between patients infected with pneumonia disease and healthy individuals. The differences are evaluated according to the presence of white hazy patches designated as "ground-glass opacity" in individuals who are suffering from the disease but absent in healthy individuals [4].

Despite the fact that RT-PCR is regarded as the most efficient recent approach for detection of COVID-19, it is time consuming, requiring the use of chemical reagents, trained experts, and often resulting in false-positive results. However, the use of clinical images such as CT scans, X-ray images, and lung ultrasounds are easier, quicker, and dependable approaches for early and timely screening of COVID-19 cases. In spite of all the advantages of radiographic images, they have some limitations which include the need for a radiologist to interpret the results, which is tedious, time-consuming, and prone to error or misinterpretation [1,5].

In order to address these challenges, scientists have explored the use of computer-aided detection based on artificial intelligence and its subtypes, such as machine learning (ML) and deep learning (DL). Currently, DL is the most effective technique that can be integrated into healthcare settings to aid in diagnosis (aka computer-aided diagnosis or CAD). Deep learning models have been shown to be an efficient, fast, reliable, and accurate approach for prediction and classification of clinical data. DL models have been applied previously for identifying health issues which include pneumonia (viral and bacterial), tuberculosis, tumours, and heart disorders using medical image datasets [6,7].

Several deep learning models such as pretrained networks, ensemble networks, and networks developed from scratch have been proposed for the screening and two-way classification of COVID-19 from normal cases (binary classification) as well as three-way and four-way classification, which include COVID-19 pneumonia, non-COVID-19 pneumonia (non-COVID-19 viral and bacterial pneumonia), and normal cases using several clinical images such as CT scans, chest X-rays, and lung images [8].

### 5.1.1 Literature Search

The current literature on the state of the art is vast, with thousands of studies that include the keywords of this chapter. The initial selection of existing researches overviewed in this study was designed by searching articles using a Google Scholar search based on the outline keywords or phrases: COVID-19 pandemic, SARS-CoV-2, COVID-19 datasets, detection/screening of COVID-19 (using artificial intelligence, deep learning, convolutional neural networks), computer-aided diagnosis of COVID-19 (from chest X-ray images, CT scans, lung ultrasounds).

In this study, more than 250 articles are reviewed, of which 72 articles were from some of the best and most popular journals selected. In terms of years of publications, we selected 64 articles published between 2015 till date, while eight are pre-2015 and four from a website. Moreover, some of the things considered for the selection of articles incorporated in this study include sound scientific contents, peer reviewed, written in English, and assigned with a DOI number except for two dataset sources and four deep learning definitions and models. Among these articles, 16 discuss DL (definition, types, supervised, unsupervised and reinforcement learning, pretrained networks or transfer learning, performance metrics, etc). Fourteen are basically on coronavirus (ranging from SARS-CoV-1, MERS-CoV, to SARS-CoV-2) as well as diagnosis using the RT-PCR technique. Twenty-one articles focus on radiographic images and datasets (which include chest X-ray, CT scans, and lung ultrasound images). Twenty-six articles reported the application of DL approaches for the classification and screening of pneumonia cases which include binary (two-way) classification of positive COVID-19 from negative cases, ternary and quaternary classification of COVID-19, non-COVID-19 such as viral and bacterial, and normal cases.

The reminder of this chapter is structured as follows: Section 5.2 offers a concise introduction to DL, classifications, transfer learning (or pretrained networks) and performance or evaluation metrics. Section 5.3 overviews

COVID-19 pneumonia, epidemics, and pandemics of coronavirus diseases and molecular testing. In Section 5.4, the classification of radiographic images reported in the current literature and the public available datasets are discussed in detail. The review of the collected literature based on application of DL models for binary and ternary classification of radiographic images is provided in Section 5.5. The chapter is concluded in Section 5.6, highlighting the need for DL models for classification of pneumonia cases as alternative or confirmatory approaches, as well as the existing limitations and future directions.

## 5.2 DEEP LEARNING (DL)

DL is a sub-branch of ML that imitates the human nervous system. Deep learning models are made up of three or more layers. Deep learning networks are stacked with multiple perceptrons, which contain input layers, hidden layers, and output layers. Unlike traditional machine learning approaches that are linear, deep learning networks are stacked in hierarchy of increasing abstraction and complexity [9].

DL models require or are fuelled by a hefty amount of dataset in order to attain higher training and testing accuracy. DL models are classified into artificial neural networks (such as recurrent neural networks that are used in speech and language recognition) and convolutional neural networks which are predominantly use in the classification of images. These networks learn parameters through forward propagation and gradient descent or back propagation. This technique allows deep learning algorithms to optimize the difference between predictive value and actual value as shown in equation (5.1). The optimization is based on estimating errors in terms of prediction and thereby adjusting both the biases and weights [9].

$$OA-OP \qquad (5.1)$$

As a sub-branch of machine ML, DL networks can be categorized as supervised, unsupervised, and reinforcements learning. In supervised learning, datasets are labelled into two or more categories in order to make predictions or classifications. This approach requires the aid of human intervention or a professional in the case of medical datasets to label input dataset correctly. In unsupervised machine learning, the input dataset is not label and does not require human intervention. Networks learn on their own through patterns and the output result in either clustering or classification is based on features or characteristics. In contrast to both supervised and unsupervised learning, reinforcements learning is a series of processes where networks learn a task in an environment over and over again in order to increase their performance and maximize rewards through a feedback mechanism [10,11].

## 5.2.1 Transfer Learning (TL)

The concept of TL has gained interest from computer scientists and other disciplines in the last decades due to the development of deep learning models and the boom of data storage such as cloud computing and big data. The first concept of transfer learning dates back to 1993 when Lorien Pratt published an article titled "Discriminability-based Transfer Between Neural Networks". This article paved the way to the application of TL in solving problems. Developing neural networks from scratch so many challenges however, and the most significant challenge is the need for a huge amount of data for training that mostly effect high performance [12].

The reuse of models previously trained on a large number of datasets for solving problems with a lower amount of dataset is the core point of TL. Therefore, TL is defined as a branch of AI and ML which applies knowledge (learned parameters such as weights, biases, features, etc.) gained from one task (i.e., source task) to a different but similar task (i.e., target task). Instead of training the neural network from scratch, scientists extract the weights and transfer them to solve problems of prediction and image classification. A pretrained model is thus define as a model designed to solve similar problems rather than building neural networks that require a large amount of data to achieve high performance [12,13]. Despite the fact that pretrained models often do not result in 100% performance, they offer several advantages over networks developed from scratch. Some of the advantages include time-saving and effort, high performance, low computation (less forward and backward iterations for the model to identify the corrects weights), the use of a low learning rate compared to the one used for initial training and they can be trained using a lower number of datasets [13].

Scientists have developed several neural networks that are currently in use today. Despite the fact that convolutional neural networks (CNNs) existed 3 decades ago, however, it was not until 2012 that they became prominent due to the development of AlexNet by Alex Krizhevsky which outperformed other models in terms of classifying the ImageNet dataset (which currently contains over 10 million high-resolution images labelled into 22,000 categories) [12,14]. Other networks that achieve high performance or best state-of-the-art models include VGGNet19, GoogleNet (Inception), ResNet, and EfficientNet [12].

### 5.2.1.1 AlexNet

AlexNet was developed by Alex Krizhevsky, Geoffrey Hinton, and Ilya Sutskever in 2012. The model achieved 84.7% accuracy and top 5-error rate of 15.3% in the ImageNet Large-Scale Visual Recognition Challenge (ILSVRC) [15,16]. The network architecture is made up eight layers in total: five convolutional layers (CLs) and three fully connected layers (FCLs). The first two CLs consist of three operations which include convolution, pooling, and normalization. The third and fourth CLs consist of only convolution and the fifth CL consists of two operations (convolution and max pooling). The sixth and seventh layers are FCLs. while the last FCL (layer 8) is designed with SoftMax classifier. Instead of the traditional tanh activation function that was common, AlexNet opted for Rectified Linear Units (ReLu) which reduce the training time and error rate. Other advantages of the AlexNet model over traditional machine learning models include the use of multiple GPUs, local response normalization, dropout, and overlapping pooling (which prevents overfitting). The model has 63.3 million parameters [16,17].

### 5.2.1.2 VGGNet

VGGNet 16 and 19 were developed by two scientists from Oxford University, Andrew Zisserman and Karen Simonyan, in 2014. In terms of performance, VGGNet is the second-best architecture in 2014 with a top-5 error rate of 7.32%. VGG-16 is comprised of 13 CLs and three FCLs, while VGG-19 has 16 CLs and three FCLs. Unlike AlexNet architecture that has A pooling layer after every convolution except for THE third and fourth convolutional layers, VGGNet has A pooling layer after TWO convolutional layers, and another pooling layer after two and four convolutional layers. The rest of the convolutional layers (nine layers for VGG-16 and 12 for VGG-19) are categorized into three, with each three layers designed with a pooling layer followed by three fully dense layers (fully connected layers). Like AlexNet, VGGNets use ReLu as an activation function and SoftMax as a classifier. Unlike AlexNet that uses 227×227×3 pixels size,

VGGNets use 224×224×3 pixels size. VGGNets can classify up to 1000 categories with 143,667,240 parameters [18, 19].

### 5.2.1.3 GoogleNet (Inception and EfficientNet)

Some of the challenges of previous architectures include the use of large kernel or filter size. This issue is addressed in GoogleNet by introducing multiple size kernels and the use of inception modules, with 1×1 convolution blocks to reduced depths. Thus, instead of going deeper like ResNet, inception networks opted for going wider. Inception models were developed by a team from Google. The model became the top-performing model in 2014 ILRSCV with a top-5 error rate of 6.67% [20]. Inception networks have 22 layers and are comprised of several modules, each consisting of different operations which include 1×1, 3×3, 5×5 convolution and max pooling operations. The model accepts input data of 229×229×3 pixel size and use ReLu as an activation function and SoftMax classifier. The model can classify objects in up to 1000 categories with 23,851,784 parameters. In order to scale up the current architecture, scientists from Google have developed the EfficientNet with 5.3 million parameters [20,21].

### 5.2.1.4 ResNet

One of the challenges of deeper models is the issue of vanishing gradients. ResNet addressed this issue by introducing shortcut connections and residual block that are repeated through the architecture. Along with the inception model, ResNet was one of the best performing models in the 2015 ILRSVC competition with a top-5 error rate of 5% due to it depths and number of layers. It was developed by scientists working at Microsoft in 2015 [22,23]. Just like the rest of the best performing models, ResNet can classify images in up to 1000 categories. The variations between ResNet models and VGGNets is the introduction of two shortcut connections known as projection and identity shortcuts. A simple example of the ResNets architecture is the ResNet-18 which has 17 CLs and a single FCL. Despite the depth of the network, it has only two pooling layers, using ReLu as an activation function and SoftMax classifier as the last FCL [22]. As an upgrade to VGGNets, it accepts images with a pixel size of 224×224×3 with 25,636,712 parameters. Since the first development of ResNet-50, the architecture has undergone upgrades which include ResNet-50 V2, ResNet-101, ResNet-101 V2, ResNet-121, ResNet-152, and ResNet-152 V2 [23]. The differences, similarities, and parameters of the top-performing architectures are presented in Table 5.1.

TABLE 5.1   The Differences, Similarities, and Parameters of the Top-Performing Architectures

| Architecture | Year | Top-5 Accuracy | Top-5 Error | Parameters | Activation Function |
|---|---|---|---|---|---|
| AlexNet | 2012 | 84.70% | 15.3% | 62 million | ReLu |
| VGGNet | 2014 | 92.30% | 7.32% | 138 million | ReLu |
| Inception | 2014 | 93.30% | 6.67%. | 6.4 million | ReLu |
| ResNet | 2015 | 95.51% | 5% | 60.3 million | ReLu |

## 5.2.2 Performance Evaluation

Evaluating the performance of deep learning models is decisive for correct classification of output. Researchers have reported the use of different performance evaluations throughout the literature. Some of these evaluations that are classified under confusion matrix include accuracy, sensitivity (i.e., recall), specificity (i.e., precision), area under the curve (AUC), ROC, F1-score, etc. [24,25].

### 5.2.2.1 Accuracy

Accuracy in ML and DL is described as the measure of how accurate (sensitive and precise) a model makes correct predictions or classifications. In order words, accuracy is termed as the sum of correctly predicted outcomes over total outcomes. For example, if a model classified 90 datasets out of 100 irrespective of positive and negative cases (i.e., 43 negative and 47 positive), the accuracy is 90 over 100 which is equal to 0.9 [24].

### 5.2.2.2 Sensitivity

Sensitivity or recall based on medical image classification is termed as the true positive rate or the amount of positive (infected or disease) cases that are predicted or classified as positive. However, not all positive cases can be predicted correctly, thus, some of the cases that are incorrectly predicted as negative cases are termed as false negative. Therefore, based on probability, the sum of true positive (sensitivity) and false positive is equal to 1. The higher score of sensitivity denotes higher score of true positive and lower value of false negative. Therefore, in healthcare settings, outcomes with higher sensitivity are more desirable [24,25].

Sensitivity can be represented mathematically by the following equation:

$$\frac{\left(\text{True Positive}\right)}{\left(\text{True Positive}\right)+\left(\text{False Negative}\right)} \tag{5.2}$$

where:

True positive: Actual cases classified as those suffering from a specific disease. In orders words, true positive is the number of individuals who are tested positive for a disease and classified correctly by the model.

False negative: Patients who are actually infected with the disease (i.e., positive or infected) but are classified as negative (i.e., healthy) by the model. In another words, false positive is the number of positive cases that are wrongly classified as normal or healthy cases.

### 5.2.2.3 Specificity

Specificity also known as precision or true negatives is the opposite of sensitivity. In this case, it is termed as the number of true negative cases that are actually or correctly predicted or classified as negative by the model. However, not all negative cases can be classified as negative, therefore some of the cases that are classified as positive when they are actually negative are called false positive. The sum of true negatives (specificity) plus false positives is equal to 1. The higher specificity score dictates a higher number of true negatives and lower value of false positive. Therefore, in healthcare settings, outcomes with higher specificity are more desirable [24,25].

Specificity can be represented mathematically by the following equation:

$$\frac{(\text{True Negative})}{(\text{True Negative}) + (\text{False Positive})} \tag{5.3}$$

where:

True negative: The actual cases that are categorized as negative by the model, in order words, true negative is the number of cases that tested negative that are categorized as negative by the model.

False positive: Patients who are actually not suffering from a specific disease (i.e., healthy) but are categorized as positive by the model. In order words, false positive is the number of negative cases that are wrongly categorized as positive by the model.

### 5.2.2.4 Receiver Operating Characteristics (ROC)

Receiver operating characteristics (ROC) is a graph of the true positive rate (sensitivity) against the false positive rate (1-specificity). The main function of ROC is to summarize the performance of a model over all potential thresholds [25].

### 5.2.2.5 Area under the Curve (AUC)

AUC is also called area under ROC or AUROC. The function of the AUC is to show how accurate or excellent the model is performing or accurately differentiating between classes (i.e., positive and negative/infected and healthy). A prediction outcome of closer to 1 (i.e., 0.95 and above) shows that the model is efficient. AUC is plotted based on the true positive rate (TPR) against the false positive rate (FPR) at various threshold values. Therefore, the higher the AUC value, the more efficient the model [25].

### 5.2.2.6 F1-Score or F Measure

This is a DL evaluation metric that is applied mostly for classification, especially when there is class imbalance. It combines both precision and recall as its basic foundation to form a single metric. F1-score can also be defined mathematically as the harmonic mean of recall and precession [25]. The formula for the F1-score is:

$$2 \times \frac{\left(\text{precession} \times \text{recall}\right)}{\left(\text{precession} + \text{recall}\right)} \tag{5.4}$$

## 5.3 COVID-19 AND PNEUMONIA

COVID-19 has been making headlines throughout 2020 as a result of the worldwide health crisis cause by the outbreak of SARS-CoV-2 on the eve of 2020 in Wuhan, China. Prior to the year of outbreak, other viruses from the same family "Coronaviridae" called SARS-CoV-1 and MERS-CoV led to epidemics with higher mortality rates [26,27]. The word "corona" means "crown" and thus the virus is named coronavirus after the spike proteins present on the surface which looks like a crown, as shown in Figure 5.1.

Like other ARDS, COVID-19 disease can be spread in the form of respiratory droplets (sneeze or cough) exhaled by an infected person, through physical contact with an infected patient, or coming into contact with a surface contaminated by the virus. Just like the pathology of common pneumonia, SARS-CoV-2 when contracted invades the alveoli present in the organs that are responsible for the exchange of $O_2$ and $CO_2$

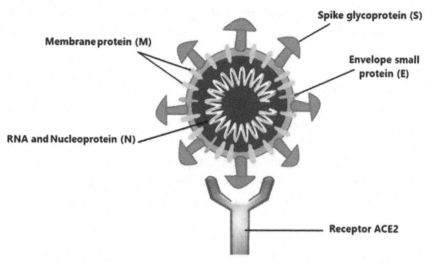

FIGURE 5.1   Structure of SARS-CoV-2

between the lungs and blood, thus leading to COVID-19 pneumonia. Symptoms associated with COVID-19 disease include: severe pneumonia, dry cough, fever, sputum secretion, fatigue, anorexia, dyspnoea, organ failure, myalgias, septic shock, etc. [27,28].

### 5.3.1  Pandemics and Epidemics of the Coronaviridae Family
#### 5.3.1.1  SARS-COV-2 Pandemic
The word "pandemic" was introduced in 2005 and it has only been declared a global health emergency five times, in 2009 as a result of the influenza virus, 2014 as a result of Ebola and polio viruses, in 2016 as a result of Zika virus, 2019 as a result of Ebola, and in 2020 as a result of SARS-CoV-2. The first reported case of this virus was declared in the city of Wuhan, Hubei Province, in mainland China on the eve of 1st January, 2020. However, it was not until 11th March 2020 that the WHO declared the disease a "pandemic" [29,30]. The virus has spread to almost all of the countries of the world and had infected more than 500 million people and caused close to 6 million deaths at the time of writing.

The mortality rate from SARS-CoV-2 is low compare to SARS-CoV-1 and MERS-CoV, currently, close to 20 million patients have recovered. The outbreak of the disease led to city lockdowns in many countries, border closures, flight cancellations, restrictions, quarantine, evacuations, and cancelations and postponements of educative, sport, cultural, and religious activities. To control the spread of the virus, governments implement the use of facemasks, hand sanitation, and social distancing based on personal hygiene [26].

### 5.3.1.2 MERS-CoV Epidemic
The first case of MERS-CoV was declared in the month of April 2012 in Saudi Arabia. The virus was reported or diagnosed in 27 different countries with the majority in the Middle East and eight countries in Europe. According to WHO, prior to 2020, there were 2500 laboratory-confirmed cases of MERS, with close to 1000 deaths, representing a 34% mortality rate. Even though the exact source of the virus remains unknown scientists have attributed the virus to the dromedary camel as the main reservoir which transmitted the virus to humans. The main symptoms of MERS include shortness of breath, fever, cough, diarrhoea, etc. [31–33].

### 5.3.1.3 SARS-COV-1 Epidemic
The first case of coronavirus (SARS-CoV-1) was declared on November 16, 2002, in Guangdong Province in southern China. Unlike MERS-CoV, bats are regarded as the reservoirs of the virus and civets are the main carriers that infect humans. The symptoms of SARS include diarrhoea, fever, dry cough, myalgia, malaise, headache, and rigorous shivering, among others. However, not all patients infected with the disease are symptomatic in the first week of illness, especially patients who are on immunosuppressants. The virus has spread to 29 countries with over 8000 confirmed cases and 774 deaths worldwide, with an estimated mortality rate of 9.675% case fatality rate (CFR) [34]. The mortality rate from infection is calculated based on the infection fatality rate (IFR), which is defined as the number of deaths over the number of infected patients multiplied by 100, and the is CFR defined as the number of deaths over the number of confirmed cases multiplied by 100 [35].

## 5.3.2 Molecular Diagnosis of Coronavirus
Currently, there are few molecular testing approaches developed by scientists. Reverse transcription-polymerase chain reaction (RT-PCR) is regarded as the most common and efficient approach for diagnosing viral diseases such as dengue, Ebola, SARS-CoV-2, HIV, influenza virus, etc. In order to detect these pathogens, RT-PCR is conducted via the following steps.

Step 1: Sample collection, which is conducted using a swab to acquire the viral sample from the throat or nose of a suspected individual.

Step 2: Extraction: different chemical reagents are added to the sample in order to remove biochemical substances such as fats and proteins to extract viral RNA without impurities.

Step 3: Reverse transcripts (RT): since SARS-CoV-2 is a virus which stores its genetic material in RNA, scientists convert the RNA into DNA prior to amplification in order to generate more copies.

Step 4: PCR amplification and detection: DNA resulting from RT is amplified using an RT-PCR device in order to generate more copies of the viral DNA for efficient detection (due to the large quantity of DNA). Detection of the virus revolves around the fragments that attach to the target part of the viral DNA with marker labels which release fluorescent dye which can be measured by the device and present the result on the device screen. One of the challenges of RT-PCR is that it requires processing time, which take between 6–24 hours to obtain the result. This waiting period can increase the spread of the disease if suspects are not isolated or quarantined [3].

## 5.4 RADIOLOGY

The advancements in imaging technology have led to the development of MRI machines, CT scans, and X-ray machines. These machines are commonly used to help doctors diagnose several conditions. Imaging techniques allow medical experts to view the internal structure of patients.

### 5.4.1 X-Ray

The X-ray is regarded as the most common imaging technique. The advantage of CXR images over other radiographic imaging techniques is that they are readily available due to their high demand, affordability, low radiation dose, and reasonable sensitivity for the diagnosis of several clinical diseases. The CXR is regarded as the first line of call for screening, diagnosis, and management of a wide range of disorders [37].

Radiologists classify chest X-rays into three main categories, which include posteroanterior, anteroposterior, and lateral views. This categorization is based on the position and orientation of the patient parallel to the X-ray source and detector panel. The lateral view, also known as the side view, differs from the frontal view (subclassified into anteroposterior

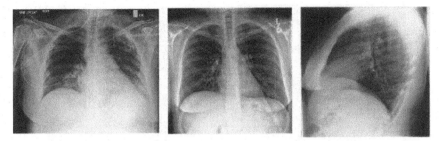

FIGURE 5.2 Left: Anterior–posterior (AP) view chest radiograph. Middle: Posterior–anterior (PA) view frontal chest radiograph. Right: Lateral chest radiograph

and posteroanterior). These two images are considered frontal due to the positioning of the X-ray source to the front or rear of the patient. Furthermore, anteroposterior and posteroanterior differ in terms of positioning, as an anteroposterior X-ray image is obtained from patients in the supine position, while posteroanterior views are obtained in an erect standing position. A lateral X-ray image is obtained as a result of the combination of posteroanterior view and projection of the X-ray from right to left (or from one side of the patient to the other), as shown in Figure 5.2 [38].

## 5.4.2 CT scans

CT scan imaging is regarded as the most efficient imaging technique for diagnosing pulmonary diseases such as pneumonia. Despite its advantages over other imaging techniques, it is hindered by many challenges such as high cost and high radiation exposure dose. Unlike X-ray images that are captured as frontal or lateral, a CT scan machine produces cross-sectional images. One of the advantages of CT scan images is that they are highly sensitive and effective in terms of imaging the lung with outstanding spatial resolution. The use of CT scans has been shown to provide clear anatomical details that are similar to those observed by gross pathological examination [39], as presented in Figure 5.3.

## 5.4.3 Lung Ultrasound

Due to the difficulty of diagnosis in critically ill patients using either CT scans or X-rays, medical experts utilize a lung ultrasound (LUS) bedside machine which is easier to use. Some of the distinct advantages of LUS over other techniques include its non-ionizing radiation technique, portability, affordability, and ease of use. The use of LUS has been shown to aid in the

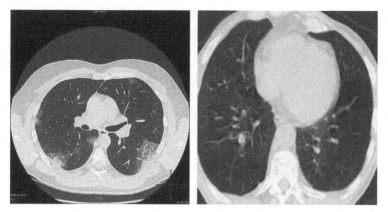

FIGURE 5.3    Left: COVID-19. Right: Non-COVID-19

detection of several pulmonary diseases (such as pneumonia, pulmonary fibrosis, pulmonary embolism, acute respiratory distress syndrome, pneumothorax lymph node of lung cancer, etc.) resulting in higher sensitivity for diagnosis of pleural effusion compared to chest X-ray [40].

Previous studies have also shown the efficiency of LUS in the diagnosis of pneumonia as well as discriminating between bacterial and viral pneumonia [40–42]. The technique behind the detection of pneumonia using LUS revolves around the presence of consolidation, which is hypoechoic or isoechoic and has a tissue-like structure and presents the loss of lung aeration. However, the hallmark for detection of pneumonia is the presence

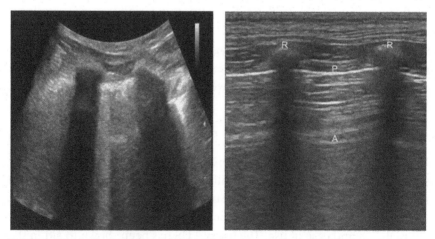

FIGURE 5.4    Left: COVID-19. Right: Normal lung ultrasound images

of branching, dynamic air bronchograms, and hyperechoic within the area of consolidation [43, 44]. Images of LUS pneumonia and normal cases are shown in Figure 5.4.

### 5.4.4 Radiological Datasets

Ever since the WHO declared the disease as a global pandemic, scientists have compiled radiographic datasets from globally diverse hospital and institutions. Some of these datasets are made available to the public and are accessible online on Kaggle, GitHub, and other repositories.

#### 5.4.4.1 COVID-19 X-Ray Images Uploaded by J Paul Cohen

The dataset prepared by Cohen et al. [45] is the most common dataset used by researchers. The dataset named "covid-chestxray-dataset" contains more than 200 COVID-19 X-ray images which are updated regularly on GitHub. The dataset is collected from several medical and scientific platforms. The dataset comprises of X-ray and CT scan images of COVID-19, MERS, SARS, ARDS, and other diseases. The images collected are comprised of four distinct views, which include lateral, anteroposterior, anteroposterior supine, and posteroanterior. The dataset is acquired from both males and females in the age range of 50–80 and is available on https://github.com/ieee8023/covid-chestxray-dataset.

#### 5.4.4.2 COVID-19 Radiography Dataset

This dataset has been made available on Kaggle (www.kaggle.com/tawsifu rrahman/covid19-radiography-database) as of January 2022 and contains different collections of pneumonia cases which include 3616 COVID-19 images, 1345 viral pneumonia X-ray images, 10,192 normal X-ray images, and 6012 lung opacity (non-COVID lung diseases). The COVID-19 Radiography Dataset has been developed by a group of scientists from different universities and medical institutions within Asia. The database is updated on a timely basis, with the first release containing 219 COVID-19, 1341 normal, and 1345 viral pneumonia chest X-ray (CXR) images. Since the first update, the database has been updated twice, in the first update, the COVID-19 CXR images were increased to 1200 images and the second update to 3616 and over 10,000 normal cases.

#### 5.4.4.3 COVIDx Dataset

This is one of the latest datasets made available by Wang et al. [46]. The dataset known as COVIDx is a collection of two public datasets which include the RSNA challenge dataset and COVID-19 Image Data Collection. The dataset enables researcher to carry out three-way (ternary) classification of normal, non-COVID-19, and COVID-19 pneumonia. The dataset contains 13,800 images in total, acquired from 13,000 people. The overall dataset is partitioned into training (13,569) and testing (231). The main source to access the images is available at https://github.com/lindawangg/COVID-Net.

### 5.4.4.4 HCV-UFPR COVID-19 Dataset
This dataset has been made available by Hospital da Cruz Vermelha in the southern part of Brazil. The dataset contains a binary collection of 281 COVID-19 and 232 healthy CXR images. Unlike the rest of the datasets listed, the HCV-UFPR COVID-19 dataset is private but can be accessed when requested [47].

### 5.4.4.5 COVIDx-US
This dataset is provided by Ebadi et al. [48] and is an open access dataset which is solely made of ultrasound images and videos of COVID-19 and normal cases. The dataset was curated from different sources and the recent version is composed of 12,943 processed images of COVID-19 (7170), non-COVID-19 (3159), other diseases related to the lungs (1636), and normal cases (978), and 150 lung ultrasound videos. The dataset is accessible at https://github.com/nrc-cnrc/COVID-US.

### 5.4.4.6 SARS-CoV-2 CT Scan Dataset
This dataset has been made available by Soares et al. [49]. It is regarded as one of the largest CT scan datasets for COVID-19 and normal CT scan images, with a total of 2481 (1252 COVID-19 and 1229 normal images). The images have been acquired from several patients in Sao Paulo, Brazil. The dataset can be access on both Kaggle and GitHub at www.kaggle.com/plameneduardo/sarscov2-ctscan-dataset and https://github.com/Plamen-Eduardo/xDNN-SARS-CoV-2-CT-Scan, respectively.

### 5.4.4.7 Radiological Society of North America (RSNA) Dataset
This dataset is made available by RSNA for the purpose of building algorithms that can detect visual signals for pneumonia from medical images. It started as a challenge or competition that allowed researchers to utilize the dataset and automatically detect lung opacities from chest

radiographs. The RSNA training dataset contains 26,684 chest radiographs and is available at https://github.com/tatigabru/kaggle-rsna.

### 5.4.4.8 Chest X-Ray Kermany et al. [50]

Prior to the pandemic, the dataset made available by Kermany et al. [50] which is accessible on the website (www.kaggle.com/paultimothymooney/chest-xray-pneumonia) was the most widely used dataset for discrimination of pneumonia cases. The dataset contains a total of 5856 images which are grouped into training, testing, and validation. The description of the dataset is curated according to X-ray images collected from retrospective paediatric patients between the ages of 1 and 5.

### 5.4.4.9 ChestX-Ray8 Uploaded by Wang et al. [51]

The ChestX-ray8 is a large dataset that comprises 108,948 frontal view X-ray images of 32,717 unique patients categorized and labelled into eight diseases, which include pneumonia, pneumothorax, effusion, mass, nodule, infiltration, atelectasis, and cardiomegaly. The database contains 24,636 X-ray images with one or more clinical diseases, while the remaining 84,312 X-ray images are healthy cases. The data are available at www.kaggle.com/nih-chest-xrays/data/home. Table 5.2 presents a summary of the publicly accessible datasets.

## 5.5 APPLICATION OF DEEP LEARNING MODELS FOR THE DETECTION OF COVID-19

The field of AI has been witnessing a remarkable rise and application over the last few decades. This exponential growth is bridging the gaps between the capabilities of machines and human intelligence. Early screening and diagnosis of disease are crucial for controlling wide spreading of diseases and timely treatment. Deep learning models have been shown to drive and enhance many biomedical applications which include diagnosis (such as classification of diseases into positive and negative in the cases of pneumonia, tuberculosis, retinopathy, etc. and grades in the cases of cancer and skin lesions or diseases), discovery of drugs to combat several diseases (such as COVID-19 drugs), predictions of the spread of disease in the case of epidemics and pandemics, and the management of medical records for decision-making [52,53].

Since the first reported cases of COVID-19 and its assignation as a pandemic by the WHO, medical experts have been on the warfront fighting

TABLE 5.2 Summary of the Datasets

| Name of Dataset | Number of Dataset | Class | Uploaded by | Accessible at |
|---|---|---|---|---|
| COVID-19 Xray Images | 200+ | COVID-19 X-ray and CT scan images | [45] | https://github.com/ieee8023/covid-chestxray-dataset. |
| COVID-19 Radiography Dataset | 21,165 | COVID-19, viral pneumonia, normal and lung opacity X-ray images | Team of researchers from different universities and medical institutions | www.kaggle.com/tawsifurrahman/covid19-radiography-database |
| COVIDx Dataset | 13,800 | Normal, non-COVID-19, and COVID-19 pneumonia | [46] | https://github.com/lindawangg/COVID-Net |
| HCV-UFPR COVID-19 Dataset | 513 | COVID-19 and normal X-ray images | Hospital da Cruz Vermelha | |
| COVIDx-US | 12,943 | COVID-19, non-COVID-19, other lung disease, normal cases, LUS | [48] | https://github.com/nrc-cnrc/COVID-US |
| SARS-CoV-2 CT Scan Dataset | 2481 | COVID-19 and normal | [49] | www.kaggle.com/plameneduardo/sarscov2-ctscan-dataset<br>https://github.com/Plamen-Eduardo/xDNN-SARS-CoV-2-CT-Scan |
| Radiological Society of North America (RSNA) Dataset | 26,684 | Normal, no lung opacity/not normal, lung opacity X-ray images | Radiological Society of North America (RSNA) | https://github.com/tatigabru/kaggle-rsna |
| Kermany et al., 2018 | 5856 | Non-COVID-19 pneumonia and normal X-ray images | [50] | www.kaggle.com/paultimothymooney/chest-xray-pneumonia |
| ChestX-ray8 | 108,948 | 8 diseases including non-COVID-19 pneumonia | [51] | www.kaggle.com/nih-chest-xrays/data/home |

against this pandemic through detection and treatment. The integration of artificial intelligence models in the detection of disease (also known as computer-aided detection or CAD) has been one of the leading battalions equipped with assisting medical experts as an alternative approach to molecular testing or as a confirmatory approach in the case of false-positive results. The literature is loaded with several studies that discriminate between COVID-19 cases and normal cases, multiclass (COVID-19, other viral pneumonia such as influenza virus, bacterial pneumonia, and normal cases) from X-ray and CT scan images. This section compiles several studies and categorizes them based on binary, ternary, and quaternary classifications, as illustrated in Figure 5.5.

### 5.5.1 Binary Classification

The use of multi-models which include AlexNet, DenseNet, GoogleNet, InceptionV3, InceptionResNetV2, ResNet18, ResNet50, ResNet-101, VGG16, VGG19, and XceptionNet and decision trees as a classifier for the discrimination of COVID-19 from X-ray images was reported by Dhiman et al. [54]. The dataset used for the study was acquired from GitHub open source and uploaded by Cohen et al. [45] and includes 50 COVID-19 X-ray and 50 normal X-ray images, and Kaggle. The efficiency of the model was evaluated according to 5k cross-validation using accuracy, recall, precision, F1-score, and specificity parameters. Among all the models used ResNet101 performed better with 97.18% accuracy, 98.64% recall, 95.86% specificity, 98.64% precision, and 97.05% F1-score.

The use of TL models for the discrimination of COVID-19 from X-ray images was reported by Vaid, Khalantar, and Bhandari [55]. Their study utilized a publicly accessible dataset made available by Cohen et al. [45] and Wang et al. [51] which contained 181 COVID-19 cases and 364 normal chest anterior-posterior X-ray images. The modification of pretrained VGG-19 was used to train (80% of the dataset) and evaluate (20% of the dataset) the model based on binary accuracy and cross-entropy. The performance evaluation of the modified model yielded 96.3% accuracy.

Ismael and Sengur [56] developed an end–end training CNN model and fine-running of pretrained networks (VGG-16, VGG-19, ResNet-18, ResNet-50, and ResNet-101) designed with an SVM classifier for two-way discrimination of COVID-19 and normal X-ray images. The models were trained using 200 normal cases and 180 cases from GitHub and Kaggle repositories. The evaluation performance of the models revealed that

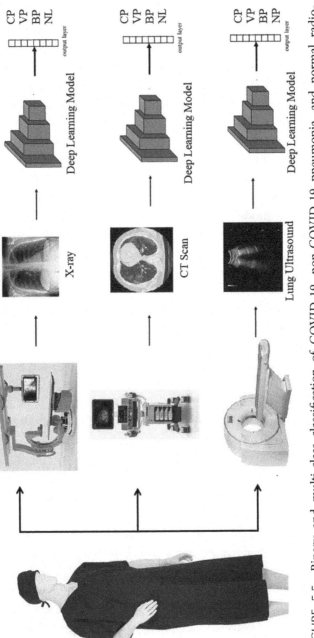

FIGURE 5.5 Binary and multi-class classification of COVID-19, non-COVID-19 pneumonia, and normal radio-graphic images

ResNet-50 designed with SVM and linear kernel function achieved the best test performance with 94.7% accuracy, 91.00% sensitivity, 98.89% specificity, 94.79% F1-score, and 0.9990 AUC value.

The study reported by Nayak et al. [57] utilized several pretrained networks, which include dAlexNet, GoogleNet, Inception-V3, MobileNet-V2, ResNet-34, ResNet-50, SqueezeNet, and VGG-16, for discrimination of COVID-19 disease from non-COVID-19 X-ray images. The dataset used for the study was acquired from the GitHub repository uploaded by Cohen et al. [45], which contained 203 COVID-19 frontal X-ray images and 500 normal X-ray images from Wang et al. [51] (Chest-Xray8). Multiple offline data augmentation (through scaling, Gaussian noise, flipping, and rotation) was conducted to increase the number of datasets and subsequently partitioned into 70:30 for training and testing, respectively. Among all the models evaluated, ResNet-34 attained the highest performance accuracy of 98.33%.

The use of a hybrid model based on incorporation of a deep belief and convolutional deep belief network (termed COVID-DeepNet system) for screening COVID-19 from chest X-ray images was proposed by Al-Waisy et al. [58]. The study utilized a dataset obtained from different sources such as Cohen et al. [45] on GitHub, Kaggle, Radiopaedia, etc. to create a large-scale dataset termed COVID19-vs.-normal which contained 24,000 chest X-ray images. In order to eliminate the noise and enhance the contrast, the images are processed using Butterworm bandpass filter and Contrast-Limited Adaptive Histogram Equalization (CLACHE). The CXR images were augmented and split into training, validation, and testing. The model performance metrics yield 99.93% accuracy, 99.90 sensitivity, 100% specificity, 100% precision, and 99.93% F1-score.

The development of a deep TL model that is faster than the RT-PCR method has been proposed by Panwar et al. [59]. The research utilized both X-ray images obtained from COVID-chest X-rays, uploaded by Cohen et al. [45], chest X-ray images (pneumonia) uploaded by Kermany et al. [50], and SARS-COV-2 CT-scans uploaded by Soares et al. [49]. The evaluation of the model showed accurate detection of COVID-19, non-COVID-19 (negative COVID-19 but positive for other pulmonary diseases), and normal cases into multiple binary classification. For two-way discrimination of COVID-19 (206 CXR images vs normal; 364 CXR images), the model achieves 88.47% overall accuracy, 76.19% sensitivity, and 97.22% specificity. For binary classification of COVID-19 vs non-COVID-19 pneumonia from CXR images, the model achieves 96.55% overall accuracy, 96.55% sensitivity, and 95.29% specificity. The uniqueness of this technique is the capacity of the model to accelerate detection within 2 seconds.

Waheed et al. [60] developed a model known as CovidGAN developed based on the Auxiliary Classifier Generative Adversarial Network that can generate synthetic chest X-ray images and VGG-16. The study utilized 1124 CXR images (403 COVID-19 and 721 normal images) acquired from three repositories (COVID-19 radiography datasets, IEEE Covid Chest X-ray by Cohen et al. [45] and Chest X-ray datasets initiative). The datasets are split into training (932 CXR images of which 601 are normal and 331 COVID-19) and testing (192 CXR images which include 120 normal and 72 COVID-19). The result has shown that the model achieves 85% accuracy, 69% sensitivity, and 95% specificity for classification of the normal dataset and 95% accuracy, 90% sensitivity, and 97% specificity after incorporation of synthetic CXR images. The summary of binary classification is shown in Table 5.3.

TABLE 5.3 Binary

| References | Model(s) | Type of Dataset | Repository | Results |
|---|---|---|---|---|
| [54] | AlexNet, DenseNet, GoogleNet, InceptionV3, InceptionResNetV2, ResNet18, ResNet50, ResNet-101, VGG16, VGG19 and XceptionNet | X-ray | [45] and other repositories | ResNet101 performed better with 97.18% accuracy |
| [55] | VGG-19 | X-ray | [45] and [51] | 96.3% accuracy |
| [56] | VGG-16, VGG-19, ResNet-18, ResNet-50 and ResNet-101 | X-ray | GitHub and Kaggle repository | ResNet-50+SVM+ linear kernel with 94.7% accuracy |
| [57] | AlexNet, GoogleNet, Inception-V3, MobileNet-V2, ResNet-34, ResNet-50, SqueezeNet and VGG-16 | X-ray | [45] and [51] | ResNet-34 attained the highest performance accuracy of 98.33% |
| [58] | COVID-DeepNet | X-ray | [45] Kaggle, Radiopaedia | 99.93% accuracy |
| [59] | Pretrained models | X-ray | [45], [49] and [50] | 96.55% overall accuracy |
| [60] | CovidGAN | X-ray | [45], [50], and COVID-19 radiography datasets | 85% accuracy |

## 5.5.2 Ternary Classification

The combination of two techniques based on fuzzy colour technique and deep learning models (SqueezeNet and MobileNetV2) for detection of COVID-19 was proposed by Togacar, Ergen, and Comet [61]. The study utilized three classes of datasets which include 76 COVID-19 cases (acquired from GitHub website uploaded by Cohen et al. [45] which contain MERS, SARS-CoV-1, SARS-CoV-2, and non-Coronavirus pneumonia cases). The second COVID-19 dataset was obtained from the Kaggle website (created by researchers from Bangladesh, Malaysia, Pakistan, and Qatar Universities which contains 219 X-ray images). The second dataset contained 98 pneumonia (non-COVID-19 viral and bacterial) and 65 normal X-ray images obtained from 53 patients. Prior to training, the images undergo pre-processing steps based on a fuzzy colour reconstruction technique and stacking. The collection of the three datasets were partitioned into 70:30 for training and testing, respectively. The datasets trained using the two models designed with SVM as a classifier resulted in 97.06% accuracy using SqueezeNet and 97.06% accuracy using MobileNetV2 Model. The uniqueness or the innovative aspect of this study is based on the notion that MobileNetV2 model can be incorporated into portable smart devices.

The study conducted by Zhao et al. [62] utilized a modified version of the pretrained ResNet-V2 model (where group normalization was replaced with batch normalization and weight standardization for all the convolutional layers) to classify COVID-19 as a novel coronavirus pneumonia (NCP), normal pneumonia (NP), and normal cases or controls (NC) from CT scan images. The study utilized COVIDx CT-2A datasets which contain over 190,000 CT scan images obtained from close to 4000 patients. The modified networks based on Random, Bit-S, and Bit-M achieved 97.9%, 98.8%, and 99.2% accuracy, respectively. The study also reported higher sensitivities and specificities of the models against normal, novel coronavirus pneumonia, and normal pneumonia.

The binary and ternary discrimination of COVID-19, non-COVID-19 pneumonia, and normal lung ultrasound imagery was proposed by Diaz-Escobar et al. [63]. Unlike most of the current state-of-the-art studies which utilize either X-ray or CT scans, this study utilized 3326 lung ultrasound frames of a COVID-19, non-COVID-19 pneumonia, and healthy dataset which is publicly accessible on POCUS. In order to discriminate these classes, the research utilized several pretrained DL models which include ResNet-50, Xception Inception V3, and VGGNet19. The models were evaluated based on per-class classification metrics (which include F1-score, precision, and recall) and overall metrics (which include AUC, accuracy, and balanced accuracy). Among all the pretrained models, inception V3 accomplished the highest result with 89.1% accuracy, 89.3% balanced accuracy, and 97.1% AUC-ROC for ternary classification.

Ko et al. [64] reported the use of a 2D deep learning model for classification of COVID-19 pneumonia from CT scan images. The model named Fast-Track COVID-19 Classification Network (FCONet) developed using either one of the pretrained networks (inception-V3, ResNet-59, VGG-16, and Xception) was trained and evaluated using a total of 3993 CT images of COVID-19, non-COVID-19 pneumonia, and normal CT scan images acquired from Chonnam National University, Wonkwang University Hospital, and the Italian Society of Medical and Interventional Radiology public database. The outcome of the model's performances has shown that FCONet-ResNet-50 achieved the best performance with 99.87% accuracy, 99.58% sensitivity, and 100% specificity.

The use of the ensemble CNN model (DenseNet, Inception-V3, InceptionResNet-V2, and Xception) for detection of COVID-19, non-COVID-19 pneumonia, and normal chest X-ray images was proposed by Bhardwaj and Kaur [65]. The model was trained and evaluated using 2161 COVID-19 X-ray images, 2022 non-COVID-19 X-ray images, and 5863 normal X-ray images obtained from Kaggle and other online repositories. Cross-validation of 5k folds was used for evaluating the efficiency of the model. The result of the model performance has shown that the ensembled network achieved 98.33% accuracy for two-way classification and 92.36% for three-way classification.

Aminu et al. [66] developed a model known as COVIDNet for the binary and ternary discrimination of COVID-19 pneumonia, non-COVID-19 pneumonia, and normal X-ray images. The peculiarity of this model compared to other pretrained models is that it required a smaller number of parameters using greyscale images directly instead of RGB that causes inefficiencies when fine-tuning the models on COVID-19 X-ray images which are mostly greyscale images. The research utilized two different datasets which included X-ray and CT scan images acquired from a public repository which included a total of 1226 X-ray images (321 COVID-19, 500 non-COVID-19, and 445 normal), while the study utilized a CT scan dataset made available by Soares et al. [49] which contained 2482 CT scans (1252 COVID-19 and 1230 non-COVID-19). The performance evaluation of the model based on five splits resulted in 95.81% average accuracy, 88.09% average sensitivity, 98.41% average specificity, and 91.90% average F1-score for ternary classification and 99.87% average accuracy, 100% sensitivity, 99.78% specificity, and 99.84% F1-score for binary classification.

The use of two pretrained DL models which included ResNet-50 and ResNet-101 for multi-class classification of COVID-19 pneumonia, non-COVID-19 pneumonia, and normal X-ray images was conducted by Jain et al. [67]. The research utilized a dataset curated from two repositories, namely that of Cohen et al. [45] (shared on GitHub) which contained 250 COVID-19 cases and the Kaggle website which contained non-COVID-19 pneumonia (350 viral and 300 bacterial) and 315 normal chest X-ray images totalling 1215 images. Image augmentation was carried out based on rotation and Gaussian blurring increasing the dataset to 1832. The two models were trained and evaluated based on a mean of 5-k fold cross-validation which resulted in 99.77% average accuracy, 97.14% for average recall, and 97.14% for average precision for ResNet-50 and 98.93% averaged accuracy, 98.93 averaged recall, and 98.66% average precision for ResNet-101.

Luz et al. [47] utilized the EfficientNet model for three-way classification of COVID-19, non-COVID-19 pneumonia, and normal X-ray images. The study utilized 13,569 X-ray images (183 COVID-19, 8614 non-COVID-19 pneumonia, and 8066 normal cases acquired from Cohen et al. [45] (on GitHub) and RSNA pneumonia detection challenge dataset). The images undergo a pre-processing step based on simple intensity normalization to adjust the images' pixel size between the range of 0 and 1 and augmentation to increase the datasets based on rotation (clockwise and anti-clockwise), zooming, and flipping. The result of the model performance based on hierarchical classification has shown that the model achieved 93.9% accuracy, 97.8% COVID-19, sensitivity and 100% positivity prediction with more than 30 times computational efficiency.

Discrimination of COVID-19 using a DL model from CT scan images was proposed by Javadi-Moghaddam and Gholamalinejad [68]. The uniqueness of this study is the use of a deep learning network. The study utilized dataset acquired from two hospitals which included two from Union Hospital and one from Liyuan Hospital. The datasets are categorized into three areas: (1) 5795 non-informative CT scan images (without king parenchyma); (2) 4001 positive CT scan images with features related to COVID-19 pneumonia; and (3) negative CT scan images. In order to optimize the performance of the COVID-19 diagnosis and convergence time, the model pooling and Squeeze Excitation Block layer employed Mish function and batch normalization. The performance evaluation of the model result in 99.03 accuracy, 98.71 average precession, and 98.91 average recall.

The use of a pretrained AlexNet Model for binary, ternary, and quaternary classification of X-ray images of COVID-19, viral, bacterial, and healthy images was proposed by Ibrahim et al. [53]. The study made used of 153 COVID-19 images obtained from GitHub titled "Covid-19-chestxray-datasets" and 219 X-ray images acquired from Kaggle (Covid-19-radiography-database). The study also utilized 1341 normal X-ray images, 1345 non-COVID-19 viral pneumonia, and 1341 normal, non-COVID-19 viral pneumonia, 4274 bacterial pneumonias from Kaggle, and 5856 (non-COVID-19 pneumonia and normal X-ray images made available by [50]). The evaluation performance of the model has shown that for the ternary classification, the model achieved 94.00% accuracy, 91.30% sensitivity, and 84.78% and for the quaternary classification, the model achieved an accuracy of 93.42%, sensitivity of 89.18%, and specificity of 98.92%.

The study proposed by Hussain et al. [69] developed "CoroDet", a CNN model for discrimination of COVID-19 cases from both CT scan and X-ray images. Unlike many researchers that reported the use of DL for binary classification, this study conducted three-way and four-way classifications of different pneumonia cases which include COVID-19, non-COVID-19 (viral and bacterial), and normal images. The datasets utilized were obtained from eight repositories, including Chestxray-dataset by Cohen et al. [45], COVID-CT, Covid-Chestxray-dataset, etc., leading to 3108 normal images, 2843 COVID-19 images, and 1439 non-COVID-19 images. The performance evaluation has shown that the model achieved 99.1% accuracy for binary classification, 94.2% for ternary classification, and 91.2% for quaternary classification.

The application of prune DL model ensembles for multi-class discrimination of pneumonia caused by SARS-CoV-2, non-COVID-19 pneumonia, and normal cases using X-ray images was proposed by Rajaraman et al. [70]. The study utilized custom CNN and pretrained networks such as DenseNet-20, Inception-V3, Inception-ResNet-V2, MobileNet, NashNet-mobile, VGG-16, VGG-19, and Xception using publicly available datasets which included paediatric chest X-ray images, RSNA chest X-ray dataset, Montreal Covid-19 dataset, and Twitter Covid-19 dataset. The performance metrics showed that the inception-V3 model achieved the best perform-ance with 99.01% accuracy and 0.9972 AUC.

Sakib et al. [71] applied a DL-based radiograph classification (DL-CRC) for binary and three-way classification of COVID-19, non-COVID-19 pneumonia, and normal cases using X-ray images. The uniqueness of this study was the generation of a synthetic COVID-19 dataset from four public domains through the use of data augmentation of radiograph images (DARI) algorithms using generative adversarial network (GAN) and generic data augmentation. The model was trained using both actual and synthetic images and evaluated based on augmentation and without augmentation. The result shows that the model achieved 93.94% accuracy with augmentation and 54.55% without augmentation. Based on indi-vidual performance, the CNN model (DL-CRC) achieved 95.91% accuracy for normal cases, 88.52% for non-COVID-19 pneumonia, and 93.94% for COVID-19 pneumonia.

The use of optimized VGGNet-19 and other networks (DenseNet121, Inception V3, InceptionResNet V2, NASNetLarge, ResNet-50 V3, and Xception) for the discrimination of OVIDd-19 from X-rays, CT scans, and ultrasound images was proposed by Horry et al. [72]. The study utilized a dataset obtained from different sources such as COVID-19 Chest X-ray uploaded by Cohen et al. [45], Chest X-ray dataset by Wang et al. [51], COVID-CT scan dataset by Yang et al. [73], and PROCOVID-Net dataset which contains ultrasound images uploaded by Born et al. [74]. Datasets were trained on the basis of binary and three-way classification. The model performance resulted in 84% precision for CT scans, 86% for X-rays, and 100% for ultrasound for the discrimination of COVID-19 against pneu-monia or normal cases. Another important input of this research was the implementation of a pre-processing pipeline in order to decrease undesir-able signal noise and increase quality.

In order to offer an inclusive and comprehensive system for the monitoring and detection of disease by integrating fog and cloud com-puting, wireless body area network, and clinical decision support system, El-Rashidy et al. [74] developed an end-to-end model which not only aided in the detection of COVID-19 but also tracked patients using wearable sensors and the use of cloud and fog computing for data storage and trans-mission. The study utilized X-ray images acquired from GitHub uploaded by Cohen et al. [45] and El-Rashidy et al. [75]. The model achieved 97.95% accuracy and 98.85% specificity. The summary of the multi-class classifica-tion is shown in Table 5.4.

TABLE 5.4  Multi-Class Classification of COVID-19 and Non-COVID-19 Radiographic Images

| References | Model | Type of Dataset | Repository | Result |
|---|---|---|---|---|
| [61] | SqueezeNet and MobileNetV2 | X-ray | Cohen et al., 2020 (GitHub) and Kaggle | 97.06% accuracy using SqueezeNet and 97.06% accuracy using MobileNetV2 Model |
| [62] | pretrained ResNet-V2 (for Bit-S and for Bit-M) | CT scans | COVIDx CT-2A datasets | 97.9%, 98.8% for Bit-S, and 99.2% accuracy for Bit-M |
| [63] | Pretrained ResNet-50, Xception Inception V3, and VGGNet19 | Lung ultrasound | Accessible on POCUS | 89.1% accuracy, 89.3% balanced accuracy and 97.1% AUC-ROC for ternary classification using inception V3 |
| [64] | Fast-Track COVID-19 Classification Network (FCONet) | X-ray | Collection | FCONet-ResNet-50 achieved the best performance with 99.87% accuracy, 99.58% sensitivity, and 100% specificity |
| [65] | DenseNet, Inception-V3, InceptionResNet-V2 and Xception | X-ray | Kaggle and other online repositories | 98.33% accuracy for binary classification and 92.36% for multi-class classification |
| [66] | COVIDNet | X-ray and CT | X-ray from online repository and CT scan dataset made available by [49] | 95.81% average accuracy |
| [67] | ResNet-50 and ResNet-101 | X-ray | [45] and Kaggle website | 98.93% averaged accuracy for ResNet-101 |
| [47] | EfficientNet | X-ray | Cohen et al.; 2020 and RSNA pneumonia detection challenge dataset | 93.9% accuracy |

| Ref | Model | Image type | Dataset | Results |
|---|---|---|---|---|
| [68] | Proposed CNN | CT scans | Union hospital and Liyuan hospital | 99.03 accuracy |
| [53] | Pretrained AlexNet | X-ray | Kaggle, GitHub, and [50] | 94.00% accuracy for ternary classification, 93.42% for quaternary classification |
| [69] | Proposed CoroDet CNN | CT and X-ray images | 8 online repositories | 99.1% accuracy |
| [70] | DenseNet-20, Inception-V3, Inception-ResNet-V2, MobileNet, NashNet-mobile, VGG-16, VGG-19 and Xception | X-ray | Paediatric chest X-ray images, RSNA chest X-ray dataset, Montreal COVID-19 dataset, and Twitter COVID-19 dataset | 99.01% accuracy and 0.9972 AUC |
| [71] | CNN model (DL-CRC) | X-ray | 4 online repositories | 93.94% accuracy with augmentation and 54.55% without augmentation |
| [72] | DenseNet121, Inception V3, InceptionResNet V2, NASNetLarge, ResNet-50 V3 and Xception | X-ray | [45], [51], [73], and [74] | 84% precision for CT-scan, 86% for X-ray and 100% |
| [75] | Proposed CNN | X-ray | [45] and [76] | 97.95% accuracy |

## 5.6 CONCLUDING REMARKS

### 5.6.1 Conclusions

The detection and treatment of COVID-19 continue to be an issue due to the continuous identification of new variants. The pandemic cause by SARS-CoV-2 continues to pose serious issues to the global healthcare system. Currently, the virus has infected over half a billion people, with millions of deaths globally. Healthcare experts rely on the application of the RT-PCR method for diagnosis of COVID-19 disease, which revolves around the use of nasal swab samples and amplification using a PCR machine. Even though this approach is regarded as the gold standard technique, it is hindered by many challenges, such as high cost, irritation in terms of sample collection, time consuming and processing time, and false-positive results.

In an attempt to address the challenges posed by the RT-PCR approach, scientists have turned to a radiographic imaging technique based on chest X-ray, lung ultrasound, and CT scan images. These methods have becoming confirmatory tests or an alternative, especially in healthcare settings with limited molecular kits. The interpretation of radiographic images can be very tedious for radiologists, especially in this pandemic. The approach can also be very harmful due to the use of ionizing radiation.

In order to address these challenges, medical experts in collaboration with biomedical engineers and computer scientists have developed deep learning models which serve as computer-aided detection methods of COVID-19 from normal cases and non-COVID-19 cases using various radiographic datasets. Several models, especially pretrained networks, reported in the literature have shown high accuracy, sensitivity, specificity, recall, and precession in the case of discriminating between COVID-19 and non-COVID-19 pneumonia and normal radiographic images.

A systematic review on the application of DL models for the classification of pneumonia cause by COVID-19 and non-COVID-19 viral and bacterial strains from radiographic images such as chest X-ray, CT scans, and lung ultrasound are presented in this study. We first provided an overview on the significance of the review by addressing challenges posed by molecular diagnosis and limitations of radiographic images. An overview of deep learning, TL, and evaluation metrics was presented. Previous coronavirus epidemics and the current pandemic were discussed. The use and mechanism of radiographic images and various public online datasets are provided. The review of so many articles based on the application of DL to addressed the global pandemic has shown the significance of the machine learning system for aiding in the diagnosis of clinical images.

### 5.6.2 Open Research Issues

Scientists all over the world continue to develop or enhance previous approaches by using hybrid models, ensemble models, augmentation, and optimization techniques to help in accurate screening of COVID-19. Consequently, one of the areas that is unsaturated is the application of the Internet of Things (IoT) or Internet of Medical Things (IoMT) using sensors and monitors to collect, process, and store data related to COVID-19 diseases. Few researches in the literature have attempted to merge IoMT, cloud computing, and edge computing with clinical detection of COVID-19. Nevertheless, few researches have demonstrated how images acquired from mobile phones can be uploaded to an online platform or mobile or computer application for classification of radiographic images into positive and negative cases. Moreover, medical experts continue to discover new variants as a result of mutations. Molecular approaches such as DNA-based biosensors have shown precision in discriminating between different strains and variants of pathogens. Currently, computer-aided detection has shown efficiency in discriminating between COVID-19, non-COVID-19 viral pneumonia and bacterial pneumonia. Future studies could explore the use of deep learning models to discriminate between different variants of COVID-19 from radiographic images.

## REFERENCES

1. Long C, Xu H, Shen Q, Zhang X, Fan B, Wang C, Zeng B, Li Z, Li X, Li H. Diagnosis of the Coronavirus disease (COVID-19): rRT-PCR or CT?. European Journal of Radiology 2020; doi: 10.1016/j.ejrad.2020.108961

2. World Health Organization. Coronavirus disease (COVID-19) Pandemic. 2022A. www.who.int/emergencies/diseases/novel-coronavirus-2019. Accessed on 22 Jan 2022.

3. Tahamtan A, Ardebili A. Real-time RT-PCR in COVID-19 detection: issues affecting the results. Expert review of molecular diagnostics 2020; doi: 10.1080/14737159.2020.1757437

4. Yang W, Yan F. Patients with RT-PCR-confirmed COVID-19 and normal chest CT. Radiology 2020; doi: 10.1148/radiol.2020200702

5. Fang Y, Zhang H, Xie J, Lin M, Ying L, Pang P, Ji W. Sensitivity of chest CT for COVID-19: comparison to RT-PCR. Radiology 2020; doi: 10.1148/radiol.2020200432

6. Jaiswal AK, Tiwari P, Kumar S, Gupta D, Khanna A, Rodrigues JJ. Identifying pneumonia in chest X-rays: a deep learning approach. Measurement 2019; doi: 10.1016/j.measurement.2019.05.076

7. Ni Q, Sun ZY, Qi L, Chen W, Yang Y, Wang L, Zhang X, Yang L, Fang Y, Xing Z, Zhou Z. A deep learning approach to characterize 2019 coronavirus disease (COVID-19) pneumonia in chest CT images. European Radiology 2020; doi: 10.1007/s00330-020-07044-9

8. Umar Ibrahim A, Ozsoz M, Serte S, Al-Turjman F, Habeeb Kolapo S. Convolutional neural network for diagnosis of viral pneumonia and COVID-19 alike diseases. Expert Systems 2021; doi: 10.1111/exsy.12705

9. Voulodimos A, Doulamis N, Doulamis A, Protopapadakis E. Deep learning for computer vision: A brief review. Computational Intelligence and Neuroscience 2018; doi: 10.1155/2018/7068349

10. Guo Y, Liu Y, Oerlemans A, Lao S, Wu S, Lew MS. Deep learning for visual understanding: A review. Neurocomputing 2016; doi: 10.1016/j.neucom.2015.09.116

11. Alloghani M, Al-Jumeily D, Mustafina J, Hussain A, Aljaaf AJ. A systematic review on supervised and unsupervised machine learning algorithms for data science. Supervised and unsupervised learning for data science, 2020; doi: 10.1007/978-3-030-22475-2_1

12. Tammina S. Transfer learning using VGG-16 with deep convolutional neural network for classifying images. International Journal of Scientific and Research Publications (IJSRP) 2019; doi: 10.29322/IJSRP.9.10.2019.p9420

13. Li H, Parikh NA, He L. A novel transfer learning approach to enhance deep neural network classification of brain functional connectomes. Frontiers in Neuroscience 2018; doi: 10.3389/fnins.2018.00491

14. Wang J, Zhu H, Wang SH, Zhang YD. A review of deep learning on medical image analysis. Mobile Networks and Applications 2021; doi: 10.1007/s11036-020-01672-7

15. Alom MZ, Taha TM, Yakopcic C, Westberg S, Sidike P, Nasrin MS, Van Esesn BC, Awwal AA, Asari VK. The history began from alexnet: A comprehensive survey on deep learning approaches. arXiv preprint arXiv:1803.01164, 2018.

16. Krizhevsky A, Sutskever I, Hinton GE. Imagenet classification with deep convolutional neural networks. Advances in Neural Information Processing Systems 2012; 25.

17. Han X, Zhong Y, Cao L, Zhang L. Pre-trained alexnet architecture with pyramid pooling and supervision for high spatial resolution remote sensing image scene classification. Remote Sensing 2017; doi: 10.3390/rs9080848

18. Simonyan K, Zisserman A. Very deep convolutional networks for large-scale image recognition. arXiv preprint arXiv:1409.1556, 2014.

19. Jaderberg M, Simonyan K, Vedaldi A, Zisserman A. Reading text in the wild with convolutional neural networks. International Journal of Computer Vision 2016; doi: 10.1007/s11263-015-0823-z

20. Szegedy C, Liu W, Jia Y, Sermanet P, Reed S, Anguelov D, Erhan D, Vanhoucke V, Rabinovich A. Going deeper with convolutions. In: Proceedings of the IEEE Conference on Computer Vision and Pattern Recognition 2015.

21. Kim JH, Seo SY, Song CG, Kim KS. Assessment of electrocardiogram rhythms by GoogLeNet deep neural network architecture. Journal of Healthcare Engineering 2019; doi: 10.1155/2019/2826901

22. Targ S, Almeida D, Lyman K. Resnet in resnet: Generalizing residual architectures. arXiv preprint arXiv:1603.08029, 2016.

23. Shin HC, Roth HR, Gao M, Lu L, Xu Z, Nogues I, Yao J, Mollura D, Summers RM. Deep convolutional neural networks for computer-aided detection: CNN architectures, dataset characteristics and transfer learning. IEEE Transactions on Medical Imaging 2016; doi: 10.1109/TMI.2016.2528162

24. Shao L, Cai Z, Liu L, Lu K. Performance evaluation of deep feature learning for RGB-D image/video classification. Information Sciences 2017; doi: 10.1016/j.ins.2017.01.013

25. Li Q, Yang Y, Guo Y, Li W, Liu Y, Liu H, Kang Y. Performance evaluation of deep learning classification network for image features. IEEE Access, 2021. doi: 10.1109/ACCESS.2020.3048956

26. Huang J, Zhang L, Liu X, Wei Y, Liu C, Lian X, Huang Z, Chou J, Liu X, Li X, Yang K. Global prediction system for COVID-19 pandemic. Science Bulletin 2020; doi: 10.1016/j.scib.2020.08.002

27. Chowell G, Mizumoto K. The COVID-19 pandemic in the USA: what might we expect?. The Lancet 2020; doi: 10.1016/S0140-6736(20)30743-1

28. Zhai P, Ding Y, Wu X, Long J, Zhong Y, Li Y. The epidemiology, diagnosis and treatment of COVID-19. International Journal of Antimicrobial Agents 2020; doi: 10.1016/j.ijantimicag.2020.105955

29. Sun J, He WT, Wang L, Lai A, Ji X, Zhai X, Li G, Suchard MA, Tian J, Zhou J, Veit M. COVID-19: epidemiology, evolution, and cross-disciplinary perspectives. Trends in Molecular Medicine 2020; doi: 10.1016/j.molmed.2020.02.008

30. Pannu J, Barry M. Global health security as it pertains to Zika, Ebola, and COVID-19. Current Opinion in Infectious Diseases 2021; doi: 10.1097/QCO.0000000000000775

31. Chen X, Chughtai AA, Dyda A, MacIntyre CR. Comparative epidemiology of Middle East respiratory syndrome coronavirus (MERS-CoV) in Saudi Arabia and South Korea. Emerging Microbes & Infections 2017; doi: https://doi.org/10.1038/emi.2017.40.

32. Centre for Disease Prevention and Control. Middle East Respiratory Syndrome (MERS). 2022. www.cdc.gov/CORONAVIRUS/MERS/INDEX.HTML. Accessed on 15 Jan 2022.

33. World Health Organization. Middle East respiratory syndrome coronavirus (MERS-CoV) – United Arab Emirates. 2022B. www.who.int/emergencies/disease-outbreak-news/item/middle-east-respiratory-syndrome-coronavirus-(mers-cov)-united-arab-emirates. Accessed on 23 Jan 2022.

34. Keogh-Brown MR, Smith RD. The economic impact of SARS: how does the reality match the predictions?. Health Policy 2008; doi: 10.1016/j.healthpol.2008.03.003

35. World Health Organization. Severe Acute Respiratory Syndrome (SARS). 2022C. www.who.int/health-topics/severe-acute-respiratory-syndrome#tab=tab_1. Accessed on 25 Jan 2022.

36. Dramé M, Teguo MT, Proye E, Hequet F, Hentzien M, Kanagaratnam L, Godaert L. Should RT-PCR be considered a gold standard in the diagnosis of Covid-19? Journal of Medical Virology 2020; doi: 10.1002/jmv.25996

37. Raoof S, Feigin D, Sung A, Raoof S, Irugulpati L, Rosenow III EC. Interpretation of plain chest roentgenogram. Chest 2012 Feb; doi: 10.1378/chest.10-1302

38. Çallı E, Sogancioglu E, van Ginneken B, van Leeuwen KG, Murphy K. Deep learning for chest X-ray analysis: A survey. Medical Image Analysis 2021; doi: 10.1016/j.media.2021.102125

39. Franquet T. Imaging of pneumonia: trends and algorithms. European Respiratory Journal 2001; doi: 10.1183/09031936.01.00213501

40. Biagi C, Pierantoni L, Baldazzi M, Greco L, Dormi A, Dondi A, Faldella G, Lanari M. Lung ultrasound for the diagnosis of pneumonia in children with acute bronchiolitis. BMC Pulmonary Medicine 2018; doi: 10.1186/s12890-018-0750-1

41. Riccabona M. Ultrasound of the chest in children (mediastinum excluded). European Radiology 2008; doi: 10.1007/s00330-007-0754-3

42. Bourcier JE, Paquet J, Seinger M, Gallard E, Redonnet JP, Cheddadi F, Garnier D, Bourgeois JM, Geeraerts T. Performance comparison of lung ultrasound and chest x-ray for the diagnosis of pneumonia in the ED. The American Journal of Emergency Medicine 2014; doi: 10.1016/j.ajem.2013.10.003

43. Alzahrani SA, Al-Salamah MA, Al-Madani WH, Elbarbary MA. Systematic review and meta-analysis for the use of ultrasound versus radiology in

diagnosing of pneumonia. Critical Ultrasound Journal 2017; doi: 10.1186/s13089-017-0059-y

44. Berce V, Tomazin M, Gorenjak M, Berce T, Lovrenčič B. The usefulness of lung ultrasound for the aetiological diagnosis of community-acquired pneumonia in children. Scientific Reports 2019; doi: 10.1038/s41598-019-54499-y

45. Cohen JP, Morrison P, Dao L, Roth K, Duong TQ, Ghassemi M. Covid-19 image data collection: Prospective predictions are the future. arXiv preprint arXiv:2006.11988. 2020. https://github.com/ieee8023/covid-chestxray-dataset. Accessed on 7 Nov 2021.

46. Wang LL, Lo K, Chandrasekhar Y, Reas R, Yang J, Eide D, Funk K, Kinney R, Liu Z, Merrill W, Mooney P. Cord-19: The covid-19 open research dataset. ArXiv 2020.

47. Luz E, Silva P, Silva R, Silva L, Guimarães J, Miozzo G, Moreira G, Menotti D. Towards an effective and efficient deep learning model for COVID-19 patterns detection in X-ray images. Research on Biomedical Engineering 2021; doi: 10.1007/s42600-021-00151-6

48. Ebadi A, Xi P, MacLean A, Tremblay S, Kohli S, Wong A. COVIDx-US--An open-access benchmark dataset of ultrasound imaging data for AI-driven COVID-19 analytics. arXiv preprint arXiv:2103.10003. 2021.

49. Soares E, Angelov P, Biaso S, Froes, M H, Abe D. SARS-CoV-2 CT-scan dataset: A large dataset of real patients CT scans for SARS-CoV-2 identification. medRxiv 2020; doi: 10.1101/2020.04.24.20078584

50. Kermany DS, Goldbaum M, Cai W, Valentim CC, Liang H, Baxter SL, McKeown A, Yang G, Wu X, Yan F, Dong J. Identifying medical diagnoses and treatable diseases by image-based deep learning. Cell. 2018; doi: 10.1016/j.cell.2018.02.010

51. Wang X, Peng Y, Lu L, Lu Z, Bagheri M, Summers RM. Chestx-ray8: Hospital-scale chest x-ray database and benchmarks on weakly-supervised classification and localization of common thorax diseases. In: Proceedings of the IEEE Conference on Computer Vision and Pattern Recognition 2017; doi: 10.1109/TMI.2014.2350539

52. Singh SP, Wang L, Gupta S, Goli H, Padmanabhan P, Gulyás B. 3D deep learning on medical images: a review. Sensors 2020; doi: 10.3390/s20185097

53. Ibrahim AU, Ozsoz M, Serte S, Al-Turjman F, Yakoi PS. Pneumonia classification using deep learning from chest X-ray images during COVID-19. Cognitive Computation 2021; doi: 10.1007/s12559-020-09787-5

54. Dhiman, G., Chang, V., Kant Singh, K., & Shankar, A. (2021). Adopt: automatic deep learning and optimization-based approach for detection of novel coronavirus covid-19 disease using x-ray images. Journal of Biomolecular Structure and Dynamics 1–13. doi: 10.1080/07391102.2021.1875049

55. Vaid S, Kalantar R, Bhandari M. Deep learning COVID-19 detection bias: accuracy through artificial intelligence. International Orthopaedics 2020; doi: 10.1007/s00264-020-04609-7

56. Ismael AM, Şengür A. Deep learning approaches for COVID-19 detection based on chest X-ray images. Expert Systems with Applications 2021; doi: 10.1016/j.eswa.2020.114054

57. Nayak SR, Nayak DR, Sinha U, Arora V, Pachori RB. Application of deep learning techniques for detection of COVID-19 cases using chest X-ray images: A comprehensive study. Biomedical Signal Processing and Control 2021; doi: 10.1016/j.bspc.2020.102365

58. Al-Waisy AS, Al-Fahdawi S, Mohammed MA, Abdulkareem KH, Mostafa SA, Maashi MS, Arif M, Garcia-Zapirain B. COVID-CheXNet: hybrid deep learning framework for identifying COVID-19 virus in chest X-rays images. Soft Computing 2020; doi: 10.1007/s00500-020-05424-3

59. Nayak SR, Nayak DR, Sinha U, Arora V, Pachori RB. Application of deep learning techniques for detection of COVID-19 cases using chest X-ray images: A comprehensive study. Biomedical Signal Processing and Control 2021; doi: 10.1016/j.chaos.2020.110190

60. Waheed A, Goyal M, Gupta D, Khanna A, Al-Turjman F, Pinheiro PR. Covidgan: data augmentation using auxiliary classifier Gan for improved covid-19 detection. IEEE Access 2020; doi: 10.1109/ACCESS.2020.2994762

61. Toğaçar M, Ergen B, Cömert Z. COVID-19 detection using deep learning models to exploit Social Mimic Optimization and structured chest X-ray images using fuzzy color and stacking approaches. Computers in Biology and Medicine 2020; doi: 10.1016/j.compbiomed.2020.103805

62. Zhao W, Jiang W, Qiu X. Deep learning for COVID-19 detection based on CT images. Scientific Reports 2021; doi: 10.1038/s41598-021-93832-2

63. Diaz-Escobar J, Ordóñez-Guillén NE, Villarreal-Reyes S, Galaviz-Mosqueda A, Kober V, Rivera-Rodriguez R, Lozano Rizk JE. Deep-learning based detection of COVID-19 using lung ultrasound imagery. Plos One 2021; doi: 10.1371/journal.pone.0255886

64. Ko H, Chung H, Kang WS, Kim KW, Shin Y, Kang SJ, Lee JH, Kim YJ, Kim NY, Jung H, Lee J. COVID-19 pneumonia diagnosis using a simple 2D deep learning framework with a single chest CT image: model development and validation. Journal of Medical Internet Research 2020; doi: 10.2196/19569

65. Bhardwaj P, Kaur A. A novel and efficient deep learning approach for COVID-19 detection using X-ray imaging modality. International Journal of Imaging Systems and Technology 2021; doi: 10.1002/ima.22627

66. Aminu M, Ahmad NA, Noor MH. Covid-19 detection via deep neural network and occlusion sensitivity maps. Alexandria Engineering Journal 2021; doi: 10.1016/j.aej.2021.03.052

67. Jain G, Mittal D, Thakur D, Mittal MK. A deep learning approach to detect Covid-19 coronavirus with X-Ray images. Biocybernetics and Biomedical Engineering 2020; doi: 10.1016/j.bbe.2020.08.008

68. Ahsan M, Based M, Haider J, Kowalski M. COVID-19 detection from chest X-ray images using feature fusion and deep learning. Sensors 2021; doi: 10.1016/j.bspc.2021.102987

69. Hussain E, Hasan M, Rahman MA, Lee I, Tamanna T, Parvez MZ. CoroDet: A deep learning based classification for COVID-19 detection using chest X-ray images. Chaos, Solitons & Fractals 2021; doi: 10.1016/j.chaos.2020.110495

70. Rajaraman S, Siegelman J, Alderson PO, Folio LS, Folio LR, Antani SK. Iteratively pruned deep learning ensembles for COVID-19 detection in chest X-rays. IEEE Access 2020; doi: 10.1109/ACCESS.2020.3003810

71. Sakib S, Tazrin T, Fouda MM, Fadlullah ZM, Guizani M. DL-CRC: deep learning-based chest radiograph classification for COVID-19 detection: a novel approach. IEEE Access 2020; doi: 10.1109/ACCESS.2020.3025010

72. Horry MJ, Chakraborty S, Paul M, Ulhaq A, Pradhan B, Saha M, Shukla N. COVID-19 detection through transfer learning using multimodal imaging data. IEEE Access 2020; doi: 10.1109/ACCESS.2020.3016780

73. Yang X, He X, Zhao J, Zhang Y, Zhang S, Xie P. COVID-CT-dataset: a CT scan dataset about COVID-19. arXiv preprint arXiv:2003.13865; 2020.

74. Born J, Brändle G, Cossio M, Disdier M, Goulet J, Roulin J, Wiedemann N. POCOVID-Net: automatic detection of COVID-19 from a new lung ultrasound imaging dataset (POCUS). arXiv preprint arXiv:2004.12084; 2020.

75. El-Rashidy N, El-Sappagh S, Islam SM, El-Bakry HM, Abdelrazek S. End-to-end deep learning framework for coronavirus (COVID-19) detection and monitoring. Electronics 2020; doi: 10.3390/electronics9091439

76. Altun A, Erdogan O. A chest x-ray image: total opacification of the hemithorax. Cardiology in Review 2003; doi: 10.1097/01.crd.0000089526.05199.04

# Industry 4.0 Challenges and Applications in the Healthcare Industry with Emerging Technologies

Meenu Gupta, Rakesh Kumar, and Madhu Bala

*Chandigarh University, Mohali, Punjab, India*

## CONTENTS

| | | |
|---|---|---|
| 6.1 | Introduction | 104 |
| 6.2 | Literature Review | 105 |
| 6.3 | Self-Determination Medicine: A Healthcare Model That Could Be Delivered by 5G Wireless Technology | 107 |
| 6.4 | IoT and Big Data: A Revolution in the Biomedical Industry | 109 |
| | 6.4.1 IoT and Big Data Technology for Personalized Medicine | 110 |
| | 6.4.2 IoT and Big Data Technology for Next-Generation Healthcare | 111 |
| 6.5 | Role of Artificial Intelligence in Healthcare | 112 |
| | 6.5.1 Virtual Nurses for Monitoring Patients | 114 |
| | 6.5.2 Development of Precision Medicine | 115 |
| | 6.5.3 Digital Consultation Chatbots | 117 |
| 6.6 | Data Mining: A New Hope in the Healthcare System | 117 |
| | 6.6.1 Intelligent Heart Disease Prediction System | 118 |
| | 6.6.2 Diagnosis and Prognosis of Cancer Disease | 119 |

DOI: 10.1201/9781003322887-6

6.6.3     Customer Relationship Management (CRM)
Systems     120
6.6.4     Avoidance and Early Detection of Various
Frauds in the Healthcare Industry     123
6.7    Introduction of Cyber-Physical Systems to the Healthcare
Industry     124
6.8    Opportunities and Challenges in Healthcare Systems     125
6.9    Conclusions and Future Scope     127
References     128

## 6.1 INTRODUCTION

With the growth of the world's population, as well as growing demands for successful treatment in healthcare with Industry 4.0, the growing pressure on healthcare is piling up. Therefore, healthcare continues to be one of the world's most critical social and economic problems in the search for modern and more innovative science and technology solutions. In terms of both involvement and economy, healthcare has drawn considerable public and personal interest and fostered unparalleled levels of investment. As the founding technologies advance, healthcare progresses, thus the term's precise characterization has undergone revolutionary adjustments and requirements, the most recent ones involving the healthcare Industry 4.0 paradigm. Healthcare Industry 4.0 and the recent historical phase that has originated globally really aren't limited to the production processes of manufacturing but can be extended to many fields, such as the IoT, big data, data mining, biomedical, cyber-physical systems, artificial intelligence, self-determination medicine, 5G, healthcare industry, and personalized medicine. Healthcare Industry 4.0 has comprehensive applications in the medical field for the development of improved implants, methods, and devices. This revolution offers an enhanced way to use data, services, and manufacturing to improve quality of life. It thus presents new manufacturing possibilities and strengthens the scope of innovation through use of the IoT. Industry 4.0 strengthens the smart manufacturing infrastructure that helps boost efforts in the manufacturing, medical, and health fields. It involves digitalization, IoT, internal wired networks, processing robots, switches, sensors, actuators, PLC systems, data formats, and cryptography for many crucial components. It uses artificial intelligence to virtually exchange information in hospitals and allows for maximum operational visibility, offering a greater understanding of performance, product, content, usage, production, assets, and visibility of consumer needs, helping industries save a lot of time and money and satisfying customers. It provides a strong collaboration between the seller and the manufacturer. The industrial Internet has extreme power in the medical and related fields to meet different requirements. It utilizes artificial intelligence in which human intelligence-like systems and other technologies are coded. It generates an extremely intelligent scalable method of development. Inside the healthcare industry, Industry 4.0 creates a specific product with the aid of different applications and advanced machining technology as needed by the patient. Industry 4.0 connects both manufacturers and consumers, in which the project is sent directly to the software, enabling the conversion of information into components. Complex personalized goods and parts are easily generated in a short period of time. Thus, it decreases production by keeping items and medical records digital. Real-time data obtained from healthcare will produce new insights and evidence to improve the understanding of health and disease patterns. This will not only enhance the welfare of people, but will also eliminate informational asymmetries while improving economies and stimulating jobs, a vital concern for the well-being and welfare of the community.

## 6.2 LITERATURE REVIEW

Aceto et al. [1] gave a study about the ICT Pillars for Healthcare 4.0, with the fundamental gathering of advancements from the supposed Fourth Industrial Revolution, specifically the IoT, cloud and fog computing, and big data investigation, zeroing in on their applications in the healthcare area. As a result, researchers discovered how this field, which had been heading towards an ICT-sponsored e-well-being, would experience a more radical transformation in the healthcare 4.0 Industry. ICTs not only offer improvements for conventional cycles and frameworks, but in cloud-based health information systems, advanced monitoring of physiological and neurotic signs, drug admission, and exercises.

Further, Celesti et al. [2] discussed the Industry 4.0 standards and discovered an extraordinary agreement and reception in various mechanical areas including healthcare.

Healthcare Industry 4.0 requires changes across industry, concessions to information possession, security, legitimate issue settling, item enlistment norms, new machine-to-machine correspondence conventions, and business/abilities advancements. Moreover, Healthcare Industry 4.0 is altering the market of health administration provisioning to patients and medical administrators. Indeed, all around the world, the quantity of ventures in data and correspondence innovation (ICT) for well-being prosperity (e-health) is quickly expanding.

Further, Valerio Persico et al. [3] discussed the large number of overviews in the scientific literature that can be discovered managing the selection of one of the recognized ICT columns in the well-being area. Even though the presence of these investigations is a mark of the interest of mainstream researchers in the points this chapter discusses, supposedly none of these investigations provides a comprehensive view of how ICTs assist healthcare. The huge selection of ICTs in healthcare is nevertheless an example of the conventional pattern towards full digitalization of human activity. Consequently, a fractional perspective on ICT applications to the well-being area misses the mark regarding providing the essential all-encompassing information.

Further, Gunasekaran Manogaran et al. [4] carried out a study into the secure industrial IoT design proposed in big data security intelligence for Healthcare Industry 4.0 to store and handle versatile sensor information (large information) for healthcare services applications. The proposed Meta Cloud-Redirection (MC-R) engineering with a huge information framework is utilized and stores the sensor information (huge amounts of information) produced from various sensor gadgets. The proposed framework utilizes key administration security instruments to ensure enormous amounts of information in Industry 4.0. In the proposed framework, sensor healthcare gadgets are fixed to the human body to gather medical indications from the patient.

Further, Kotevski et al. [5] proposed that the framework offers distant capacities that improve the level of medical assistance to the patient while allowing them to be checked in their home. This is particularly significant for patients with constant infections and those that require regular observation of important functions.

In healthcare, customization, reduced lead time, and other surgical facilities are significant issues that cannot be overcome through conventional assembling innovations. For this, we require a savvy fabricating framework that can be joined with Industry 4.0, and this is another way to meet the necessary quality requirements. Accordingly, there is a need to attempt an investigation into various innovations and capacities of Industry 4.0 in the healthcare industry. Likewise, there are critical requirements to distinguish its broad applications in the healthcare industry (Table 6.1).

TABLE 6.1    Relative Studies of Various Researchers' Views on Healthcare Industry 4.0

| Authors | Year | Description |
|---|---|---|
| Aceto et al. [1] | 2020 | Detailed review on ICT Pillars for Healthcare Industry 4.0 in Fourth Industrial Revolution and their application in the healthcare area |
| Celesti et al. [2] | 2019 | Introduced various mechanical areas including Cloud Computing, Edge Computing, Internet of Things, and Big Data Analytics Applications for Healthcare Industry 4.0 |
| Valerio Persico et al. [3] | 2018 | Discussed the role of Information, Communication Technologies, and comprehensive view of how ICTs uphold Healthcare Industry 4.0 |
| Gunasekaran Manogaran et al. [4] | 2017 | Detailed review on Cybersecurity and Big Data Security Intelligence for Healthcare Industry 4.0 |
| Kotevski A et al. [5] | 2016 | Implemented an improved E-health monitoring system in Healthcare Industry 4.0 |

## 6.3  SELF-DETERMINATION MEDICINE: A HEALTHCARE MODEL THAT COULD BE DELIVERED BY 5G WIRELESS TECHNOLOGY

The 5G implications for healthcare are worth considering. While 5G generally means high-speed Internet for most users, there are likely to be many impacts of 5G on healthcare. Healthcare will benefit immensely from secure Internet connectivity for large items and medical devices, with greater bandwidth and excellent coverage and accessibility than offered by 4G network, in addition to faster Internet. Self-determination healthcare would come into being in the 5G era, with the greater capacity of software to handle vast quantities of data. The data transfer rate, latency, coverage, power, and network energy are important features of 5G technology, with the following unique features for healthcare: high-speed data transfer rate, super-low latency, connectivity and capacity, and high bandwidth and durability per unit area (Figure 6.1). Internet access, coverage (up to 100%), and capacity to connect devices per unit would contribute to an environment focused on 5G super bandwidth per unit area, in which an "information network" will provide real-time interactivity for large medical devices and wearable devices for patients, with cloud computing-based trade-offs between speed, latency, coverage, availability, and low-power IoT service, etc. [6].

The self-assurance medical model would extraordinarily expand the independence of the patient, rather than the general doctor-focused

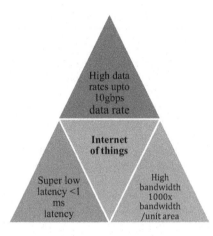

FIGURE 6.1    Basic features of 5G technology (IoT) [6]

current findings and care framework, by allowing the patient's inclusion in the whole treatment process. The safety problem is 5G, with its high speed and the capacity to transfer heavy data packets, that is supposed to transform the so-called Internet of Things radically. The Internet of Things is defined as a system of devices that can use the Internet to share details.

The applications of 5G technology in healthcare promise to deliver faster data speed as compared to other networks. 5G can be used with other developing technologies like artificial intelligence and highly distributed computing. This paradigm can be applied to the healthcare sector. There is a great need for transmission speed increases, thus it is not surprising that most people believe that 5G's core feature will be fast data transfer. In comparison to the current 4G association, 5G is expected to increase data transfer speed by many times; 5G is undoubtedly the front-line far-off framework organization progression. The significant advances brought about by 5G are, at the very least, its tremendous bandwidth and low lethargy (Figure 6.2).

5G is most likely to benefit directly from the fields of virtual reality and augmented reality, with possible contributions to intelligence healthcare as 5G networks develop. 5G is not a standalone system, as stated, but rather a mixture of cutting-edge technologies, such as big data, cloud computing, and machine intelligence [6].

From 2030 onward, 6G is a potential communication technology that will dominate the entire health business. It will dominate not only

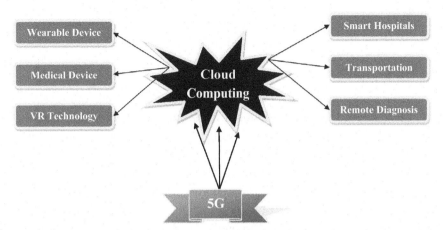

FIGURE 6.2 Schematic drawing illustrating applications of 5G technology in healthcare (virtual reality)

the health sector, but also a variety of other industries. Many industries, including healthcare, are projected to be transformed by 6G. Healthcare will be entirely AI-driven and reliant on technology. The 6G communication technology will alter our vision of the world and way of life. Currently, time and space are the most significant impediments to progress. These obstacles will be overcome via healthcare and 6G. Furthermore, 6G will be demonstrated to be a game-changing technology for healthcare. As a result, we envision healthcare in this light. For the era of 6G communication technologies, we've created a system. Moreover, various new approaches must be introduced to improve our way of life. Quality of life is one of the issues addressed in this perspective.

## 6.4 IOT AND BIG DATA: A REVOLUTION IN THE BIOMEDICAL INDUSTRY

Huge amounts of information are produced, prepared, and investigated by different public and private area enterprises to upgrade their work and processes. Different huge information sources in the medical services area include emergency clinic reports, patient clinical records, clinical test results, and applications that are essential for the Internet of Things. A critical segment of big data identified with public medical services is likewise delivered by biomedical examinations. This is the reason why medical care suppliers should be outfitted with adequate assets to regularly create and assess large amounts of information to enable important techniques to be developed to improve general well-being. By opening new avenues for present-day medical services, fruitful administration, examination, and comprehension of enormous information will change the game [7].

In the region of medical services, the IoT has become a developing system. IoT gadgets produce a persistent stream of information when following a patient's well-being, making these gadgets a critical supporter of medical services with enormous amounts of information. Continuously, we should deal with the information inflow from IoT apparatuses and investigate it constantly. Partners in the medical care area endeavour to reduce expenses and improve the nature of therapy by examination to information both at the location and remotely. The quality and cost of medical care can be improved by applying IoT innovations to medical care frameworks [7,8].

## 6.4.1 IoT and Big Data Technology for Personalized Medicine

This innovation has expanded in new ways, and a great deal of information has an impact on how pharmaceuticals are tested and utilized by helping to create more fruitful preliminary studies. Due to delays in developing persistent pools, difficulties locating pools with the appropriate hereditary cosmetics, the need to extend the length of preliminary studies to find drugs that will be effective for larger, more diverse areas of the population, the cost and duration of developing prescriptions that expand, pharmaceutical companies strive to make more successful medication preliminary studies. Unparalleled developments in the mechanized collection of vastly varied sub-atomic and clinical data provide great challenges in the inspection and interpretation of all data, necessitating the development of novel diagnostic techniques to address the situation.

It will be necessary to build incredible structures for the successful use of biomedical big data in personalized medicine. This will require significant logical and innovative advancements in areas like innovation, design, venture, and budgetary management [8]. Utilizing the IoT and vast amounts of data to carry out medication to exploratory therapies and examination will likely result in lower costs, enable quicker recommending of the correct medication, and improve results at lower costs. The medical and healthcare industry is working to change how preliminary therapy information is organized and communicated. The application of vast amounts of information specific to the field of medicine has led to the discovery of organic indicators and fundamental advances in the study of cancer, among other unusual issues like neurodegeneration, diabetes, and cardio-vascular diseases [8,9].

### 6.4.2 IoT and Big Data Technology for Next-Generation Healthcare

The Internet of Things (IoT) is a physical object reference, with access to the network used for data collection and sharing. "Thing" relates to software that is connected to the Internet and passes information about the system to other applications. The Internet's IPv6 is one of the most significant IoT connectivities, as billions of computers can be added to the IPv4 Internet to ensure successful contact between the devices. Using special representing mechanisms, objects communicate with each other to arrive at a shared target. Most protocols have been designed to allow the operation of IoT devices in all the layers of the ISO stack. Low Power and Lossy Networks Routing Protocol for Constrained Application Protocol messaging protocols are more knowledgeable. These protocols are for energy-saving purposes with low computing and memory requirements in mind. As shown in Figure 6.3, the security layer places an emphasis on protecting objects, communications, and software. The embedded security layer

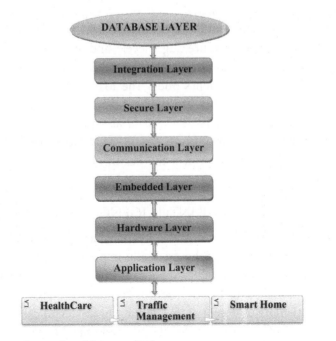

FIGURE 6.3   Layered architecture [11]

TABLE 6.2    Main Benefits and Challenges from the Adoption of Industry 4.0 Pillars in Healthcare

| Benefits | Challenges |
|---|---|
| **IoT:** | • Energy imperatives |
| • Upgraded electro medical gadgets (shut circle plan, prescient upkeep, new helplines) [12] | • Security |
| • Interoperability, evolvability on account of open correspondence standards [13] | • Versatility |
| **Big Data:** | • Foundation accessibility |
| • New experiences and significant data from new information sources [14] | • Outrageous heterogeneity |
| • Regular change of expressive investigation into prescient and prescriptive one [15] | • Murkiness of examination |

focuses on the creation of security features for embedded objects, such as wearable, controllers, and sensors products. The security layer of communication is used to secure the transferring of data between items. The security layer of the database focuses on data security and safeguarding of remote databases or cloud links for servers. Layer applications are deployed and secured in this with the help of various tools for web protection [10]. Wireless Mobile with the IoT plays an integral role in the daily routine to check a person's health status. Therefore, several experts are currently using the IoT in the application of healthcare, which involves continuous tracking of pulse, blood pressure, sugar levels, and body temperature of the human body. IoT devices are normally connected to continuously monitor the health status of the patient's body. The IoT devices sense the health status of the patients and then the medical data are passed to physicians and other healthcare workers. These data are most widely used for the diagnosis of diseases and healthcare. Useful information derived from the clinical database is used to protect the health of patients in emergencies (Table 6.2) [10,11].

## 6.5 ROLE OF ARTIFICIAL INTELLIGENCE IN HEALTHCARE

In healthcare, the sophistication and increase in data research have revealed that artificial intelligence can be gradually implemented in the industry. Several forms of artificial intelligence are now being used by revenues and health professionals, and health sciences businesses. Diagnosis and care decisions, patient involvement, implementation, and technical work are the main categories of applications. While there are many instances in which artificial intelligence can manage healthcare tasks well and even better than people, for a substantial period, development considerations may prohibit the large-scale automation of technical healthcare positions. In society and companies, artificial intelligence and related innovations are extremely pervasive and are beginning to be applied to healthcare. These innovations can change many areas of patient care including with the suppliers, providers, and pharmacy companies, as well as administrative processes. There seem to be several kinds of research indicating that in healthcare activities, such as diagnosis and treatment of illnesses, artificial intelligence can play a vital role. However, for a variety of reasons, it is agreed that for large medical process domains, it will be several years before artificial intelligence replaces humans. We explain both the opportunities that artificial intelligence provides to optimize aspects of treatment in this chapter and some of the challenges to the rapid adoption of artificial intelligence in healthcare. Here are several fields that are primed and prepared to extract advantages from AI, as shown in Figure 6.4.

**Patient health record management:** With tons of data, along with the collection of patients' medical details, we are in an era of data explosion. To analyse these data, to solve health issues, and to make intelligent, accurate, and quicker decisions, industries use analytics. On-going advice and guidance for diagnosis and care as well as administrative information are provided by artificial intelligence tools and virtual assistants, enabling physicians to concentrate their attention on the very important elements of contact with patient physicians.

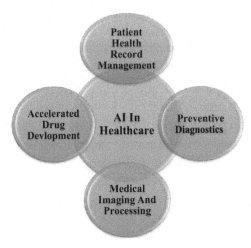

FIGURE 6.4    Areas of healthcare [16]

**Medical imaging and processing:** Medical imaging is being modified by artificial intelligence. Specifically, with the ever-growing power of deep learning technology, its image recognition power to interpret and apply data obtained from radiology images in unique medical cases is proving to be very beneficial for the medical imaging industry. By recognizing patterns, artificial intelligence algorithms read medical images, with accuracy comparable to that of radiologists. To identify what natural anatomy looks like on CT scans, magnetic resonance imaging, ultrasound, or nuclear imaging, artificial intelligence systems are trained using large numbers of tests.

**Accelerated drug development and clinical trials:** Clinical trials involve a long process that often takes more than a decade for pharma companies to develop through medical studies and costing millions and millions of dollars. The use of artificial intelligence and machine learning to discover drugs helps minimize time and expenses and is very beneficial for pharma companies. Medical imaging has the Atom Net framework for structure-based drug design and discovery, which is the first deep learning neural network of its kind. In one of its successful good news stories, medical imaging found a drug candidate that could dramatically decrease the infection rate of influenza.

**Preventive diagnostics using predictive analytics:** These techniques use laboratory results, previous medical records, and demographic and behavioural data in statistical analytics to classify health threats and problems. To better predict the occurrence of episodes for people with epilepsy, researchers are now applying machine learning technology. Remote outpatient heart rate monitoring and associated forecasts can also alert patients to the onset of a heart attack, and care can be given before chronic symptoms become a medical emergency [16,17].

## 6.5.1 Virtual Nurses for Monitoring Patients

From engaging with patients and leading patients to the most appropriate place for treatment, virtual nurses can be used. They can respond to any questions, track patients, as well as provide fast answers because virtual nurses are available around the clock. To avoid re-hospitalizations or unwanted doctor visits, most technologies of virtual nursing assistants today allow for more regular contact between patients and healthcare providers between hospital visits. Surely, in this new virtual staging area, there is a massive learning curve. However, historically, nurses have been the first adopters of innovative technology, and access to these resources has not only increased patient care but is also improving the nurses' operating area.

**Broadening flexibility for nurses**: In the healthcare industry, nurses also have to be technically minded, with the bulk of their job behind a desktop computer and largely focused on the individual's perception. However, the new virtual nurse also has greater insight and expertise in the medical skill set of neurosciences, internal medicine, emergency medicine, etc. For doctors, virtual nurses are used as a resource, which means they can get all sorts of health queries that need rapid analysis and responses. Not unexpectedly, all virtual nurses begin with at least five years of serious patient care. However, the study of a virtual nurse proceeds for a longer time.

**Serving all doctors as a valuable resource**: A nurse can be available for many patients, but he or she must be concentrated solely on an individual patient when dealing with them. With a virtual care system, nurses may feel assured that a virtual nurse may attend to them quickly or contact another nurse who is available to help provide treatment if they're dealing with one patient for an examination and another patient requires help. Nursing staff now have access to medical care at the touch of a button as well.

**Growing career period in healthcare for virtual nurses**: Nursing is a profession that is physically hard. Imagine handling 500 patients with a few hundred additional pieces of monitoring equipment required for transportation for 350 beds. These physical requirements are getting more complicated over time. Healthcare offers the chance for nurses to broaden their careers. Nurses can now expand their skills into the later years of their career.

The idea of virtual nursing is still new, and will involve adjustment by both staff and patients. While more and more patients are becoming aware of the importance of healthcare, these services are beginning to be implemented by hospitals across the world, requiring more trained nurses to operate them. Healthcare is rising and this is going to be a catalyst for healthcare systems. However, for nurses, it reflects the fact that thousands of patients obtain the treatment they required and are alive today because of virtual nurses [18].

### 6.5.2 Development of Precision Medicine

The objective of precision medicine is to utilize a massive amount of collected data from the human brain and additional research. This enables healthcare to be modified and digital medical records to be integrated on an independent and broader scale. In addition to typical clinical symptoms, decisions and procedures are adapted to the patient based on their intrinsic biology. Based on a broader biochemical understanding of issues and effective validation of medical physiological properties, the development of target-specific prescription medications has made great progress in improving the treatment response to different diseases (Table 6.3) [19].

TABLE 6.3 More Examples of Precision Medicine Applications across Medicine [20]

| Field | Disease | Examples of PM Use |
|---|---|---|
| Oncology | • Lung cancer | • Epidermal growth factor receptor (EGFR) and anaplastic lymphoma kinase (ALK) are the two most prominent mutations leading to replace chemotherapy with tyrosine kinase inhibitors |
| | • Melanoma | • BRAF mutations testing |
| | • Hairy cell leukaemia | • BRAF mutations testing |
| | • Breast cancer | • ER/PR/HER2 mutations testing Oncotype: TAILORx trial showed that over 50% of women with the most common form of breast cancer do not need chemotherapy |
| Immunotherapy | • Checkpoint inhibitors | • PD1/PDL1 expression affects the response to checkpoint inhibitors such as nivolumab, pembrolizumab, and ipilimumab, among others Mutations burden load correlates with response to checkpoint inhibitors T-cell infiltrates correlate with outcome in solid tumours receiving checkpoint inhibitors FDA-approved pembrolizumab in patients with microsatellite instability (MSI)-high or mismatch repair (MMR)-deficient solid tumours, as a first across tumour types Microbiome impacts +++ Response to checkpoint inhibitors |
| Cardiovascular | • Clopridogel • Statins | • CYP2C19 polymorphisms affect metabolism of antiplatelet agent clopidogrel impacting antiplatelet treatment recommendations for prevention and treatment of stroke and infarcts • Multiple polymorphisms impact the efficacy or toxicity profile of statins |
| Neurology | • Alzheimer's/ dementia | • Neurology Alzheimer's/dementia Major genetic risk factor for Alzheimer's in individuals with a specific copy of the APOE gene |

### 6.5.3 Digital Consultation Chatbots

Chatbots are applications intended to advance and start discussions with a client with AI strategies, including normal language handling to give constant advice to patients. Without truly knowing, numerous people speak with chatbots on their gadget's day in day out. Chatbots are changing the way we live, from getting up to speed with sports news to exploring bank applications. Medical care experts, including clinical aides, are presently beginning to use these AI-empowered instruments. We see a medical care chatbot in real life when a patient starts up a discussion with a clinical agent who may sound human, yet underneath is a clever conversational machine [21].

## 6.6 DATA MINING: A NEW HOPE IN THE HEALTHCARE SYSTEM

Data mining is a non-negligible processing of implicit, formerly inherent, unidentified, and possible knowledge about data that is useful. In brief, it is a method of evaluating and collecting information about data from various viewpoints. The information found can be used for various purposes, such as in the healthcare industry. The healthcare industry now produces vast volumes of patient knowledge, disease diagnosis, etc. Data mining offers a variety of methods for finding hidden data patterns. The quality of service is a big problem facing the healthcare industry. Service quality means correctly diagnosing illnesses and delivering a successful diagnosis. Poor diagnosis may contribute to tragic outcomes that are unacceptable.

Data mining isn't new, it has been rigorously used for consumer credit, banking firms, detection and fraud, advertisers, targeted marketing and known security vulnerabilities, marketing strategies, and by retailers for quality management and quality control. Data mining is becoming important in healthcare. Therefore, many areas have promoted the use of data mining software in healthcare. The occurrence of fraud and misuse of medical insurance, for instance, has resulted in several healthcare insurers trying to significantly decrease their losses by using software for data mining to help them identify and monitor offenders.

Another reason is that it is too complicated and voluminous for the vast quantities of data produced by healthcare transactions to be processed and analysed by conventional methods. By finding patterns and trends in large volumes of complex data, data mining will enhance decision-making. Such evaluation has become increasingly relevant as the need for the healthcare industry to make decisions based on medical and financial data collection has been enhanced by financial pressures. Insights gained from data mining, while maintaining a high level of service, can affect expense, revenue, and operational performance [22].

### 6.6.1 Intelligent Heart Disease Prediction System

The heart is an essential part of the human body. It's nothing more than a pump, which moves blood through the body. If blood flow in the body is inefficient in organs such as the brain, and if the heart stops functioning completely, death happens within minutes. The word heart attack refers to a disease of the heart and blood vessel system within it. Several factors have been shown to increase the risk of heart disease (Figure 6.5) [23].

For the diagnosis of heart disease, parameters like those in Figure 6.5 are used. In certain cases, the diagnosis is based on the patient's current test results and doctor's experience. The diagnosis, therefore, is a complex task that needs a great deal of experience and high capacity.

An Intelligent Heart Disease Prediction System (IHDPS) has been developed by using naive Bayes, neural network, and decision trees. To get accurate results, each procedure has its effect. Building these hidden patterns of the system and relationships between them, data mining techniques are used [24].

The issue of recognizing restricted connections and prediction rules for heart disease was studied by Carlos Ordonez. The resulting dataset includes the records of heart disease in patients. Some constraints were introduced

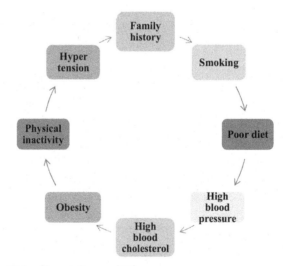

FIGURE 6.5    Risk of heart disease [23]

to decrease the number of patterns. Attributes must appear on one side of the rule only. The characteristics are divided into classes. There should be a small number of attributes [24,25].

Hospitals generally handle patient records using healthcare information systems. These systems contain a large amount of data, used to extract personal information to create a smart medical diagnosis. The Intelligent Heart Disease Predictive System uses a historical heart database to diagnose heart disease [26].

## 6.6.2 Diagnosis and Prognosis of Cancer Disease

Lately, huge advances have been made in treating cancers and other diseases because of rapid gains on various fronts. Presently, trial drugs can be planned and focused on various tissues in the body, or to explicit cancers. Changes or movements in cell digestion or sub-cell structure that occur in diseases, transformations, or cancer-causing events are routinely evaluated. The fast advancement in fundamental science and applied medical exploration for diagnosis of cancer disease is illustrated in Table 6.4.

TABLE 6.4  Novel Biochemical Markers for the *ex vivo* Monitoring of Cell Death [27]

| Biochemical Marker | Disease or Pathology |
| --- | --- |
| Cytochrome c | Cancer therapy<br>• Detected in serum and plasma<br>• Accompanies cancer treatment in vivo<br>• May show in vivo tumour cell turnover and tumour mass |
| Cytochrome c | Epstein–Barr infection disease<br>• Detected in serum<br>• Virus-caused haemophagocytic lymphohistiocytosis<br>• Correlates with Epstein–Barr infection load |
| Cytochrome c | Liver illness<br>• Detected in serum and plasma<br>• Strongly associates with clinical indications of fulminant liver harm<br>• Correlates with the seriousness of hepatic trance state<br>  Harm: serum hepatocyte development factor, aspartate aminotransferase (AST), lactic dehydrogenase (LDH), and soluble phosphatase (ALP)<br>• Negatively associates with serum alpha-fetoprotein (AFP) and absolute plasma bilirubin levels |
| Cytochrome c | Neuronal harm<br>• Detected in cerebrospinal liquid<br>• Detected in extracellular space upon staurosporine- instigated neuronal cell demise, may intervene onlooker |

### 6.6.3 Customer Relationship Management (CRM) Systems

The customer relationship management (CRM) is a creative innovation that tries to improve consumer loyalty, dependability, and benefit by gaining, creating, and maintaining successful client connections, and also collaborations with partners [28]. Various investigations into CRM have gained huge ground in a few areas, for example, media communications, banking, and assembling, yet research explicit to the healthcare area is extremely restricted. Different information bases have been utilized to direct a far-reaching search of studies that analyse CRM in the healthcare climate (including clinics, facilities, and nursing homes). Our outcomes have revealed that a huge hole exists in the information on utilizing CRM in the healthcare area.

Considering Tables 6.5 and 6.6, most of the studies concerning the three fundamental classifications of CRM (e-CRM, implementing, and adopting CRMs) were able to deliver positive results for patients, clinical experts, and healthcare associations. Tables 6.5 and 6.6 give brief outlines of each CRM classification. These include brief description, types of evidence, settings, and findings for information assortment. there are also plus (+) and minus (−) symbols in the findings column which show the positive and negative results of each examination.

Figure 6.6 presents a structure for sorting CRM research in the healthcare services climate, starting with social online CRM (eCRM). This also recommends that healthcare ought to deal with all types of correspondence and associations with their patients through Web 2.0 and web-based media advances. In line with this, Kohli et al. investigated a web-based CRM application called PPS, discovering positive outcomes in a few areas, for example, the doctor healthcare relationship, medical tasks, persistent fulfilment, and also healthcare results (particularly in nourishment and nervous system science). The effects of this investigation depended on the doctor contextual analyses, and experimental information from a cost/advantage investigation and execution. It would have been more productive if patients were associated with the contextual investigation, to realize whether executing these processes has an immediate impact as well as a having relationship with patients.

Anshari et al. suggested a CRM 2.0 model to determine the needs for e-healthcare systems. This study also found a positive result for patients, with over 70% of patients wishing to check their electronic healthcare records on the web. Only one study offered a framework for establishing social CRM [43,44].

TABLE 6.5   e-CRM Studies in Healthcare

| Brief Description | Types of Evidence | Settings | Findings |
|---|---|---|---|
| Investigated e-CRM through PPS, and performed a cost- benefit examination on the quality and execution of PPS [29] | Contextual investigation | Hospital | (+) Physician–emergency clinic relationships, clinical activiti es, and patient fulfilment were improved fundamentally<br>(+) Better clinical results found in nourishment, nervous system science, and muscular health |
| Proposed e-CRM model to decide patients' desires for e-wellbeing administrations [30] | Overview | Hospital and homecare focus | (+) 80% wanted to make arrangements, instalments, and view well-being advancements on the web<br>(+) 75% wanted to see/control EMR and examine ailments in informal organizations |
| Built-up a structure and recognized the key variables for e-CRM usage [31] | Overview | Clinic centre and hospital | (+) Resistance to distinguishing e-CRM, backing, and inclusion from top administration, business objectives, IT framework, and worker preparing was discovered to be the key components |
| Proposed a structure for e-CRM selection [32] | Calculated structure | Hospital | (+) The proposed structure depended on TOE, dissemination of innovation, and institutional hypotheses<br>(+) Technological factors, for example, intricacy and relatively favourable position; authoritative factors (size and the executives uphold); and ecological variables (administrative and outside weight) are discovered to be essential for e-CRM selection |
| Proposed a system for e-CRM execution [33] | Calculated structure | Hospital | (+) The proposed structure depended on TOE, dispersion of innovation, and IS achievement speculations<br>(+) Technological factors, for example, similarity, intuitiveness, and security; hierarchical factors (the executives uphold, web-based media strategy, and initiative information) and natural variables (social trust and fleeting trend pressure) are discovered to be critical for e-CRM usage |

TABLE 6.6  Implementing CRMS in Healthcare

| Brief Description | Types of Evidence | Settings | Findings |
|---|---|---|---|
| Assessed CRM execution and adjusted a CRM scale dependent on four measurements of CRM: (i) key client centre, (ii) CRM association, (iii) innovation-based CRM, and (iv) KM [34] | Overview (post mail) | Hospital-based nursing home | (+) Hospital-based nursing homes are inclined toward getting tolerant needs and conveying brief clinical administrations through informal learning <br><br> (+) Private nursing homes zeroed in on CRM association and technology-based CRM for building connections |
| Presented a CRM usage model that comprises seven parts: customer fulfilment, dependability, trust, desires, observations, seen quality, and architecture [35] | Overview | Hospital | (+) All seven parts were discovered critical and have a relationship with one another |
| Planned a CRM usage model dependent on HR factors, for example, worker fulfilment, hierarchical culture, correspondence the board, strengthening, hierarchical responsibility, and hierarchical structure and change the executives [36] | Overview | University hospital | (+) HRM assumes an urgent part in the execution of CRM. <br><br> (+) All of the explored factors have impacted the execution of CRM <br><br> (+) Employee fulfilment had the most noteworthy impact <br><br> (−) The organizational mission had the most reduced impact |
| Dissected the elements that impact the usage of CRM based on programming perspectives [37] | Overview | Hospital | (+) Operational productivity, centralization of information, the executives of existing clients, and clinic picture were found to affect the execution of CRM |

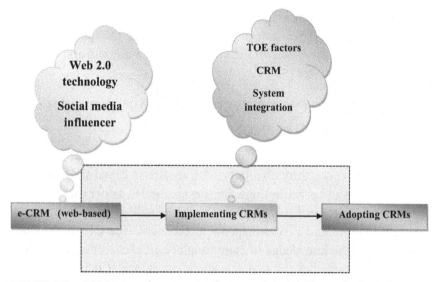

FIGURE 6.6    CRM research categories framework in healthcare [45]

### 6.6.4 Avoidance and Early Detection of Various Frauds in the Healthcare Industry

The United States spent more than $1 trillion in the healthcare industry. The extent of annual healthcare costs lost to fraud and misuse remains unknown because such instances are not methodically counted. Since 1992, when healthcare change became an issue of public discussion, the issue of fraud control has gained much consideration. For instance, healthcare fraud remains the main concern of the U.S. Division of Justice, with criminal proceedings in 1997 being triple those in 1992 [46]. The Federal Bureau of Investigation (FBI) has uniquely expanded the number of specialists appointed to its healthcare fraud unit [47].

The numerous occasions of healthcare fraud indicate that current control frameworks don't work how we envision they should. Frequently, the way fraud is uncovered is more down to luck than procedures. In one case, a drug specialist from California had been charging Medicaid for unrealistically high volumes of professionally prescribed medications. In another case, Medicaid paid for more than 142 lab tests and 85 remedies in 18 days [48]; every one of these exchanges was found to be fraudulent, yet none was discovered by routine observing or identification endeavours. Therefore, notwithstanding the degree of political, authoritative, and regulatory consideration paid to the fraud issue in the last a few years, upsetting and astonishing omissions in control continue [49–51].

Fraud control – in any area – is a hopeless business. The inability to identify fraud is terrible news, as is uncovering extortion. The following seven criteria help to illustrate why fraud control is such a difficult and complex test in any environment [51].

## 6.7 INTRODUCTION OF CYBER-PHYSICAL SYSTEMS TO THE HEALTHCARE INDUSTRY

CPS is a formula that joins the real cycles of PC enterprises with the cyber world. The real cycles through input circles are also screened and controlled by inserted PCs and organizations. Sensors are used to gather various information types from verifiable sources. The digital world is then informed of this information, and it is managed and reviewed. The CPS is designed to coordinate the knowledge in commonplace articles/administrations to carry out fundamental tasks. A few social assistance structures that are built on data innovation can greatly benefit from the CPS idea. This might very well be used in social administrations, especially in applications for clinical and medical care. It holds the key to determining the system's management capacity and registering advancements to provide the MCPS with a sufficient foundation. These developments monitor a person's health and alert the appropriate medical professionals to provide the best care with the correct administration in emergency situations [52,53].

Large-scale financial problems arise as a result of CPS errors, which affect the functioning of the comparison system. The versatility, aptitude, adaptability, usability, strength, security, and well-being of CPSs will be engaged, giving an unanticipated framework in comparison to the simplest established frameworks. In tele-medication, for instance, the end clients, i.e., doctors and patients, are joined through the web (Figure 6.7).

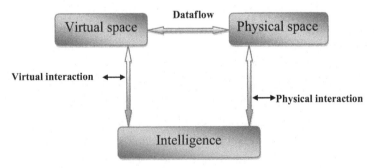

FIGURE 6.7   Interactions in the CPS system [54]

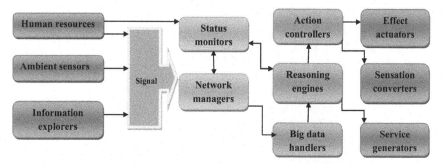

FIGURE 6.8    The cyber-physical systems standard architecture [55]

Understanding the actual communication channels, i.e., the actual sensor contributions, as well as the external cycle channels, such as human administrators' reactions to the system, where the MCPS, clinical sensors, and gadgets are integrated, is essential. High-certainty CPS and MCPS take into account the looming framework issue for security and protection. For instance, when more connected clinical devices and sensors are used on Internet of Things frameworks in collaboration with the real world and people, the requirements for security, constancy, protection, and well-being at MCPS grow significantly. In a CPS, clients may be both aware of current events and in the circle, which makes these frameworks useful. The IoT collects data from connected things that exchange information to provide a foundation for common figuring circumstances in the future. As seen in Figure 6.8, the CPS concept is thus shown via the Internet of Things (IoT).

## 6.8  OPPORTUNITIES AND CHALLENGES IN HEALTHCARE SYSTEMS

Although there has been a significant improvement in healthcare administrations in India post-independence, there remains far to go before India can give reasonable and opportune health opportunities to all of its citizens. Alongside the financial developments over the last couple of years, there has likewise been a flood of infections affecting the health of the Indian population. Although the numbers of individuals living in destitution has decreased, there has been an increase in transmittable and non-transferable infections and lifestyle illnesses. The following are the challenges and opportunities for healthcare as shown in Figure 6.9 [56]:

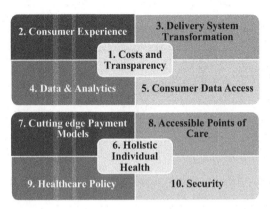

FIGURE 6.9    Challenges and opportunities for healthcare

1. Costs and Transparency: Implementing techniques and strategies to address the development of clinical and drug costs and effects on access to and the nature of care.

2. Consumer Experience: In order for health to seamlessly integrate into each person's, family's, and community's everyday activities, it is important to recognize, address, and ensure that all consumer interactions and outcomes are simple, practical, timely, streamlined, and coherent.

3. Delivery System Transformation: Using partnerships and collaborations between healthcare and community-based organizations, operationalizing and scaling coordination and delivery system transformation of medical and non-medical services can help overcome obstacles like social health factors and produce better results.

4. Data and Analytics: Utilize cutting-edge analytics and new sources of fractious, non-standard, unorganized, widely varying data (history, laboratories, Rx, devices, m-Health, IoT, social-economic, geographic, genomic, demographic, and lifestyle behaviour patterns) to support the transition from volume to value and enhance the efficiency of individuals, providers, and payers.

5. Consumer Data Access: Combining and expanding the transmission of membership, supplier, patient, and provider data and procedures to effectively distribute the value of aggregated information and systems, i.e. related to EHRs, HIEs, commercial, administrative, and clinical data, etc.) to all stakeholders equally.

6. Holistic Individual Health – Identifying, tending to, and improving the part/patient's general clinical, way of life/conduct, financial, social, monetary, instructive, geographic, and ecological prosperity for a frictionless and associated medical care insight.

7. Cutting Edge Payment Models: Developing and incorporating specialized and operational foundations and projects for a more cooperative and fair way to deal with overseeing costs, sharing danger, and upgraded quality results in the progress from volume to esteem.

8. Accessible Points of Care: Telehealth, mHealth, wearables, computerized gadgets, retail centres, locally situated considerations, micro-hospitals; and acknowledgment of these and different activities drawing care nearer to the home and office.

9. Healthcare Policy: Dealing with repeals/supplants/changes to current medical care strategies, guidelines, political vulnerability/opposition, and absence of a trained administrative cycle. Government medical care for all, single-payer, Medicare/Medicaid purchase in, block awards, unexpected expenses, supplier indexes, affiliation well-being plans, and momentary approaches, FHIR norms, and different commands.

10. Security: Staying ahead of network safety dangers for the protection of purchaser and other medical care data to improve client trust in sharing information. Remaining current with the changing scene of government and state protection laws [56,57].

## 6.9  CONCLUSIONS AND FUTURE SCOPE

The healthcare industry may gain a significant amount of leeway from this new upheaval. It uses cutting-edge manufacturing techniques to produce high-quality medical equipment and components that meet the needs of every patient. Providing patients with a well-monitored framework can help with expanding overall performance in the healthcare industry. It embraces mass customization successfully to fulfil the necessary conditions. With the help of several advanced manufacturing companies, this change improves the climate by reducing resources and labour. It provides the patient with a proper diagnostic process through the use of additional material production, sensors, big data, robotics, AI, vast information, and IoT devices. Industry 4.0 will open the way for future developments that make use of integrated innovative planning, manufacturing, and services. It will play a crucial role in completing the prerequisite of healthcare during inventive work. Industry 4.0 allows the manufacturing of more innovative medical devices with less expense and time.

## REFERENCES

1. Aceto, G., Persico, V. and Pescapé, A. 2020. Industry 4.0 and health: Internet of things, big data, and cloud computing for healthcare 4.0. Journal of Industrial Information Integration, 18, p.100129.
2. Celesti, Antonio, Oliver Amft, and Massimo Villari. 2019. Guest Editorial Special Section on Cloud Computing, Edge Computing, Internet of Things, and Big Data Analytics Applications for Healthcare Industry 4.0. IEEE Transactions on Industrial Informatics 15.1, pp.454–456.
3. Aceto, G., Persico, V. and Pescapé, A. 2018. The role of Information and Communication Technologies in healthcare: taxonomies, perspectives, and challenges. Journal of Network and Computer Applications, 107, pp.125–154.
4. Manogaran G, Thota C, Lopez D, Sundarasekar R. 2017. Big Data Security Intelligence for Healthcare Industry 4.0. In: Cybersecurity for Industry 4.0, 715, p.103e126
5. Kotevski A, Koceska N, Koceski S. 2016. E-health monitoring system. In: International Conference on Applied Internet and Information Technologies. https:// doi.org/10.20544/AIIT2016.32.
6. Dong Li. 2019. 5G, and intelligence medicine—how the next generation of wireless technology will reconstruct healthcare?, Precision Clinical Medicine, 2(4), pp.205–208.
7. Waterson, James. 2015. Big data and the internet of medical things a revolution in communication and information. Arab Health Quarterly.
8. Jagadeeswari, V., Subramaniyaswamy, V., Logesh, R. and Vijayakumar, V. 2018. A study on medical Internet of Things and Big Data in personalized healthcare system. Health information science and systems, 6(1), p.14.
9. Cirillo, Davide & Valencia, Alfonso. 2019. Big data analytics for personalized medicine. Current Opinion in Biotechnology. 58. 161–167.
10. Bhatt, Chintan, Nilanjan Dey, and Amira S. Ashour, eds. 2017. Internet of things and big data technologies for next generation healthcare, pp.978–3.
11. Dey, N., Hassanien, A.E., Bhatt, C., Ashour, A. and Satapathy, S.C. eds. 2018. Internet of things and big data analytics toward next-generation intelligence (pp. 3–549). Berlin: Springer.
12. M. McKnight. 2017. IoT, industry 4.0, industrial IoT why connected devices are the future of design, KnE Eng. 2(2), pp.197–202.

13. S. Movassaghi, M. Abolhasan, J. Lipman, D. Smith, A. Jamalipour. 2014. Wireless body area networks: a survey, IEEE Commun. Surv. Tutor. 16(3), pp.1658–1686.

14. K. Jee, G.-H. Kim. 2013. Potentiality of big data in the medical sector: focus on how to reshape the healthcare system, Healthc Inform. Res. 19(2), pp.79–85.

15. H. Chang, M. Choi. 2016. Big data and healthcare: building an augmented world, Healthc. Inform. Res. 22(3), pp.153–155.

16. Mishra, S., et al. 2017. Role of artificial intelligence in health care. BioChemistry: An Indian Journal 11(5), pp.1–14.

17. Aghada, Dharmesh, and Varun Agrawal. 2019. Role of Artificial Intelligence in Healthcare. Research & Reviews: A Journal of Bioinformatics 6(1), pp.20–24.

18. Alice Larsen Sneed. 2020. www.philips.com/a-w/about/news/archive/ blogs/innovation- matters/the-virtual-nurse-is-here.html

19. Dugger, Sarah A., Adam Platt, and David B. Goldstein. 2018. Drug development in the era of precision medicine. Nature Reviews Drug Discovery 17(3), p.183.

20. National Cancer Institute Press Office. 2018. TAILORx trial finds most women with early breast cancer do not benefit from chemotherapy, National Cancer Institute, 3 June. www.cancer.gov/news- events/press-releases/2018/tailorx-breast-cancer-chemotherapy

21. Bates, Mary. 2019. Health care chatbots are here to help. IEEE pulse 10(3), pp.12–14.

22. Koh, Hian Chye, and Gerald Tan. 2011. Data mining applications in healthcare. Journal of healthcare information management 19(2), p.65.

23. Dangare, Chaitrali S., and Sulabha S. Apte. 2012. Improved study of heart disease prediction system using data mining classification techniques. International Journal of Computer Applications 47(10), pp. 44–48.

24. Sellappan Palaniappan, Rafiah Awang. 2008. Intelligent Heart Disease Prediction System Using Data Mining Techniques, IJCSNS International Journal of Computer Science and Network Security, 8(8).

25. Shantakumar B. Patil, Y.S. Kumaraswamy. 2009. Intelligent and Effective Heart Attack Prediction System Using Data Mining and Artificial Neural Network. 31(4), pp.642–656

26. Dr. Yashpal Singh, Alok Singh Chauhan. 2005–2009. Neural networks in data mining. Journal of Theoretical and Applied Information Technology.

27. Anderson, J.E., Hansen, L.L., Mooren, F.C., Post, M., Hug, H., Zuse, A. and Los, M. 2006. Methods and biomarkers for the diagnosis and prognosis of cancer and other diseases: towards personalized medicine. Drug Resistance Updates, 9(4–5), pp.198–210.

28. Yahia Baashar et al. 2020. Customer relationship management systems (CRMS)in the healthcare environment: A systematic literature review. In:Com-puter Standards Interfaces 71, p. 103442.

29. R. Kohli, F. Piontek, T. Ellington, T. VanOsdol, M. Shepard, G. Brazel. 2001. Managing customer relationships through E-business decision support applications: a case of hospital–physician collaboration, Decis. Supp. Syst. 32 (2), pp.171–187.

30. M. Anshari, M. N. Almunawar, P. K. Low, and Z. Wint. 2012. Customer Empowerment in Healthcare Organisations Through CRM 2.0: Survey Results From Brunei Tracking a Future Path in e-Health Research, arXiv:1207.6164.

31. M. Hosseinianzadeh. 2015. A Framework for e-CRM Implementation in health service industry of a developing country, Int. J. Eng. Innov. Technol. 4(8).

32. A.N. Jalal, M. Bahari, A.K. Tarofder. 2018. Investigating the Crucial Factors Affecting the Social CRM Implementation and Its Benefits in Iraqi Healthcare Industry, 1st Malaysia Doctoral Consortium for Information Systems, Association for Information Systems – Malaysia Chapter 1, p.50.

33. A.N. Jalal, M. Bahari, A.K. Tarofder, W.M.N.M.W. Musa. 2019. Factors influencing customer social relationship management implementation and its benefits in healthcare industry, Polish J. Manag. Stud, 19.

34. M.-L. Wang. 2013. An evaluation of customer relationship management in hospital-based and privately run nursing homes in Taiwan, Total Qual. Manag. Bus. Excell. 24(9–10), pp.1004–1021.

35. L.Y. Sin, C. Alan, F.H. Yim. 2005. CRM: conceptualization and scale development, Eur. J. Mark. 39(11/12), pp.1264–1290.

36. E. Zamani, M.J. Tarokh. 2016. Analysis of customer relationship management in hospitals and present an efficient model for CRM implementation in hospitals, Bull. Soc. R. Sci. Liège 85, pp.1448–1456.

37. S. Taghavi, L. Riahi, A.A. Nasiripour, K. Jahangiri. 2017. Modeling customer relationship management pattern using human factors approach in the hospitals of Tehran university of medical sciences, Health Scope 6(2).

38. P. Gandhi, N. Tandon. 2017. Study to analyze the variables that affect the CRM implementation in the hospitals, Adv. Comput. Sci. Technol. 10(5) pp.933–944.

39. M. Yaghoubi, H. Asgari, M. Javadi. 2017. The impact of the customer relationship management on organizational productivity, customer trust and satisfaction by using the structural equation model: A study in the Iranian hospitals, J. Educ. Health Promot. 6.

40. S.-Y. Hung, W.-H. Hung, C.-A. Tsai, S.-C. Jiang. 2010. Critical factors of hospital adoption on CRM system: Organizational and information system perspectives, Decis. Supp. Syst. 48(4), pp.592–603

41. A.R. Alkhazali, S. Hassan. 2015. Factors affecting customer relationship management perception: a study of Jordanian hospital sector, J. Manag. Sustain. 5(3), p.126.

42. A.R. Alkhazali, S. Hassan. 2015. The effect of customer relationship management system adoption and perception on organization performance: Study of Jordanian hospital sectors, J. Manag. Sustain. 5, p.141.

43. R. Kohli, F. Piontek, T. Ellington, T. VanOsdol, M. Shepard, G. Brazel. 2001. Managing customer relationships through E-business decision support applications: a case of hospital–physician collaboration, Decis. Supp. Syst. 32(2), pp.171–187.

44. M. Anshari, M. N. Almunawar, P. K. Low, and Z. Wint. 2012. "Customer Empowerment in Healthcare Organisations Through CRM 2.0: Survey Results From Brunei Tracking a Future Path in e-Health Research," arXiv:1207.6164.

45. M. Hosseinianzadeh. 2015. A Framework for e-CRM Implementation in health service industry of a developing country, Int. J. Eng. Innov. Technol. 4(8).

46. Health Care Financing Administration, Financial Report for Fiscal Year 1996, Washington, D.C.: U.S. Department of Health and Human Services, Health Care Financing Administration, 1997; Health Care Financing Administration, Financial Report for Fiscal Year 1997, Washington, D.C.: U.S. Department of Health and Human Services, Health Care Financing Administration, 1998.

47. U.S. Department of Justice, 1997. Annual Report, Washington, D.C.: U.S. Department of Justice, 1997: 27.

48. Jagger, Sarah F. 1995. "Medicare and Medicaid: Opportunities to Save Program Dollars by Reducing Fraud and Abuse," Testimony before the Subcommittee on Human Resources and Intergovernmental Relations, Committee on Government Reform and Oversight, House of Representatives, Washington, D.C., March 22.

49. Reiss, A. J., Jr., and A. D. Biderman. 1980. "Data Sources on White-Collar Law-Breaking," Washington, D.C.: U.S. Department of Justice, National Institute of Justice, September, p.91.

50. Morey, Larry. 1993. Deputy Inspector General for Investigations, Office of Inspector General, Department of Health and Human Services, statement to the Subcommittee on Health of the Committee on Ways and Means, House of Representatives. 103rd Congress, 1st Session, March 8.

51. Bongomin, O., Yemane, A., Kembabazi, B., Malanda, C., Chikonkolo Mwape, M., Sheron Mpofu, N. and Tigalana, D. 2020. Industry 4.0 Disruption and Its Neologisms in Major Industrial Sectors: A State of the Art. Journal of Engineering.

52. Neuman C. 2009. Challenges in security for cyber-physical systems. InDHS Workshop on Future Directions in Cyber-Physical Systems Security 22, pp.22–24.

53. Kocsis I, Tóth ÁR, Szatmári Z, Dabóczi T, Pataricza A, Guta G. 2016. Towards cyber-physical system technologies over Apache VCL. International Journal of Cloud Computing 5(1–2), pp.1–111.

54. Sampigethaya K, Poovendran R. 2013. Aviation cyber–physical systems: Foundations for future aircraft and air transport. Proceedings of the IEEE 101(8), pp.834–55.

55. Horvath I. 2012. Beyond advanced mechatronics: new design challenges of Social-Cyber-Physical systems. In: Proceedings of the 1st Workshop on Mechatronic Design, Linz (Austria), 27–29 June. ACCM Austrian Center of Competence in Mechatronics.

56. Lakeville, Minnesota. 2020. https://homebusinessmag.com/lifestyles/health-and-fitness/8- challenges-faced-healthcare-india/

57. Jasmine Pennic. 2020. https://hitconsultant.net/2019/09/13/top-10-challenges-issues-and-opportunities-healthcare-executives-will-face-in-2020/ #.X7vXoFUzaT8

# Cyber-Security Countermeasures and Vulnerabilities to Prevent Social-Engineering Attacks

## Ramiz Salama and Fadi Al-Turjman

*AI and Robotics Institute, Near East University, Nicosia, Turkey*

## CONTENTS

7.1 Introduction 133
    7.1.1 AI Techniques against Cyber-Security Risks 134
    7.1.2 Describing Social Engineering 136
7.2 The Role of Social Engineering in Cyber Theft 139
7.3 Social Engineering Approach 140
7.4 Preventative Steps against Social Engineering 141
7.5 Conclusions 142
References 142

## 7.1 INTRODUCTION

Securing the systems, networks, and data that we rely on has grown increasingly important, as technology is refined it becomes reliantly connected with the different aspects of human nature. Because it is a primary medium

DOI: 10.1201/9781003322887-7

for terrorism, cybercrime is a huge threat to the economy, individual safety, and even the broader population. In fact, according to Europol's 2016 Internet Organized Crime Threat Assessment, cyber criminality has accelerated to the point that it has exceeded traditional crime in some EU countries. Assisting in the fight against a wide range of dangers, including the use of technology to commit criminal behaviours on digital systems or networks in order to steal valuable company information or personal data and generate profit [1,2].

### 7.1.1 AI Techniques against Cyber-Security Risks

The concept of human hacking, also known as social engineering, involves tricking consumers and workers into disclosing sensitive information, such as login credentials, which are then used to gain access to accounts and networks that are meant to be safe. It is a hacker's cunning use of trickery or exploitation of people's inherent propensity to believe, cooperate, or just look at and be intrigued. Even the most advanced IT security measures are unable to completely protect computers from hackers or block what seems to be authorized access. People are ideal targets for cyberattacks because they are simple to exploit and their social media posts are easy prey. Most of the time, infecting a company's network or mobile devices is as simple as getting customers to visit bogus websites, tricking them into clicking on dangerous links.

Research conducted in 2013 by T-N-S-Global by Halon, an email encryption company, concluded that 30% of 1,000 people surveyed in the United States said that even knowing that an email contained a virus or was questionable, they would be inclined to open it. Despite extensive efforts warning users about the potential risks of opening questionable e-mails, the vast mass of email users is still susceptible to social engineering cyber-attack attempts. To address the issues faced by social engineering assaults, research-based recommendations provide strategies for reducing the likelihood of a successful social engineering attack. Users and businesses have not effectively installed protections to deter cyber-security incidents, which are increasing dramatically in damage to organizations and their prestige in their specific industry.

The overall objective of this research is to ascertain how susceptible an organization's information technology infrastructure is to cyber intrusions, which includes hardware and software systems, transmission media, local area networks, wide area networks, enterprise networks, intranets, and

Internet use, according to F.B.I. Director James Comey in an interview from 2013: To do this, the study aims to describe the significance and function of social engineering in network invasions and cyber-theft. It also goes into great detail regarding the causes behind the exponential increase in cybercrime. The paper also provides a thorough explanation of social engineering, its definition, and the justification for its application in network espionage and online identity theft.

As virtual technology flourishes and the online universe turns becomes steadily indistinguishable from actual life, cybercrime grows to turn out to be part of everyone's everyday lives. Attacks in the direction of corporations and international locations have turned out to so drastically affect those companies in such a way that they are unable to respond to the vast quantity and extent of those probable cyber-attacks. With the aid of the B-O-A (Bank of America), Merrill-Lynch Global Research estimated that cybercrimes cost the worldwide economic system as much as 540 billion euros each year, proving that during the worst possible scenario regarding cybercrime, it should doubtlessly extract a fifth of the turnover created with the aid of the Internet. Cyber safety incidents are growing exponentially, both in frequency and damage, and sadly customers and agencies no longer have properly deployed defences to deter the criminals. In the last two months of 2015 alone, the ISACA1 and RSA22 Conferences performed an internationally conducted research of 461 cyber-attack precautionary practitioners and managers. The research peers showed that a vast quantity of safety breaches concentrated on personal and corporation statistics remained unchecked, with assault methods even progressing to be increasingly sophisticated.

The modern notion of worldwide cyber safety remains chaotic, with the frequency of assaults not generally anticipated to decrease, and nearly 75% of respondents anticipated falling prey to a cyber-assault in 2016. Cybercriminals who utilize social engineering as a preliminary step before initiating an electronic attack are the most hazardous. Cyber-criminals have moved from computerized attacks and are working on the human factor. Using methods to infect systems by stealing passwords and shifting money to manipulate people into creating vulnerabilities. Across all attack surfaces, chance actors employed social engineering to manipulate people into performing actions that had previously relied on malicious code [2]. The most famous hacker in the world, Kevin Mitnick, was imprisoned when he was a young teenager for breaking into and abusing computer networks, typically by using his charm and seduction rather than his technical talents.

The best known cyber attackers, taking into consideration an early grasp of the technological know-how when it comes to social engineering, have proven that despite the employment of protective programs, there is still a lack of understanding and awareness of the notion of social engineering. As proven by numerous research studies, social engineering is a deception method that takes advantage of human error to obtain sensitive information, access, or assets. Such studies will perceive why cyber-theft keeps increasing at an exponential rate. Mental aspects that make contributions to weak security have been discussed. Research can be supplied that perceives the main concerns concerning social engineering, factors such as how customers can be taught to avoid potential assaults and providing reliable techniques to reduce device and consumer risks [3–6].

## 7.1.2 Describing Social Engineering

Social engineering is described as one of the most effective strategies to collect statistics by manipulating human weak spots, which differs from organization to organization. In reality, social engineering refers back to the layout and alertness of nefarious strategies to intentionally target human victims. In a cyber-protection context, in most cases it is used to cause individuals to disclose personal data, or to carry out moves that breach protection protocols, unknowingly infecting structures or releasing categorized statistics. The foundation of a social engineering assault is to keep away from cyber-protection structures by manipulating the weakest human link.

During the interplay, victims are ignorant when it comes to the damaging nature of their own steps. Social engineering manipulates harmless instincts, with actions that are no longer criminal. Explicit strategies, inclusive of afflicted threats or bribery, are now no longer considered to be categorized within the scope of social engineering. A gifted hacker in this area is aware of and relies on social interplay skillsets to govern the mental factors concerning the human decision-making skills. Using this skill set, the attacker can exploit a weakness to gain access to the database with little effort or financial expense, as opposed to paying a lot of money to circumvent technological security measures. Although social engineers are aware of social information that indirectly aids in the hacking process, they also use technology methods to successfully finish the hacking process.

When it comes to the human side of social engineering, we see that although it may be classified as a primitive attack, it nonetheless succeeds in its goal of coercing victims into disclosing personal information by exploiting their vulnerabilities. Through deceptive faults in human reasoning and comprehension as a cognitive foundation, social engineering as a technique uses tactics to gain access to personal information. Human factors are a weak point in security methods that aim to improve the safety of information devices, and these weaknesses are exploited during a social engineering attack.

According to the results of several studies, the term "social engineering" encompasses a wide range of evil intentions. These studies also identify 13 of the most novel ways to target victims using social engineering, including:

1. **Pretexting:** Threat actors generally seek victims for specific information during pretexting assaults, claiming that it is required to authenticate the victim's identity. In practice, the threat actor steals this information and uses it to launch secondary attacks or commit identity theft. Advanced assaults try to take advantage of a weak spot in any company or organization. Such an approach calls for the assailant to construct a reputable tale that leaves no clues to cause confusion with the aid of using a goal. The approach is to apply worry and urgency whilst constructing a feeling of consideration with a sufferer to verify or achieve sought information [7].

2. **Baiting:** This is much like a phishing assault; however it lures the victim by attraction strategies. Cyber-attackers use the trap of assured items if the person gives away their login credentials to particular sites. A malicious attachment with a tempting name could be used as the trap [8].

3. **Phishing:** The term "phishing" refers to a fraud in which thieves attempt to steal personal or financial account information by sending false electronic messages that fool unsuspecting users into providing personal information [9].

4. **Tailgating:** Tailgating (also known as piggybacking) in physical security is one of the most common and sometimes unnoticed security breaches affecting enterprises today. Tailgating is merely the forced or unintentional passage of an unauthorized individual behind an authorized user [10].

5. **Quid pro quo:** Quid pro quo means "something in exchange for something." A quid pro quo attack occurs when a social engineer promises a service, typically "tech support," in exchange for access to secure information [11].

6. **Categories:** Hunting and farming are the two basic categorizations of any probable social engineering attack [12].

7. **Hunting:** This type of approach is implemented to carry out a social engineering attack using the least interaction with the intended victim or firm possible. As soon as the required goal is completed or a safety breech is made, verbal exchange is in all likelihood terminated. The hunting approach is the most commonly opted technique to assist cyber assaults [13].

8. **Pharming:** Pharming, a combination of the words "phishing" and "farming", is an online scam similar to phishing in which the traffic on a website is manipulated and personal information is obtained. It is essentially the unlawful act of creating a bogus website and then diverting consumers to it [14].

9. **Impersonation:** This tactic implies that the attacker provides a fake identity to increase their credibility as a foundation to perform nefarious actions. Further tailgating, the cyber-attacker tries to advance towards physical access to secure personal areas. In such a situation however, the hacker acquires access from the person with a valid entry key using impersonation, such as employees that have security clearance. Impersonating an expert entity, the assailant tries to gain access through protection protocols in place and gains entry to private and secure information. Quid pro quo, with inside knowledge of social engineering and protection, is an assault typically provided to the end-goal of a technical false carrier that calls for sensitive data to be properly secure. The assailant impersonates a helpful IT technician, attempting to infect a gadget by claiming to be helping the individual experiencing technical difficulties [15].

10. **Multiple phases:** In order to acquire a particular goal, social-engineering assaults can vary from a chain of actions, probably related to numerous risk factors, meant to acquire fragments of associated records from unique collections. Assaults of such nature, although depending on a sole interaction, commonly include four related phases: research, hook, play, and exit [16].

11. **Hook:** In this phase of cyber warfare, the threat intender starts communication with the victim. The attacker engages the victim,

provides a concocted story, creates a scenario forming a level of trust, and takes over the interaction [17].

12. **Play:** This phase of cyber warfare avails a reason of the assault, ranging from extracting crucial information or used to guide the intended victim to willingly provide the security access to a system [18].

13. **Exit:** The interaction with the targeted victim is ended in this element of social engineering without raising any red flags. Since the attacker deceives the victim into believing their bogus trail, this final stage ensures that the cyberattacker is very difficult to identify [19,20].

## 7.2 THE ROLE OF SOCIAL ENGINEERING IN CYBER THEFT

Information security is described as "defensive statistics and statistics structures from unauthorized provisions, disclosure, use, disruption, destruction or modification" in line with United States laws.

increasingly sophisticated and skilled social engineering assaults are being carried out by hackers. They can piece together disparate data from various sources, including social media, business blogs, and records. They can also painstakingly extract crucial and key data from well-meaning employees, which they can then use to attack networks, steal valuable data, hold organizations hostage, and occasionally damage the object of their targets. Regarding the rise of cybercrime and robbery, there are significant factors in the rise and motivation for cybercrime, which financially affects both individuals and organizations. The benefit of robbing someone while exploiting ambiguity is one factor attracting people to cybercrime. Thousands of cybercriminals commit crimes online, yet only a small number are caught and imprisoned.

Additionally, digital thieves do not need to be informed to be successful, and they are willing to take risks due to the advantages of being able to remain distant from a victim while placing themselves in a low-risk and low-exposure environment. International cyber thefts are common, yet law enforcement agencies are only able to pursue cybercriminals who operate inside their jurisdictional borders. The investigation also requires cooperating with law enforcement organizations from jurisdictions outside of the country. While getting foreign help to fight transnational theft is still challenging for law enforcement in the United States, it is becoming less difficult on a local level. The vast majority of foreign nations essentially don't cooperate. Evidence is a further component, and deficiencies in timely available evidence are a contributing factor to the dearth of successful convictions [21,22].

## 7.3 SOCIAL ENGINEERING APPROACH

Social engineering attackers can use a variety of human or technical approaches, such as phishing and diving into social privacy, to acquire visibility or obtain secret information. A synergy of human and technological approaches may be used by aggressive and effective attackers to get abundant information about an individual or gain access to an organization.

In regards to the stages involved in acquiring information and executing a social engineering assault, in Figure 7.1, it is graphically illustrated that the use of a step-by-step strategy to carrying out social engineering assaults means the process begins with a research and information collecting phase, followed by the establishment of a connection. The attacker gains access to the system during the exploitation phase, and the attack is carried out during the final phase.

Attacks using social engineering can be carried out through human or technical deployments. You can learn about some important issues through education and social engineering penetration testing. Most importantly, education paired with further social engineering testing decreases the success of social engineering assaults, reducing the susceptibility of information systems and networks, according to the 2011 Columbia University study described in this research report.

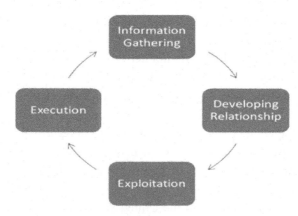

FIGURE 7.1    The four fundamental steps of social engineering

On the other hand, the 2011 Columbia University study makes no mention of how frequently training and testing could be required to maintain the same results. In conclusion, it is difficult to draw a clear conclusion that the same outcomes would be anticipated by more testing due to the flaws in the Columbia University study. The usage of recurrent training models will now be tested to see if users can sustain similar outcomes over time [23,24].

## 7.4 PREVENTATIVE STEPS AGAINST SOCIAL ENGINEERING

It is evident that the human aspect will always be a vulnerability, regardless of how technologically secure a network appears to be. Social engineering gives malicious actors a lot of anonymity, which increases the success rate and volume of cybercrimes, which are both rising rapidly. To respond correctly, businesses need to be aware of the various threat actors and the variety of assaults they use. To bring the risk of social engineering down to a reasonable level, both technological and non-technical safeguards might be taken. Businesses are increasing the number of layers in their security systems so that, in the case of an outer layer failure, at least one inner layer method will help avert a catastrophe (Table 7.1) [25].

TABLE 7.1   Measures to Stop Social Engineering

| | |
|---|---|
| **A Secure Policy** | A proper policy must contain nontechnical and technical access that is solely controlled by administration |
| **Network Management** | Corporations should protect their network by whitelisting only authorized websites |
| **Audits and Compliance** | Organizations must actively check to see if their security policy is being followed. Checking desktop setups at least twice a month and revalidating employee rights are a few investigative controls |
| **Training** | Employees should be initially trained during their orientation and further trained through refresher training |
| **Technical Procedures** | To safeguard data and the network's basic architecture, the network should have several levels of definitions. Every device ought to have firewalls, intrusion detection systems, and intrusion prevention systems installed |
| **Guidance** | A wide range of solutions for safeguarding the assets of a firm. Mantraps (access control), security officers, and security cameras work well together to spot invaders |

## 7.5 CONCLUSIONS

The modern technological era is exponentially becoming increasingly vulnerable as there are countless cyber-attacks being carried out every day. Such attacks are targeting people's ability to trust or to gain access to crucial information and credentials to attack their personal bank accounts and in doing so these cyber criminals have the best opportunity because they are physically far from the victims and probably carrying out this crime in the safety of their own premises and are able to leave a fake digital footprint to misguide the authorities trying to track them. Even though technology is aided by a surge in Internet usage, humankind is progressing quickly as the expansion of publicly accessible information is grown and facilitated. You can virtually gather information about anyone by tracking their online profiles. As an example, if someone chose their banking information's recovery questions to be their pet's name and they post a picture of their pet mentioning their pet's name, they are in reality handing out crucial credential information without even realizing it. Therefore, this chapter aims to inform the general public about the many ways in which they are vulnerable and to consider thinking twice about what information they post or provide someone with, either willingly or unknowingly. While social engineering attacks are an element of solving cyber-security issues, research demonstrates that the best defence is a knowledgeable computer user. Think of the people who were shown to be the most vulnerable in this study as brand-new employees of a company, with the attacker looking to collect personally identifiable information (PII) from them. Threat actors today prey on human flaws to commit cybercrime, although they do not necessarily have a thorough technical expertise of information systems. According to recent studies, the great majority of cyber-attacks place people at the centre of the infection chain. The use of social engineering is growing both in the public and private sectors.

## REFERENCES

[1]  Conteh, N. Y., & Schmick, P. J. (2021). Cybersecurity risks, vulnerabilities, and countermeasures to prevent social engineering attacks. In Ethical hacking techniques and countermeasures for cybercrime prevention (pp. 19–31). IGI Global.

[2]  Siddiqi, M. A., Pak, W., & Siddiqi, M. A. (2022). A Study on the Psychology of Social Engineering-Based Cyberattacks and Existing Countermeasures. Applied Sciences, 12(12), 6042.

[3] Alhayani, B., Mohammed, H. J., Chaloob, I. Z., & Ahmed, J. S. (2021). Effectiveness of artificial intelligence techniques against cyber security risks apply of IT industry. Materials Today: Proceedings.

[4] Holovkin, B. M., Tavolzhanskyi, O. V., & Lysodyed, O. V. (2021). Corruption as a cybersecurity threat in conditions of the new world's order. Linguistics and Culture Review, 5(S3), 499–512.

[5] Kuzlu, M., Fair, C., & Guler, O. (2021). Role of artificial intelligence in the Internet of Things (IoT) cybersecurity. Discover Internet of things, 1(1), 1–14.

[6] Kuzlu, M., Fair, C., & Guler, O. (2021). Role of artificial intelligence in the Internet of Things (IoT) cybersecurity. Discover Internet of things, 1(1), 1–14.

[7] Pimentel, A., & Steinmetz, K. F. (2022). Enacting social engineering: the emotional experience of information security deception. Crime, Law and Social Change, 77(3), 341–361.

[8] Fancourt, B. A., Augusteyn, J., Cremasco, P., Nolan, B., Richards, S., Speed, J., ... & Gentle, M. N. (2021). Measuring, evaluating and improving the effectiveness of invasive predator control programs: Feral cat baiting as a case study. Journal of Environmental Management, 280, 111691.

[9] Rifat, N., Ahsan, M., Chowdhury, M., & Gomes, R. (2022, May). BERT Against Social Engineering Attack: Phishing Text Detection. In 2022 IEEE International Conference on Electro Information Technology (eIT) (pp. 1–6). IEEE.

[10] Wang, Z., Zhu, H., Liu, P., & Sun, L. (2021). Social engineering in cybersecurity: a domain ontology and knowledge graph application examples. Cybersecurity, 4(1), 1–21.

[11] Myers, P. (2021). Merit-Based Karma and Social Engineering in Germany and France. In Spiritual Empires in Europe and India (pp. 157–190). Palgrave Macmillan, Cham.

[12] Pharris, L., & Perez-Mira, B. (2022). Preventing social engineering: a phenomenological inquiry. Information & Computer Security.

[13] Li, M. (2021). Environmental factors affect social engineering attacks (Doctoral dissertation, Purdue University Graduate School).

[14] Vlachos, G. L. (2022). Agricultural Cooperatives as Social-Engineering Mechanisms: Fragments of Evidence from Two Case Studies from the Interwar Greek Macedonia. Hiperboreea, 9(1), 69–94.

[15] Rodriguez, R. M., & Atyabi, A. (2022). Social Engineering Attacks and Defenses in the Physical World vs. Cyberspace: A Contrast Study. arXiv preprint arXiv:2203.04813.

[16] Montañez, R., Atyabi, A., & Xu, S. (2022). Social engineering attacks and defenses in the physical world vs. cyberspace: A contrast study. In Cybersecurity and Cognitive Science (pp. 3–41). Academic Press.

[17] Bhusal, C. S. (2021). Systematic Review on Social Engineering: Hacking by Manipulating Humans. Journal of Information Security, 12, 104–114.

[18] Li, T., Wang, X., & Ni, Y. (2022). Aligning social concerns with information system security: A fundamental ontology for social engineering. Information Systems, 104, 101699.

[19] Chebii, P. J. (2021). Securing Mobile Money Payment and Transfer Applications Against Smishing and Vishing Social Engineering Attacks (Doctoral dissertation, University of Nairobi).

[20] Wang, Z., Zhu, H., & Sun, L. (2021). Social engineering in cybersecurity: Effect mechanisms, human vulnerabilities and attack methods. IEEE Access, 9, 11895–11910.

[21] Conteh, N. Y., & Jackson, A. B. (2021). Evaluating the Impact of Cybertheft Through Social Engineering and Network Intrusions. In Ethical Hacking Techniques and Countermeasures for Cybercrime Prevention (pp. 44–53). IGI Global.

[22] Mashtalyar, N., Ntaganzwa, U. N., Santos, T., Hakak, S., & Ray, S. (2021, July). Social engineering attacks: Recent advances and challenges. In International Conference on Human-Computer Interaction (pp. 417–431). Springer, Cham.

[23] Venkatesha, S., Reddy, K. R., & Chandavarkar, B. R. (2021). Social engineering attacks during the COVID-19 pandemic. SN computer science, 2(2), 1–9.

[24] Grassegger, T., & Nedbal, D. (2021). The role of employees' information security awareness on the intention to resist social engineering. Procedia Computer Science, 181, 59–66.

[25] Sekaran, K., Abas, H., & Bakar, N. A. A. (2021). A Study of Social Engineering: Threats, Awareness and Measures. Open International Journal of Informatics, 9(2), 57–63.

# CHAPTER 8

# Development of a COVID-19 Tracking System

Olusegun Odewole, Fadi Al-Turjman,
Auwalu Saleh Mubarak,
and Zubaida Sa'id Ameen

*AI and Robotics Institute, Near East University, Nicosia, Turkey*

## CONTENTS

| | | |
|---|---|---|
| 8.1 | Introduction | 145 |
| 8.2 | Related Works | 147 |
| 8.3 | Methodology | 148 |
| | 8.3.1 The Dataset | 148 |
| | 8.3.2 COVID-19 Detection | 148 |
| | 8.3.3 Functional Requirements | 149 |
| | 8.3.4 Class Diagram | 149 |
| | 8.3.5 Hardware and Software Requirements | 151 |
| 8.4 | Results and Implementation | 151 |
| 8.5 | Conclusion | 156 |
| Acknowledgements | | 156 |
| References | | 156 |

## 8.1 INTRODUCTION

COVID-19, popularly referred to as coronavirus disease, is an extremely contagious viral disease that surfaced in China in December 2019. This

DOI: 10.1201/9781003322887-8

disease is caused by "severe acute respiratory syndrome coronavirus 2" (SARS-CoV-2), a virus that is of the family of coronaviruses. COVID-19 originated in Wuhan, Hubei Province of China, in December 2019 and in a short time turned out to be a worldwide epidemic, spreading to 220 countries and becoming the first pandemic of the twenty-first century [1,2].

The detection of coronavirus (COVID-19) has turned out to be the foremost demanding situation in the world due to its fast spread [3,4]. As of 3:06 pm GMT, 28 February 2022, 434,154,739 verified worldwide cases of COVID-19, had been collected by WHO, including 5,944,342 mortalities [2].

Human movement is a key factor advancing the fast spread of COVID-19 across geographic boundaries [5–7]. COVID-19 has a highly contagious rate amongst humans and can be transmitted even before the onset of its symptoms. To date, restricting and tracking human movement has been effective in curtailing the proliferation of the COVID-19 plague across the globe [6].

Common COVID-19 symptoms include cough, sore throat, fever, anosmia, etc. [1,8]. The usual diagnostic technique is the RT-PCR nucleic acid amplification test (NAAT) [9]. Also, chest CT is a verified, rapid, and dependable alternative to RT-PCR for the detection of COVID-19 in highly common territories [10,11]. Most COVID-19 symptoms show signs of respiratory and lung abnormalities, which radiologists can identify. In addition, several studies have advocated the use of CT scans instead of RT-PCR in countries with inadequate testing kits [10].

It is challenging and time-consuming for skilled radiologists [12] in clinical care to interpret bulk chest X-ray images to detect COVID-19 pneumonia amidst non-COVID-19 pneumonia. It is challenging because COVID-19 and other viral and bacterial pneumonias have closely related imaging features [10]. Rapid diagnosis technologies can curb and prevent the spread of pandemics, and assist doctors and radiologists to facilitate the treatment of patients [13].

Machine learning is an aspect of artificial intelligence that develops programs that automatically learn from previous data and can make decisions with minimum human intervention [3]. Machine learning has proven useful for a very large number of applications and has been widely used in radiology [3]. Also, a world coupled with the Internet of Things (IoT) signifies a remarkable advancement. Hence, we design advanced diagnostic and tracking systems that utilize machine learning/ artificial intelligence (AI) tools to distinguish COVID-19-infected people from healthy people based on uploaded chest (CT scan) images and track their location for effective quarantine. The main contributions of this study are:

- Enhanced speed of CT image analysis by reducing the challenges of CT scans and assisting in evaluating COVID-19 CT scan images quickly.
- Reducing the spread of the virus by tracking of COVID-19-positive patients' locations.
- Reduction in virus spread. Early detection helps to reduce the spread of COVID-19.

## 8.2 RELATED WORKS

Stemmed by the need for quick analysis of radiology images during the COVID-19 pandemic, there have been several studies on detecting COVID-19 from chest X-ray and CT images using the 2D convolutional neural network deep learning-based model. Zhang et al. [14] trained an 18-layer residual convolutional neural network deep learning-based model that can distinguish COVID-19 chest X-ray images from non-COVID-19 chest X-ray images with good sensitivity (range of 70.65% to 96.00%) for non-COVID and COVID cases, respectively.

Wang et al. [15] proposed a COVID-Net network architecture that was pre-trained on the ImageNet43 dataset and obtained a good test accuracy of 93.3%. Narin et al. [16] used five pre-trained CNN models to detect coronavirus patients from chest X-ray images and achieved a high classification accuracy, the highest (99.5–99.7%) gotten from the pre-trained ResNet50 model. Jin et al. [17] within a short time developed an AI system that automatically analyses CT images to detect COVID-19 pneumonia features.

Chen et al. [18] built a deep learning system to distinguish COVID-19 pneumonia CT images from non-COVID-19 ones and went further to develop a cloud-based open-access system that accepts CT scan image uploads and provides assistance in detecting COVID-19. In all these systems, none have aimed at tracking COVID-19-positive users after the

AI system analysis, hence the impetus for this research. We developed a system that allows users worldwide to upload CT scans and the system tracks the users from the location in which the system was accessed.

## 8.3 METHODOLOGY

### 8.3.1 The Dataset

In this study, two datasets were merged to efficiently classify COVID-19 and healthy individuals. The CT images of Yang et al. [19] contain 349 and 397 COVID-19-positive class and health individuals, respectively, while those of Soares et al. [20] contain 1972 and 1608 COVID-19-positive class and healthy individuals, respectively. The data were augmented to increase the number of training images to 8000. Figure 8.1 shows the samples of CT scans

### 8.3.2 COVID-19 Detection

The model of COVID-19 used is based on VGG16 – a type of convolutional neural network (CNN) model – modelled to detect COVID-19 using CT-scan images. VGG16 is one of the highest-quality vision-model architectures currently available. It generates patterns by stacking convolutional layers with tiny filters (3×3) rather than using a single layer with larger filter sizes (5×5 and 7×7). Transfer learning feature extraction (the weights of the VGG16 model pre-trained on some IMAGE dataset) was used to enhance the results of classification. The proposed model (COVID-19 Analyzer) is trained with 8000 CT-scan images of COVID-19-infected and healthy individuals from a pool of the dataset obtained, four-fifths of which was used for training and the remaining fifth was separated for

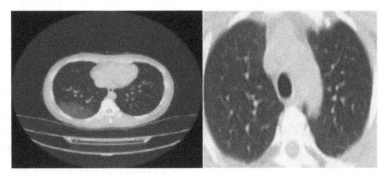

FIGURE 8.1    CT scan images

testing. The weights of the CNN were initialized at random, the learning rate at the start was set to 0.1 and different batch sizes were used and empirically set to 25 to achieve high training accuracy and prevent model over-fitting.

### 8.3.3 Functional Requirements

**User module:** The user can register on the COVID system, login to their dashboard, upload their CT-scan images, and check the result within 24 hours.

The administrator can analyse CT scan images, delete users' images if not correctly uploaded, and track COVID-19-positive users, as shown in Figure 8.2. Figure 8.3 illustrates the sequence diagram for the COVID tracking system (user), while Figure 8.4 illustrates the entity relationship diagram of the developed system.

Figure 8.2 shows the sequence of information between the user, COVID-19 tracking system, and the Admin. A user can register and afterwards login, thereafter upload the CT scan image after granting the system access to their location, the system immediately sends an email to the admin that an image has been uploaded and the admin analyses each CT image using the system. Once the analysis is complete, the system updates the COVID status of the user and the user can view the result.

Figure 8.3 shows the Internet of Things architecture model of the COVID-19 tracking system. Uploads can be made into the system via mobile/desktop platforms; the uploads are then analysed in the analysis and tracking system by the admin, after which the system alerts the quarantine admin agent. All data are stored on the cloud via the Internet.

### 8.3.4 Class Diagram

The class diagram (Figure 8.4) illustrates the data/information transfer within this COVID-19 tracking system. It reveals its implementation in a relational database.

This system has five classes: user, admin, patient, data, and COVID classes. Both admin and patient inherit from the user class. Each patient can have one or more data and each data, at a particular period, has the COVID-19 status.

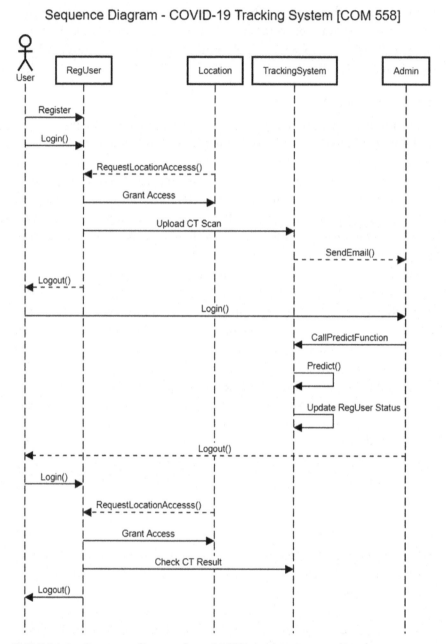

FIGURE 8.2  Sequence diagram for a COVID tracking system (User)

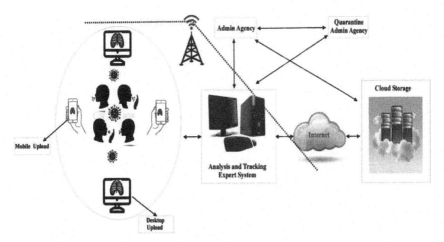

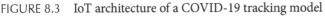

FIGURE 8.3   IoT architecture of a COVID-19 tracking model

### 8.3.5 Hardware and Software Requirements

1. *Hardware requirements:*

    Processor: Intel(R) Core(TM) i3-4005U CPU @ 1.70GHz. CPU

    RAM: 6 GB. System type: 32-bit/64-bit operating system, ×32- or ×64-based processor. Operating system: Windows 7/8/10.

2. *Software requirements:*

    Front end: HTML, CSS, Bootstrap, JQuery

    Back end: Py thon (Django)

    Local/production access link: localhost:8000

## 8.4  RESULTS AND IMPLEMENTATION

In this study, CT scans were used to train a VGG convolutional neural network to classify COVID-19 CT scan images, the trained model will be saved and deployed into a server to give medical practitioners access to uploaded CT scan images. In Table 8.1 it can be observed that the model achieves an accuracy, precision, recall, and F1-score of 80%, 80%, 80.3%, and 80%, respectively. Based on the model's observed performance, it performed very well in detecting COVID-19. Figures 8.5 and 8.6 show training/validation loss and training/validation accuracy, respectively.

Figure 8.7 shows the home page after the user logs in. It has a description on the main page welcoming the user and instructing them on how to use

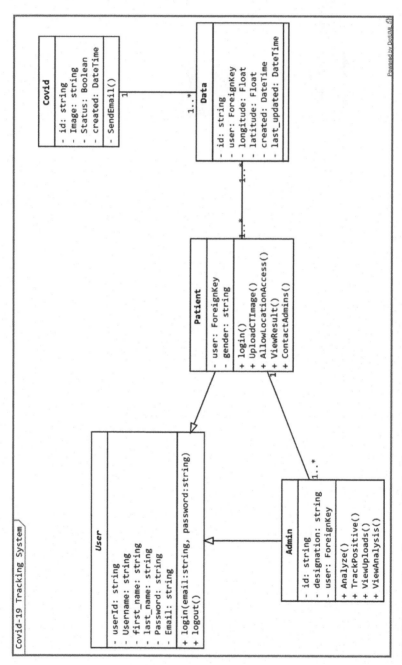

FIGURE 8.4   Class diagram of a developed system

TABLE 8.1   Employed Model Performance Evaluation

| Performance criteria | Values (%) |
| --- | --- |
| Accuracy | 80 |
| Recall | 80.3 |
| Precision | 80 |
| F1-Score | 80 |

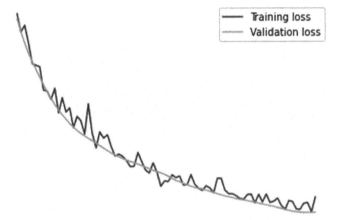

FIGURE 8.5   Training loss and validation loss of the model

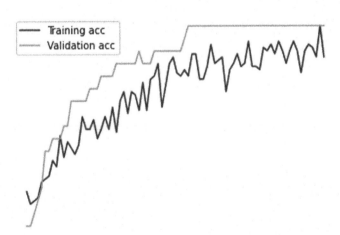

FIGURE 8.6   Training accuracy and validation accuracy of the model generated

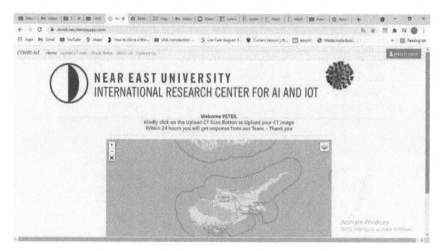

FIGURE 8.7    Landing page after user login to the system

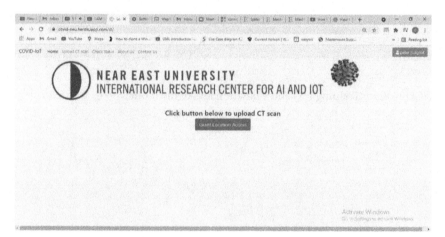

FIGURE 8.8    Location request page that collects the user's geolocation

the app. This is the page from which the user is directed to the page where they uploads the CT-scan image.

Figure 8.8 shows the next page (user's location request page) when they click on the upload CT scan from the previous screen (see Figure 8.7). The user is not allowed to upload the CT scan image unless they grant the system access to track his current location. This is the page from which the user is directed to the page where they upload the CT scan image.

Figure 8.9 shows the CT scan upload page where users are allowed to upload their CT scan image. The user is automatically directed to this page

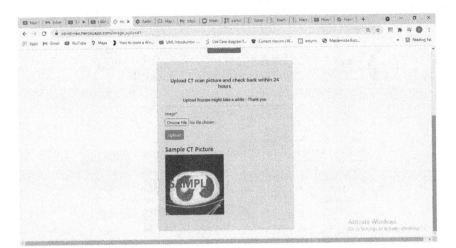

FIGURE 8.9    CT-scan upload page

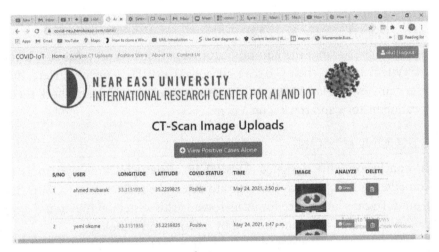

FIGURE 8.10    Admin CT-scan analysis page

once the access to user's location (see Figure 8.8) is successful and within a few minutes of granting the system access to the location, else the user is redirected again to the user's location page (see Figure 8.8).

Figure 8.10 shows the administrator page after login. This page allows the administrator to analyse a CT-scan image. A row corresponds to the fata of a user and an analyse button shows on the same row as the uploaded image on which the admin clicks to analyse the image. Once the analysis is complete, the COVID status of the analysed image is shown in the COVID status row and the analysis status removes the analyse/predict button and

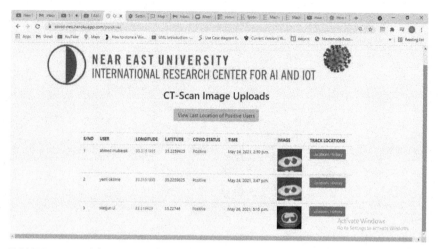

FIGURE 8.11    Admin page that displays positive coronavirus user's geolocation

displays "Done". The administrator could also delete the analysis here if a wrong image has been uploaded.

Figure 8.11 shows the administrator page that lists all users in which the system analyses their CT-scan images as COVID-19 positive. Here, the user can view the last location the user uploaded the CT scan, check their location history, and track it on a map.

## 8.5 CONCLUSION

In conclusion, this designed COVID-19 analysis/tracking system is a computer-aided approach that helps to detect the incidence of COVID-19 from CT scans and hence lower its spread. This system is free to use and can be used as an adjuvant method by patients and radiologists.

It is successfully developed to meet the basic COVID-19 CT-scan analysis and provide the features required for tracking COVID-infected users promptly with a user-friendly interface.

## ACKNOWLEDGEMENTS

This work was supported by the Department of Artificial Intelligence, Faculty of Engineering, Near East University, Nicosia, TRNC.

## REFERENCES

[1] Elibol, E. (2021). Otolaryngological symptoms in COVID-19. European Archives of Oto-Rhino-Laryngology, 278(4), 1233-1236.

[2] World Health Organization. (2022, February 28). WHO Coronavirus Disease (COVID-19) Dashboard. https://covid19.who.int/

[3] Noguerol, T. M., Paulano-Godino, F., Martín-Valdivia, M. T., Menias, C. O., & Luna, A. (2019). Strengths, weaknesses, opportunities, and threats analysis of artificial intelligence and machine learning applications in radiology. Journal of the American College of Radiology, 16(9), 1239–1247.

[4] Alazab, M., Awajan, A., Mesleh, A., Abraham, A., Jatana, V., & Alhyari, S. (2020). COVID-19 prediction and detection using deep learning. International Journal of Computer Information Systems and Industrial Management Applications, 12, 168–181.

[5] Hu, B., Qiu, J., Chen, H., Tao, V., Wang, J., & Lin, H. (2020). First, second and potential third generation spreads of the COVID-19 epidemic in mainland China: an early exploratory study incorporating location-based service data of mobile devices. International Journal of Infectious Diseases, 96, 489–495.

[6] Pascarella, G., Strumia, A., Piliego, C., Bruno, F., Del Buono, R., Costa, F., ... & Agrò, F. E. (2020). COVID-19 diagnosis and management: a comprehensive review. Journal of internal medicine, 288(2), 192–206.

[7] Zhou, Y., Xu, R., Hu, D., Yue, Y., Li, Q., & Xia, J. (2020). Effects of human mobility restrictions on the spread of COVID-19 in Shenzhen, China: a modelling study using mobile phone data. The Lancet Digital Health, 2(8), e417–e424.

[8] Larsen, J. R., Martin, M. R., Martin, J. D., Kuhn, P., & Hicks, J. B. (2020). Modeling the Onset of Symptoms of COVID-19. Frontiers in public health, 8, 473.

[9] World Health Organization. (2020). Laboratory testing for coronavirus disease 2019 (COVID-19) in suspected human cases: interim guidance, 2 March 2020 (No. WHO/COVID-19/laboratory/2020.4). World Health Organization.

[10] Dai, W. C., Zhang, H. W., Yu, J., Xu, H. J., Chen, H., Luo, S. P., ... & Lin, F. (2020). CT imaging and differential diagnosis of COVID-19. Canadian Association of Radiologists Journal, 71(2), 195–200.

[11] Zali, A., Sohrabi, M. R., Mahdavi, A., Khalili, N., Taheri, M. S., Maher, A., ... & Hanani, K. (2021). Correlation between low-dose chest computed tomography and RT-PCR results for the diagnosis of COVID-19: A report of 27,824 cases in tehran, Iran. Academic Radiology, 28(12), 1654–1661.

[12] Wang, K., Zhang, X., Huang, S., & Chen, F. (2019, November). Automatic detection of pneumonia in chest X-ray images using cooperative convolutional neural networks. In Chinese Conference on Pattern Recognition and Computer Vision (PRCV) (pp. 328–340). Springer, Cham.

[13] A. A. Ardakani, A. R. Kanafi, U. R. Acharya, N. Khadem, and A. Mohammadi, "Application of deep learning technique to manage

COVID-19 in routine clinical practice using CT images: Results of 10 convolutional neural networks," Comput. Biol. Med., vol. 121, no. March, p. 103795, 2020, doi: 10.1016/j.compbiomed.2020.103795.

[14] Zhang, J., Xie, Y., Li, Y., Shen, C., & Xia, Y. (2020). COVID-19 screening on chest x-ray images using deep learning based anomaly detection. arXiv preprint arXiv:2003.12338, 27.

[15] Wang, L., Lin, Z. Q., & Wong, A. (2020). Covid-net: A tailored deep convolutional neural network design for detection of COVID-19 cases from chest x-ray images. Scientific Reports, 10(1), 1–12

[16] Narin, A., Kaya, C., & Pamuk, Z. (2021). Automatic detection of coronavirus disease (COVID-19) using x-ray images and deep convolutional neural networks. Pattern Analysis and Applications, 24(3), 1207–1220.

[17] Jin C, Chen W, Cao Y, Xu Z, Tan Z, Zhang X, Deng L, Zheng C, Zhou J, Shi H, Feng J. Development and evaluation of an artificial intelligence system for COVID-19 diagnosis. Nat Commun. 2020 Oct 9;11(1):5088. doi: 10.1038/s41467-020-18685-1. PMID: 33037212; PMCID: PMC7547659.

[18] Chen, J., Wu, L., Zhang, J., Zhang, L., Gong, D., Zhao, Y., ... & Yu, H. (2020). Deep learning-based model for detecting 2019 novel coronavirus pneumonia on high-resolution computed tomography. Scientific reports, 10(1), 1–11.

[19] X. Yang, X. He, J. Zhao, Y. Zhang, S. Zhang, and P. Xie, "COVID-CT-Dataset: A CT Image Dataset about COVID-19," pp. 1–14.

[20] E. Soares, P. Angelov, S. Biaso, M. Higa Froes, and D. Kanda Abe, "SARS-CoV-2 CT-scan dataset: A large dataset of real patients CT scans for SARS-CoV-2 identification," pp. 1–8, 2020, doi: 10.1101/2020.04.24.20078584.

# An Overview of Autonomous Perception for a Robotic Arm

Auwalu Saleh Mubarak, Zubaida Sa'id Ameen, and Fadi Al-Turjman

*AI and Robotics Institute, Near East University, Nicosia, Turkey*

## CONTENTS

| | | |
|---|---|---|
| 9.1 | Introduction | 160 |
| 9.2 | Overview | 161 |
| | 9.2.1 Artificial Neural Networks | 161 |
| | 9.2.2 Convolutional Neural Network | 162 |
| | 9.2.3 Recurrent Neural Network | 162 |
| 9.3 | Grasp Representation | 163 |
| | 9.3.1 Object Detection | 163 |
| |     9.3.1.1 Analytical Approach | 163 |
| |     9.3.1.2 Empirical Approach | 164 |
| |     9.3.1.3 Empirical Grasp Approach | 165 |
| 9.4 | Conclusions | 168 |
| | Acknowledgements | 169 |
| | References | 169 |

DOI: 10.1201/9781003322887-9

## 9.1 INTRODUCTION

Kevin Ashton of MIT's Auto-ID Center developed the term "Internet of Things" to describe a worldwide intelligent network that connects a variety of things with the ability to observe, compute, execute, and communicate with the Internet [1]. The Internet of Things (IoT) is a critical infrastructure for a variety of applications, including smart homes, smart transportation, smart grids, smart tourism, and smart healthcare [2–7]. The IoT sector is forecast to contribute $2.7 to $6.2 trillion to the global economy by 2025, according to a McKinsey estimate. A perception layer, a network layer, and an application layer are the three levels of a typical IoT design [8]. The perception layer is made up of a variety of sensors, actuators, and devices that collect data and send them to higher levels. Different networks (e.g., local area networks [LANs], cellular networks, and the Internet) and devices are enabled by different communication technologies such as Bluetooth, Wi-Fi, LTE, and 5G at the network layer. The top IoT layer is the application layer, which is driven by cloud computing platforms and provides customers with customized services. The age of artificial intelligence of things (AIoT), in which AI meets IoT, is rapidly approaching. According to a white paper published by Cisco [9], 99.4% of physical things are linked. Several AIoT applications have now been built that provide services and generate revenue. Here, we show how artificial intelligence (AI) may give things intelligence and improve applications.

Researchers have been trying their best to make robots perform tasks autonomously, with little human intervention, with the introduction of computer vision, researchers have achieved mimicking human vision with appreciable performance accuracy by employing machine learning. With the recent advancements in computers, vision robots can achieve an assigned task in structured and unstructured environments independently. The employment of deep learning in the field of computer vision proves that robots can achieve a lot more and even compete with humans in the future; the backbone of deep learning is artificial neural networks, which perform a task similar to that of the human neural system. Although there have been advancements in the field, researchers have developed advanced models like deep neural networks (DNNs), also referred to as convolutional neural networks (CNNs), etc.

Computer vision-based grasp control is one of the developing areas in computer vision, where researchers attempt to make robotic arms with grippers and sensors to emulate the way humans identify an object, object's pose orientation and also perform grasping with high quality [10]. In computer vision grasping there are several ways to perform the grasping of an object, there is an analytical approach which relies on heavy coding and an empirical approach which relies on training from previous success attempts [6,11–13].

Object detection, localization, and pose estimation is another task to be considered, with the use of reference rectangles, oriented reference rectangles, anchor boxes, and oriented anchor boxes defining the coordinates of the object and pose orientation, which helps in achieving end-effector position and orientation. Fast detection has been the major concern when it comes to detection, and several approaches are being carried out such as the sliding window approach [14] in which a window is slid across the whole image. This approach is time-consuming and has a high computational cost, and so a fast approach was proposed which is the region proposal, in which the target regions are proposed faster than the sliding window technique because only the selected regions are fed into the network [15,16]. The "You Only Look Once" approach (YOLO) was later proposed which applies to global image detection, and is applicable in real-life situations. YOLO is faster than the region proposal because it sends one image at a time to the network [17]. The state-of-the-art detection method is the Single Short Detection (SSD), which is an advancement of YOLO. It is faster, accurate, and also achieves 59 frames per second on the Cornell dataset for object grasp detection [18].

In this overview, we concentrate on computer-based grasp control techniques performed in previous works. We also provide an overview of how a robot initiates, performs, and evaluates the performance of a grasping task in a human-like way based on some works achieved on popular datasets. To mimic human vision requires quite a lot of tasks, with image recognition and pose estimation being the backbone tasks in achieving a good grasp, and the secondary task being getting hold of the object to achieve the assigned task.

## 9.2 OVERVIEW

### 9.2.1 Artificial Neural Networks

Artificial neural networks can be described as computational tools which are composed of interconnected adaptive processing elements commonly referred to as neurons [19]. The ANN architecture is presented in Figure 9.1.

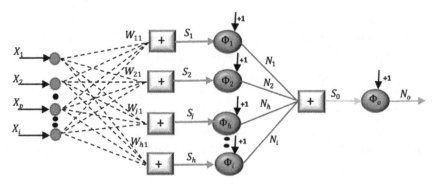

FIGURE 9.1    Artificial neural network architecture

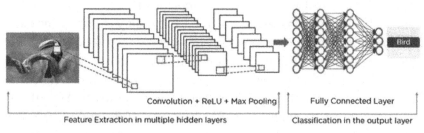

FIGURE 9.2    CNN architecture

## 9.2.2 Convolutional Neural Network

A CNN [20] is a feed-forward neural network that is generally used for image recognition and object classification. CNN considers only the current input and has four layers, namely:

1. Convolution layer
2. ReLU layer
3. Pooling
4. Fully connected layer.

Every layer has its functionality and performs feature extractions and finds out hidden patterns. CNN cannot handle sequential data. The architecture of CNN is presented in Figure 9.2.

## 9.2.3 Recurrent Neural Network

An RNN works on the principle of saving the output of a layer and feeding this back to the input in order to predict the output of the layer. RNN

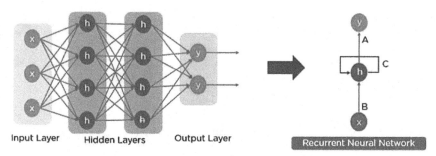

FIGURE 9.3    Recurrent neural network architecture

considers the current input and also the previously received inputs. It can memorize previous inputs due to its internal memory. There are four types of RNN namely: one to one, one to many, many to one, and many to many. RNN can handle sequential data. The architecture of RNN is presented in Figure 9.3.

## 9.3  GRASP REPRESENTATION

Grasp representation can be achieved by identifying the grasp point in an object. In some earlier works, points were identified on objects as the grasp point and also the orientation of the object so that it could match the end-effector orientation of the robotic gripper; in planning grasp there is a global approach which recognizes the whole image point cloud [21–23], boundary of the object [16,24], and also the texture of the image [24].

### 9.3.1  Object Detection

#### 9.3.1.1  Analytical Approach
Analytical methods are carried out in some works in which they rely on hardcore manual programming of robots and are mostly applied to a known environment to perform a specific task based on what is expected to be achieved. The analytical approach relies on the assumption that the object is known. This method also causes task drift. The performance in an environment complementary to that and a new task make it not applicable in every situation, which is a major drawback. To achieve the desired output in a structured and unstructured environment, the empirical method (data-driven approach) makes the robot perform better by feeding the robot with abundant information for learning so that it can achieve what is expected of it. This method is more adaptive and robust. Figure 9.4 shows a summary of the analytical approach.

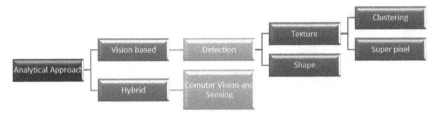

FIGURE 9.4   Visual summary of the analytical approach

### 9.3.1.2 Empirical Approach

9.3.1.2.1 Deep Learning   Detection in computer vision is the detection of an object in a bounding box, and segmentation is the probable isolation of pixels that belong to an object in an image by using their boundary. In detection some work is being carried out on an analytical method whereby the task is mainly carried out based on how the robot is programmed, and it is assumed that the geometry of the object, physical models, and force analytics are known [10,14,21–23,25,26]. Due to the drawbacks of the analytical methods, the empirical method is preferred due to the uncertainty of the environment, object shape, texture, and changes that are developing in the robot's environment, and so the empirical methods are more robust and can achieve high performance on objects and environments they are not familiar with. The data-driven approach relies on previous training success achieved in the detection of the object. There are two empirical method approaches:

1. The method that uses learning for grasp detection and uses separate planning in planning grasp
2. Direct image to grasp which is visuomotor

Detection of the object under the empirical approach can be categorized into two categories:

1. Global object detection
2. Local object detection

In global object detection, the whole object's physical and geometric model is considered. Baumgartl and Henrich [21] report that they made use of geometry to detect grasp poses in 3D point clouds. A pair of point contacts with friction is antipodal if and only if the line connecting the contact points lies inside both friction cones.

9.3.1.2.2 Classical Deep Learning Approach    The Hough transform (HT) was introduced more than half a century ago but remains a popular method in image processing and computer vision, having been extended to detect features, objects, or shapes of any type. HT is a process of summing up evidence (accumulating votes) for a shape from multiple, local, image elements that could be constituent parts of that shape. Evidence is summed in an accumulator array in which different cells represent different combinations of parameters (such as the location, scale, orientation, etc.) for possible instances of the shape. Following this voting process, cells with high values will correspond to those instances of the shape for which there is the most evidence. Shape detection thus involves finding the peaks in the accumulator array. To identify grasp on a flat surface, RANSAC performs very well, and can isolate point cloud clusters in this way to identify the whole object.

### 9.3.1.3 Empirical Grasp Approach
9.3.1.3.1 Global Detection    Kanoulas et al. [23] employ random sample consensus (RANSAC) for extraction of maximum point clouds, and the centre of mass of the object is detected using the point cloud of the object. The final grasp localization is estimated in two iterative stages until a termination threshold criterion is met, using exteroceptive and proprioceptive perception (Figure 9.5). Duan et al. [16] apply RANSAC for ellipse detection RANSAC which was applied in both the horizontal and vertical directions to locate the centre and boundary of the ellipse. The main advantage of this method is easy computation. Also, self-calibration can be realized. Lippiello et al. [22] place a virtual elastic surface reconstruction around the object, then this surface is shrunk at every iteration step until the hull intercepts with some points on the object. Attractive forces with respect to the border of the visual hull are generated so as to compensate for the elastic force. The line is drawn using the Hough transform (HT) which the gripper will identify in the optimal location of grasp [27]. With contact-reactive grasping of objects with partial shape information, in this work, grasp was achieved by the contact reactive method of sensor noise and contact error. The point cloud cluster is identified as the object and bounded by a box, to achieve the grip the bounding box line and the point cloud edge are considered as the collision point, with this a grasp of that area can be achieved [14], by using multiple view measurements. The quadric is estimated in each 2D view. The robot arm will already start moving towards the unknown object after the first quadric estimation is obtained, which results in a fast-real-time grasping algorithm. Baumgartl and Henrich [21]

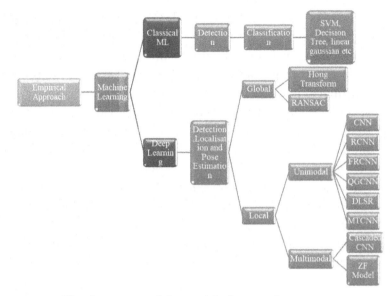

FIGURE 9.5    Visual summary of the empirical approach

perform fast vision-based grasp and delivery planning for unknown objects; they make use of Hough transform techniques to find lines on an unknown object that will match the gripper width. Then, planning of delivery was based on tracking the bounding box of the delivery area, which it can achieve in real time.

9.3.1.3.2  Local Detection    Dunet et al. [14] applied K-means clustering to build a dictionary learning for learning features and then deep learning using CNN to predict the recognition and pose estimation of objects [28]. In this work, for the detection of an object, a reference rectangle with five elements was used to find the probable grasp point and also a convolutional neural network was applied which was a train on ImageNet and also a loss function base on IoU matrices was proposed, which improves the state-of-the-art procedure and achieved a mean accuracy of 73.4% [29]. This was applied to the unstructured environment and a low-cost 2D camera can be used. Ren et al. [30] report real-time image recognition by implementing a region proposal on FRCNN, which achieves 9–17 fps and obtains the highest accuracy of 91.3% on the Cornell dataset. This method is a little slow in detection. Zhang et al. [26] employ a multi-task convolutional neural network to achieve real-time perception, reasoning, and grasping of an object, and although it is not fast it achieves 6.5 frames per second. Zhang et al. [31] oriented anchor boxes that were applied with a method called angle matching, where the oriented anchor box provides a better grasp and is faster in training on the grasp network. The accuracy of previously seen objects is 90% and for unseen ones it is 84%, with real-time recognition it achieves 67 fps. Guo et al. [32] apply a reference rectangle with an aspect ratio of 4:1 using the Ziglar and Fergus method (ZF) in which the images were rotated for K samples and the image is fed into the network and the IoU region was captured as the graspable region. This method achieves 80 frames per second FCNN that has five shared convolutional layers to extract features from the input image. Transfer learning feature extraction (the weights of the VGG16 model pre-trained on some IMAGE dataset) was used to enhance the results of classification. As per the presented work in this paper, Guo et al. [32] achieved the fastest object detection with 80 fps.

Object detection and localization were performed using an oriented reference rectangle [33], a cascaded two-layer DNN was used for training, and for recognition an inference layer was applied to find a single rectangle with maximum probability in the first network and the second network was used to validate. In this work, recognition can be achieved without any supervision. The first network has fewer features, is faster to run, and can effectively prune out unlikely candidate grasps. The second, with more features, is slower but has to run only on the top few detections. Second, we need to handle multimodal inputs effectively, for which we present a method that applies structured regularization on the weights based on multimodal group regularization. The two-layer network is efficient and gives high accuracy when it comes to detection. Trottier et al. [34] made use of dictionary learning and sparse representation; this method is fast in feature extraction and localization, and the accuracy on the Cornell dataset was improved by 3.16% on the state-of-the-art methods using CNN in which the highest the dataset achieves was89.40%, and so it could be a viable option for computer vision base grasp detection [35]. The dictionary is built by using K-means clustering for the colour component of the images with background and objects. Clustering is a way to separate groups of components and apply max-pooling convolutional neural network (MPCNN) for pose estimation in vision-based robotic grasp [36]. In this method, cognitive vision was used to estimate the size of the gripper and grasp using a high-level controller and EMG to control position/force open, close, and hold using a low-level controller. In this work, an accuracy of 93% was achieved because the reasoning capability of the user of the prosthetic hand could provide a good grasp with minimal prior training background [37].

Image recognition on the dual network eases the deep neural network instead of leaving unreferenced functions and provides comprehensive empirical evidence showing that the residual network is easier to optimize and can gain accuracy by considering the increase in depth; an assembly of the net achieves a 3.57% error on image net set [10]. The grasp quality convolutional neural network (GQ-CNN) model rapidly predicts the probability of success of grasps from depth images, where grasps are specified as the planar position, angle, and depth of a gripper relative to an RGB-D sensor. GQ-CNN trained with only synthetic data from Dex-Net 2.0 can be used to plan grasps in 0.8 s with a success rate of 93% on eight known objects with adversarial geometry and is three times faster than registering point clouds.

Using oriented rectangles, they find the best rectangle by matching the width of the gripper and the rectangle with the highest score, applying a spatial histogram to improve the fast search [39]. Sumra and Kanan [40] achieved 89.21% on the Cornell dataset, with the detection and localization being done using a reference rectangle, and deep learning was applied using ResNet architecture. Park et al. [17] report having performed grasp detection using the You Only Look Once technique and employing fully convolutional neural network (FCNN) for training. This approach can achieve real-time object detection, grasp points are detected and localize, and the orientation of the object is known, which the robot uses to manipulate the end effector to a position of grasp. On the Cornell dataset, the accuracy achieved on novel objects is up to 96.1%. This is a remarkable achievement as YOLO is amongst the fastest detection techniques. Liu et al. [18] employed Single Shot Detection (SSD) on multi-scale convolutional bounding box outputs attached to multiple feature maps at the top of the network, the SSD outperforms Faster RCNN with a real-time detection of 59 fps when tested on the nPASCAL VOC and COCO. So far, SSD is the state of the art when it comes to detection.

## 9.4 CONCLUSIONS

As discussed in the previous sections, object detection, localization, and pose estimation play a huge role in object grasp detection and control. Based on the accuracies presented in Table 9.1, on the most popular dataset (i.e. Cornell dataset), the highest accuracy achieved in real time is 96.1%

TABLE 9.1    Model's Performance Summary on Different Datasets

| Dataset | Network | Architecture | Accuracy (%) |
|---|---|---|---|
| Cornell [24] | DCNN | ResNet | 89.29 |
| THU [15] | FRCNN | ZF | 93.2 |
| VMRD [26] | MTCNN | | 94.2 |
| DexNet [10] | QGCNN | | 93 |
| CMU [32] | ZF | FCNN | 82 |
| Cornell [31] | FCNN | ResNet | 90 |
| Cornell [29] | CNN | ImageNet | 73.4 |
| Cornell [34] | DLSR | | 92.65 |
| PASCAL VOC [23] | FRCNN | | 91.3 |
| Cornell [33] | DNN | ImageNet | 92 |
| Cornell [17] | FCNN | | 96.1 |

and 59 fps during the detection process using Single Shot Detection [17]. The approach with the fastest detection is the ZF model which achieved 80 fps though the accuracy was 82% on the THU dataset, but still it could perform better and achieve greater accuracy in detection if improved [32]. To mimic human vision fast detection of objection detection and the ability to make a decision are important.

## ACKNOWLEDGEMENTS

The authors would like to acknowledge the support of the Near East University Research Center for AI and IoT, and the AI and Robotics Institute of Near East University.

## REFERENCES

[1] A. Kevin, That 'Internet of Things' Thing, RFiD J., p. 4986, 2010, www. itrco.jp/libraries/RFIDjournal-That Internet of Things Thing.pdf

[2] L. Catarinucci et al., An IoT-Aware Architecture for Smart Healthcare Systems, IEEE Internet Things J., vol. 2, no. 6, pp. 515–526, 2015.

[3] Z. Guan, J. Li, L. Wu, Y. Zhang, J. Wu, and X. Du, Achieving Efficient and Secure Data Acquisition for Cloud-Supported Internet of Things in Smart Grid, IEEE Internet Things J., vol. 4, no. 6, pp. 1934–1944, 2017, doi: 10.1109/JIOT.2017.269052.

[4] S. Aslam, M. P. Michaelides, and H. Herodotou, Internet of Ships: A Survey on Architectures, Emerging Applications, and Challenges, IEEE Internet Things J., vol. 7, no. 10, pp. 9714–9727, 2020.

[5] J. Contreras-Castillo, S. Zeadally, and J. A. Guerrero-Ibanez, Internet of Vehicles: Architecture, Protocols, and Security, IEEE Internet Things J., vol. 5, no. 5, pp. 3701–3709, 2018.

[6] A. S. Mubarak, Z. Sa'id Ameen, P. Tonga, and F. Al-Turjman, Smart Tourism: A Proof of Concept For Cyprus Museum of Modern Arts In The IoT Era, pp. 49–53, 2021.

[7] A. S. Mubarak, Z. S. Ameen, P. Tonga, C. Altrjman, and F. Al-Turjman, A Framework for Pothole Detection via the AI-Blockchain Integration, in 2021 International Conference on Forthcoming Networks and Sustainability in AIoT Era (FoNeS-AIoT), IEEE, 2022, pp. 398–406.

[8] J. Lin, W. Yu, N. Zhang, X. Yang, H. Zhang, and W. Zhao, A Survey on Internet of Things: Architecture, Enabling Technologies, Security and Privacy, and Applications, IEEE Internet Things J., vol. 4, no. 5, pp. 1125–1142, 2017.

[9] Joseph Bradley, J. Barbier, and D. Handler, Embracing the Internet of Everything To Capture Your Share of $ 14.4 Trillion, Cisco Ibsg Gr., 2013, www.cisco.com/web/about/ac79/docs/innov/IoE_Economy.pdf

[10] J. Mahler et al., Dex-Net 2.0: Deep Learning to Plan Robust Grasps with Synthetic Point Clouds and Analytic Grasp Metrics, 2017, doi: 10.15607/RSS.2017.XIII.058.

[11] A. S. Mubarak, Z. S. Ameen, P. Tonga, C. Altrjman, and F. Al-Turjman, A Framework for Pothole Detection via the AI-Blockchain Integration BT – Forthcoming Networks and Sustainability in the IoT Era, 2022, pp. 398–406.

[12] M. A. Saleh, Z. S. Ameen, C. Altrjman, and F. Al-Turjman, Computer-Vision-Based Statue Detection with Gaussian Smoothing Filter and Efficient Detection, pp. 1–10, 2022.

[13] S. Caldera, A. Rassau, and D. Chai, Review of Deep Learning Methods in Robotic Grasp Detection, 2018, doi: 10.3390/mti2030057.

[14] C. Dune, E. Marchand, C. Collowet, and C. Leroux, Active rough shape estimation of unknown objects Active rough shape estimation of unknown objects, January 2008, doi: 10.1109/IROS.2008.4651005.

[15] D. Guo, F. Sun, H. Liu, T. Kong, B. Fang, and N. Xi, A Hybrid Deep Architecture for Robotic Grasp Detection, pp. 1609–1614, 2017.

[16] F. Duan, L. Wang, and P. Guo, Neural Information Processing. Models and Applications, 6444, November 2010, doi: 10.1007/978-3-642-17534-3.

[17] D. Park, Y. Seo, and S. Y. Chun, Real-Time, Highly Accurate Robotic Grasp Detection using Fully Convolutional Neural Networks with High-Resolution Images, 2011.

[18] W. Liu et al., SSD: Single Shot MultiBox Detector.

[19] R. Laezza, Deep Neural Networks for Myoelectric Pattern Recognition An Implementation for Multifunctional Control, 2018.

[20] Z. S. Ameen, A. Saleh Mubarak, C. Altrjman, S. Alturjman, and R. A. Abdulkadir, C-SVR Crispr: Prediction of CRISPR / Cas12 guideRNA activity using deep learning models, in 2021 International Conference

on Forthcoming Networks and Sustainability in AIoT Era (FoNeS-AIoT), Dec. 2021, vol. 60, no. 4, pp. 9–12.

[21] J. Baumgartl and D. Henrich, Fast Vision-based Grasp and Delivery Planning for unknown Objects Fast Vision-based Grasp and Delivery Planning for unknown Objects, June, 2014.

[22] V. Lippiello, F. Ruggiero, and B. Siciliano, Visual Grasp Planning for Unknown Objects Using a Multi-Fingered Robotic Hand, January 2019, doi: 10.1109/TMECH.2012.2195500.

[23] D. Kanoulas, J. Lee, D. G. Caldwell, and N. G. Tsagarakis, Center-of-Mass-Based Grasp Pose Adaptation Using 3D Range and Force/Torque Sensing, pp. 1–26, 2018.

[24] A. Saxena, J. Driemeyer, and A. Y. Ng, Robotic grasping of novel objects using vision, Int. J. Rob. Res., vol. 27, no. 2, pp. 157–173, 2008.

[25] A. Pas and R. Platt, Using Geometry to Detect Grasp Poses in 3D Point Clouds Using Geometry to Detect Grasp Poses in 3D Point Clouds, September, 2015.

[26] H. Zhang, X. Lan, L. Wan, C. Yang, X. Zhou, and N. Zheng, RPRG: Toward Real-time Robotic Perception, Reasoning and Grasping with One Multi-task Convolutional Neural Network, no. 1.

[27] K. Hsiao, S. Chitta, M. Ciocarlie, and E. G. Jones, Contact-reactive grasping of objects with partial shape information Contact-Reactive Grasping of Objects with Partial Shape Information, June 2014, doi: 10.1109/IROS.2010.5649494.

[28] P. Bezak, P. Bozek, and Y. Nikitin, Advanced Robotic Grasping System Using Deep Learning, Procedia Eng., vol. 96, pp. 10–20, 2014.

[29] L. Bergamini, M. Sposato, and M. Peruzzini, Deep Learning-Based Method for Vision- Guided Robotic Grasping of Unknown Objects, September 2018, doi: 10.3233/978-1-61499-898-3-281.

[30] S. Ren, K. He, R. Girshick, and J. Sun, Faster R-CNN: Towards Real-Time Object Detection with Region Proposal Networks, vol. 8828, no. c, pp. 1–14, 2016.

[31] H. Zhang, X. Zhou, X. Lan, J. Li, Z. Tian, and N. Z. Fellow, A Real-time Robotic Grasp Approach with Oriented Anchor Box, pp. 1–11.

[32] D. Guo, F. Sun, T. Kong, and H. Liu, Deep vision networks for real-time robotic grasp detection, February, pp. 1–8, 2017.

[33] I. Lenz, H. Lee, and A. Saxena, Deep learning for detecting robotic grasps, vol. 34, pp. 705–724, 2015.

[34] L. Trottier, P. Giguere, and B. Chaib-Draa, Sparse dictionary learning for identifying grasp locations, Proc. – 2017 IEEE Winter Conf. Appl. Comput. Vision, WACV 2017, pp. 871–879, 2017.

[35] J. Yu, K. Weng, G. Liang, and G. Xie, A Vision-based Robotic Grasping System Using Deep Learning for 3D Object Recognition and Pose

Estimation, 2013 IEEE Int. Conf. Robot. Biomimetics, no. December, pp. 1175–1180, 2013.

[36] S. Do, C. Cipriani, M. Controzzi, M. C. Carrozza, and D. B. Popovi, Cognitive vision system for control of dexterous prosthetic hands: Experimental evaluation, pp. 1–14, 2010.

[37] K. He, X. Zhang, S. Ren, and J. Sun, Deep residual learning for image recognition, in Proceedings of the IEEE Computer Society Conference on Computer Vision and Pattern Recognition, 2016, vol. 2016-Decem, pp. 770–778.

[38] E. Johns, S. Leutenegger, and A. J. Davison, Deep Learning a Grasp Function for Grasping under Gripper Pose Uncertainty, pp. 4461–4468, 2016.

[39] Y. Jiang, S. Moseson, and A. Saxena, Efficient Grasping from RGBD Images: Learning using a new Rectangle Representation, pp. 3304–3311, 2011.

[40] S. Kumra and C. Kanan, Robotic grasp detection using deep convolutional neural networks, IEEE Int. Conf. Intell. Robot. Syst., vol. 2017-Sept, pp. 769–776, 2017.

# CHAPTER 10

# Artificial Intelligence-Based Methods for SARS-CoV-2 Detection with CRISPR Systems

Zubaida Sa'id Ameen, Auwalu Saleh Mubarak, Fadi Al-Turjman, and Sinem Alturjman

*AI and Robotics Institute, Near East University, Nicosia, Turkey*

## CONTENTS

| | | |
|---|---|---|
| 10.1 | Introduction | 174 |
| 10.2 | CRISPR Overview | 175 |
| 10.3 | COVID-19 Diagnostic Tools Based on Cas12 | 176 |
| 10.4 | COVID-19 Diagnostic Tools Based on Cas13 | 179 |
| 10.5 | Application of Artificial Intelligence for SARS-CoV-2 Detection Using CRISPR-Based Methods | 181 |
| 10.6 | Conclusions | 184 |
| References | | 185 |

DOI: 10.1201/9781003322887-10

## 10.1 INTRODUCTION

CRISPR technology, meaning clustered regularly interspaced short palindromic repeats, is a powerful method for changing the genome [1]. It makes it simple for scientists to manipulate DNA sequences and correct gene function. CRISPR and CRISPR-associated proteins known as Cas proteins have a wide range of potential uses, including the correction of genetic abnormalities, disease treatment, and disease prevention [1,2]. Researchers have been able to put CRISPR to good use in both therapeutics of several infectious illnesses and molecular diagnostic applications due to recent advancements [3,4]. Coronaviruses (CoVs) are single-stranded RNA viruses that contain four structural proteins: the envelope, the spike, the nucleoprotein, and finally the membrane [56]. The six CoVs known to be pathogenic to humans are SARS-CoV, MERS-CoV, HCoV-OC43, HCoVHKU1, HCoV-NL63, and HCoV-229E, the first two of which are highly transmissible and pathogenic [7–9]. The novel (new) global coronavirus pandemic has resulted in a dramatic increase in deaths. SARS-CoV-2 is the third extremely pathogenic coronavirus in the human population, after SARS-CoV and MERS-CoV [10]. One of the most popular methods for detecting COVID-19 infection is to identify the genome of SARS-CoV-2 [11]. For SARS-CoV-2 detection, nucleic-acid-based assays are widely considered a useful tool. SARS-CoV-2 is commonly detected using one of two molecular methods: reverse-transcription polymerase chain reaction (RT-PCR) or metagenomic next-generation sequencing (mNGS) [12–14]. However, the applicability of mNGS is hampered by its high cost and a roughly one-day detection time. As a result, it is unsuitable for applications in diagnosis for SARS-CoV-2 [15]. In relation to mNGS-based techniques, the RT-PCR test was reported to be quicker and less expensive. Despite this, the requirement for a thermocycler makes them difficult to utilize in poor settings and limits assay productivity, as a result, both techniques are ineffective for diagnosing SARS-CoV-2, especially at the point of care [16]. Due to the lack of a fast and promising detection techniques and the urgent need for rapid diagnostic tests, novel techniques such as CRISPR technology could be a good option for SARS-CoV-2 infection detection and treatment platform. CRISPRs were first described in the genome of *Escherichia coli* as a collection of short repetitive sequences interspersed with short sequences by Japanese researchers in 1987 [17]. CRISPRs were later discovered in a variety of bacteria and archaea [18], prompting speculation about their potential functions in the repair of DNA as well as gene regulation [19]. It was later suggested that CRISPR is a defensive mechanism based on the discovery that CRISPR loci undergo transcription and that the proteins expressed by Cas genes have two domains, helicase and nuclease [1]. The CRISPR RNA (crRNA) forms a complex together with Cas protein that can interfere with the activities of foreign viral DNA serving as a means of an adaptive defence mechanism. The use of CRISPR in gene editing was made possible after the components needed were first synthesized in vitro to target any gene of interest [20]. After that, CRISPR was utilized around the world for various applications that were not possible before and that brought about a new era in gene editing.

In addition, CRISPR has recently been utilized to identify nucleic acids [21]. According to recent studies, CRISPR methods may detect SARS-CoV-2 with good sensitivity and specificity [22,23] making it a promising technique for COVID-19 detection. In the detection process, the CRISPR complex cuts the desired location first, which initiates the next phase, that is, collateral cleavage of the surrounding nucleic acids. The collateral cleavage effect is seen in a variety of CRISPR types such as types III, V, and VI systems utilizing Csm, Cas12 or Cas14, and Cas13 proteins, respectively. The collateral cleavage capacity of CRISPR Cas12, the Cas13, and the Cas14 proteins allows them to indiscriminately cut neighbouring nucleic acid after they attach to the target site.

For diagnosing 2019 novel coronavirus infection, Cas13 and Csm employ the Specific High-Sensitivity Enzymatic Reporter unlocking (SHERLOCK) technology, while Cas12 and Cas14 utilize DNA endonuclease-targeted CRISPR trans reporter (DETECTR) technology to provide quick and reliable SARS-CoV-2 diagnostic tests based on CRISPR methods with high sensitivity as well as specificity [24]. Because CRISPR detection methods are very sensitive and specific, and do not require specialized equipment for analysis, they may be used to identify SARS-CoV-2 in hospitals and at the point of care. The variety of CRISPR approaches utilized for SARS-CoV-2 detection and their detection processes are the focus of this study.

## 10.2 CRISPR OVERVIEW

The CRISPR system, which was identified in bacteria and archaea, was needed to fight phages as well as other mobile genetic elements such as plasmids and transposons [25]. Adaptation, crRNA processing, and interference are the three primary processes in this CRISPR system. First, adaptation entails inserting the foreign invading genomic segments as spacer sequences inside the CRISPR array [26]. Next, during crRNA processing, the CRISPR array is translated into pre-crRNA, which is subsequently processed into mature crRNAs, which form complexes with Cas proteins, and finally CRISPR interference, were the crRNA–Cas complexes catalyse sequence-specific destruction to recognize and delete foreign genomic regions [1]. CRISPR systems are very diverse and their classification is based on a number of characteristics, including unique Cas genes, Cas operon architecture, and Cas protein phylogenies [27]. Due to the overall nature of the interference complex and the number of Cas genes, CRISPR systems are grouped into two classes, 1 and 2. Class 1 includes the I, III, and IV types with various subtypes, and the CRISPR ribonucleoprotein effector nucleases in these subtypes employ several Cas proteins, whereas class 2 includes the II, V, and VI types with various subtypes and uses a single Cas protein [27,28].

The most well-studied and characterized are the class 2 systems that include Cas9 from the type II system, Cas12 from the type V system, and Cas13 from the type VI system. Cas9 was the first utilized specifically for gene editing [29]. Cas9 uses RuvC and HNH as two DNA-cutting domains to generate blunt double-stranded DNA (dsDNA) breaks at the target location [30]. Cas12 is closely related to Cas9, but it introduces staggered dsDNA breaks using a single RuvC domain [31]. Cas12a has been discovered to degrade nonspecific single-stranded DNA (ssDNA) in response to specific binding of crRNA to either ssDNA or dsDNA [32]. Cas13 is a protein with two higher eukaryotes and prokaryotes nucleotide-binding (HEPN) domains that are believed to target RNA rather than DNA [33]. Cas13 cleaves RNA targets that are complementary to the crRNA, but it also causes non-specific RNA to be degraded [34]. The non-specific cleavage, also called collateral cleavage, performed by some of the Cas proteins has immense applications in the detection of nucleic acids. The binding of crRNA with the SARS-CoV-2 gene can cause collateral cleavage of a reporter molecule, which can be detected in a variety of ways.

## 10.3 COVID-19 DIAGNOSTIC TOOLS BASED ON CAS12

The CRISPR/Cas12 system causes single-stranded DNA cleavage after the guide RNA binds to the target location. The ability to produce collateral cleavage in single-stranded DNA can be employed to detect fluorescent single-stranded reporter molecules because the Cas12 complex and target association triggers indiscriminate single-stranded DNase activity [32]. As a result, CRISPR-Cas12-related techniques can be employed as a tool to detect SARS-CoV-2 in real time. Figure 10.1 depicts the whole process for the assay using the Cas12 detection platform. The major processes include reverse transcription (RT) amplification, Cas12 reaction, and signal readout. After isolating viral RNA from the samples obtained, reverse transcription and amplification of the target RNAs are performed. Then the DNA that was amplified will be added to the Cas12a/guideRNA complex in the Cas12a reaction step. After binding to the target DNA, Cas12a would carry out collateral cleavage on non-target reporters in the vicinity. Finally, due to the cleavage of single-stranded DNA (ssDNA) reporter molecules, the detection may be easily noticed. ssDNA that has been fluorophore quencher (FQ) or fluorophore biotin (FB) labelled is commonly used as a reporter and a fluorescence-based reaction or a colorimetric reaction can be used to read the signal once the non-targeted ssDNA reporter has been cleaved.

Using the CRISPR/Cas12a technology, an attempt was made to detect SARS-CoV-2 precisely, sensitively, and quickly [23]. The researchers were able to identify SARS-CoV-2 RNA recovered from patient respiratory tract swab samples in under 40 minutes using a DNA endonuclease-targeted CRISPR trans reporter (DETECTR). This method was developed by combining the CRISPR/Cas12a DETECTR system with isothermal amplification for pure RNA from nasopharyngeal or oropharyngeal swabs, which performs reverse transcription and isothermal amplification by loop-mediated replication at the same time (RT-LAMP). When Cas12a recognizes specific viral sequences, the reporter molecule cleaves, revealing the presence of a virus [23].

Similarly, the effective CRISPR method of diagnosis show that the DETECTR diagnostic system may be used as a quick, low-cost, and easy alternative to PCR [35]. A 95% relationship was observed when the DETECTR method was compared to qRT-PCR in 378 individuals for SARS-CoV-2 diagnosis. Furthermore, the DETECTR system for the diagnosis does not require specialist equipment and can be utilized to diagnose SARS-CoV-2 and the technology was 100% specific for recognizing SARS-CoV-2. This CRISPR diagnostic systems show that the DETECTR diagnostic system may be used as an easy, low-cost, and quick alternative to qRT-PCR, without sacrificing sensitivity or specificity for molecular detection [35]. Lalla et al. [36] utilized Cas12 for the detection of SARS-CoV-2 using two types of crRNAs to target different locations; the binding of the

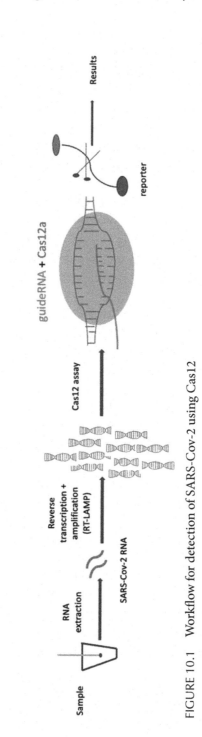

FIGURE 10.1  Workflow for detection of SARS-Cov-2 using Cas12

crRNA to their targets activates the collateral cleavage of ssDNA reporter molecules. This reaction was carried out at room temperature in one test tube and the results can be seen with the naked eye within 40 minutes [36]. Another system based on two crRNAs for SARS-CoV-2 detection was reported by Ma et al. [37], this method involves the addition of manganese ($Mn^{2+}$) to further increase the detection sensitivity of the Cas12a system. The use of Cas12-based systems for SARS-CoV-2 detection is commonly used due it its sensitivity and simplicity, as it does not require sophisticated instruments or trained personnel and the duration is less an hour and it can be carried out in isothermal conditions. Other studies have reported Cas12 detection with high sensitivity. Although numerous studies have reported the use of Cas12a, another assay was carried out using Cas12b [38]. For the Cas12b-based system, RNA was first extracted from a sample and amplified using recombinase-aided amplification after producing the cDNA with reverse transcription. Then, the amplified product was mixed together with Cas12b complex in a single tube, which leads to binding of the modified crRNA to the SARS-CoV-2 gene and cleavage of the reporter molecule labelled with fluorophore which was visualized under blue LED light or UV light. This reaction was carried out within 10–30 min at 37–42°C with a high sensitivity since the detection limit was around 10 copies/µL [38].

## 10.4 COVID-19 DIAGNOSTIC TOOLS BASED ON CAS13

SHERLOCK, called specific high-sensitivity enzymatic reporter unlocking, is a nucleic acid detection tool developed by Feng [39]. Unlike DETECTR which is based on Cas12 system [32], SHERLOCK is normally used with the Cas13a system as well as Cas12a and Csm6 [39]. SHERLOCK is widely used to detect RNA viruses because the activation of Cas13 components leads to cleavage of RNA molecules which were bound to the reporter molecule, confirming the presence of the virus. Figure 10.2 depicts the whole process for the assay using a Cas13a detection platform. Similar to the Cas12-based detection system, amplification, Cas13a assay, and signal readout are the main stages involved. The amplification procedure is first carried out after viral RNA extraction from raw samples using recombinase polymerase amplification (RPA). This amplification step is important as it serves as a substitute for the PCR amplification method that is normally used. Then the target amplicons will be added to the Cas13a/crRNA complex in the Cas13a assay step. The Cas13a would become activated after binding to the SARS-CoV-2 gene and undertake collateral cleavage

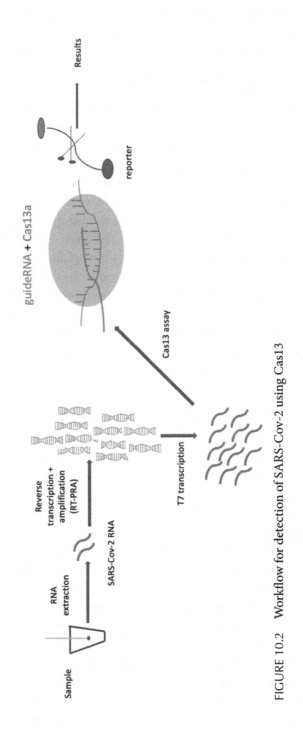

FIGURE 10.2 Workflow for detection of SARS-Cov-2 using Cas13

on the surrounding non-target reporters. Finally, the detection can be easily observed by the cleavage of single-stranded RNA (ssRNA) reporter molecules since they are coupled to a fluorescent molecule. Although the Cas13a-based detection system is used to detect RNA viruses it can also be used to detect DNA molecules after incorporation of the T7 RNA polymerase reaction which will convert the DNA into an RNA molecule that is recognized by the Cas13a components.

Feng [40] developed an improved Cas13-based method for detection of the SARS-CoV-2 gene. This system is a very rapid and sensitive method of detection that can be carried out without the need for laboratory equipment. The improved method can be used to detect the presence of the SARS-CoV-2 gene from clinical samples in less than an hour with a simple experimental setup [40]. Another SHERLOCK-based method called SHERLOCK testing in one pot (STOP) that can be utilized at the point of care because the whole assay can be carried out in a single tube in less than an hour [41] was able to detect COVID-19 from nasopharyngeal swabs of patients within 70 min for lateral flow readouts and 40 min for fluorescence [41]. CREST, known as Cas13a-based rugged equitable scalable testing, can be utilized also for the detection of SARS-CoV-2 with good sensitivity and can be deployed in point-of-care settings [42]. This method can be carried out within 2 hours using simple reagents and instrumentation and can manage the issue of scalability of CRISPR-based methods [42]. In order to handle the problem of SARS-CoV-2 detection due to virus mutations in the PCR method, the Variant Nucleotide Guard (VanGuard) method was developed by Ooi et al. [43]. This method is able to detect the SARS-CoV-2 gene even when it has undergone mutations. VanGuard can be utilized at point-of-care settings with an assay time within 30 min [43]. In an effort to eliminate the nucleic acid extraction step from samples prior to amplification, a detection method called heating unextracted diagnostic samples to obliterate nucleases (HUDSON) was combined with SHERLOCK with high sensitivity and can be used at the point of care [44].

## 10.5 APPLICATION OF ARTIFICIAL INTELLIGENCE FOR SARS-COV-2 DETECTION USING CRISPR-BASED METHODS

One of the challenges of utilizing this CRISPR-based detection method is the design and selection suitable guideRNA that will bind to the specific region of the SARS-CoV-2 gene that will trigger the collateral cleavage and hence confirmation of the presence of the virus, therefore without an active guideRNA molecule the whole SARS-CoV-2 detection will not be possible. Computational methods such as machine learning or deep learning methods are needed to design good guideRNAs and to predict their activity before carrying out the assay (Figure 10.3).

Machine learning algorithms automatically uncover patterns in data, which is suitable for data-driven sciences like genomics [45]. In medical imaging for COVID-19 analysis, a variety of DL frameworks were employed [46–50]. In CRISPR-based COVID-19 applications, the creation of innovative machine learning models for prediction and analysis tools is in great demand.

Cas12a crRNA is a single-guide RNA with a total length of 40–44 bases, a 20–24nt protospacer region that is specific to the target gene, and a continuous stem-loop region 20nt in length. The Cas12a protospacer adjacent motif is TTTY region where Y represents either G, C, U, or A [31]. Cas12a proteins have a loop domain that is unique to them, but the target region can be redesigned to match a target gene. Machine learning models can be utilized for the design of good guide RNAs that will bind to the target location on the SARS-CoV-2. Recently, Ameen et al. [51] developed a deep learning tool based on the combination of support vector regression (SVR) and convolutional neural network (CNN) in a single model, that will assist in choosing appropriate guideRNA that will successfully target a specific region on the SARS-CoV-2 gene using the Cas12a system. Another deep learning model was developed for predicting active and inactive guideRNAs using CNN [52]. Similarly, CINDEL, a machine learning tool, was utilized for predicting Cas12a guideRNA activity [53]. Also, a support vector machine was used for designing Cas12a guideRNAs [54]. In another work Metsky and Freije [55] created a set of test designs and experimental techniques for use in diagnostic systems that centred on CRISPR and might be beneficial for long-term monitoring. The described designs were created to detect 67 different viral species and subspecies, including SARS-CoV-2. Metsky's methods utilized machine learning algorithms to enable the creation of molecular detection assays, the results of which have the potential to enhance diagnostics for the identification of viral species [55].

Unlike the Cas12a crRNA design, Cas13a crRNA is a single guide RNA, a 22nt protospacer region that is specific to the target gene and a continuous stem-loop region also specific to the Cas13a protein with the stem loop region playing a role in the ssRNA cleavage [34]. Certain crRNAs are more

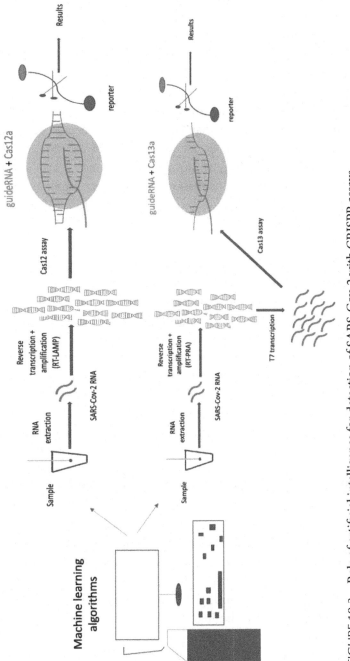

FIGURE 10.3   Role of artificial intelligence for detection of SARS-Cov-2 with CRISPR assays

active than others due to the nature of nucleotide compositions, therefore it is important to consider the protospacer flanking site (PFS). A Cas13 platform for high-throughput phenotypic screening and understanding the design concepts that support its RNA targeting effectiveness was developed by Wei et al. [56]. Different machine learning algorithms and linear regression were compared for training a CNN that can predict guideRNA activity from guideRNA sequences. The final CNN model was able to predict active guideRNA with over 90% accuracy on the test datasets. A design tool was developed from the research that can be used to design active guides for RNA detection using the Cas13 system [56]. In addition, combining Internet of Things technology with machine learning, as well as CRISPR sensing for wireless signal transmission via the cloud, might aid decision-making [57], which will enhance the application of CRISPR-based tools in the detection of SARS-CoV-2.

## 10.6 CONCLUSIONS

The escalating number of deaths associated with the COVID-19 outbreak has generated significant concerns throughout the globe. One of the most problematic aspects of COVID-19 is that it presents a range of symptoms between individuals. As a result, extremely sensitive, specific, and accurate techniques for early identification and consequently improved treatment of COVID-19 must be developed. CRISPR, a gene-editing toolset, has changed the face of medical diagnostic testing. CRISPR may be instructed to target virtually any part of the genome of interest, which is one of its most enticing properties. CRISPR technology, which is most recognized for its genome-editing capabilities, has a broad range of other applications and has recently been used to detect SARS-CoV-2. CRISPR methods of diagnosis with the Cas12a and Cas13 proteins have recently been established. The primary characteristics of this potential instrument in the battle to eradicate diseases are speed, precision, power, cheap cost, sensitivity, and diversity. Another intriguing aspect of using CRISPR as diagnostic systems is that they don't necessitate the use of specialist laboratory instruments like PCR machines, making them accessible even in low-income communities.

For a variety of reasons, using the CRISPR system to identify nucleic acids is problematic. The limited number of targetable sequences, for example, is one of the most common difficulties in CRISPR/Cas-mediated detection. The presence of a sequence known as PAM, on the other hand, is essential for the guide RNA/Cas complex to find and bind with the target location, depending on the kind of Cas protein used. In mismatch tolerance, the Cas protein family determines the tolerance of mismatches between the guideRNA sequence and the target sequence, which is another crucial problem. To develop excellent guideRNAs and predict their activity before doing the assay, computational approaches such as machine learning or deep learning are required. Recently, machine learning-based tools have shown outstanding performance in terms of guideRNA design, and they can also be used to design tests for SARS-CoV-2 detection. The application of machine learning technologies in the discovery of COVID-19 using CRISPR approaches is still in its development, although tools have been reported on Cas12a with a few on Cas13a systems, there is a need for more machine or deep learning-based tools in this regard. Standardization is another key component of the CRISPR system's effective detection. In order to make sure that all users obtain the same result, protocols must be standardized. Furthermore, artificial intelligence (AI) may be used in conjunction with point-of-care sensor technologies to improve data storage and sharing. Combining Internet of Things technology with machine learning, as well as CRISPR-based COVI9-19 detection for wireless signal transmission via the cloud, might aid the decision-making process. This will offer a lot of opportunities for improving CRISPR sensing for COVID-19 detection and management in the future.

## REFERENCES

[1] J. A. Doudna and E. Charpentier, The new frontier of genome engineering with CRISPR-Cas9, Science (80)., vol. 346, no. 6213, 2014.

[2] H. Li, Y. Yang, W. Hong, M. Huang, M. Wu, and X. Zhao, Applications of genome editing technology in the targeted therapy of human diseases: mechanisms, advances and prospects, Signal Transduct. Target. Ther., vol. 5, no. 1, 2020.

[3] F. Safari, S. Farajnia, Y. Ghasemi, and N. Zarghami, New Developments in CRISPR Technology: Improvements in Specificity and Efficiency, pp. 1038–1054, 2017, doi: 10.2174/1389201019666180209120533.

[4] R. Barrangou and P. Horvath, A decade of discovery: CRISPR functions and applications, Nat. Microbiol., vol. 2, no. June, pp. 1–9, 2017.

[5] L. Ren et al., Identification of a novel coronavirus causing severe pneumonia in human: a descriptive study, pp. 4–13, 2020, doi: 10.1097/CM9.0000000000000722.

[6] R. Lu et al., Genomic characterisation and epidemiology of 2019 novel coronavirus: implications for virus origins and receptor binding, Lancet, vol. 6736, no. 20, pp. 1–10, 2020.

[7]  S. Su et al., Epidemiology, Genetic Recombination, and Pathogenesis of Coronaviruses, Trends Microbiol., vol. xx, pp. 1–13, 2016.

[8]  S. R. Weiss, S. Navas-martin, S. R. Weiss, and S. Navas-Martin, Coronavirus Pathogenesis and the Emerging Pathogen Severe Acute Respiratory Syndrome Coronavirus Coronavirus Pathogenesis and the Emerging Pathogen Severe Acute Respiratory Syndrome Coronavirus, vol. 69, no. 4, 2005.

[9]  R. J. De Groot et al., Middle East Respiratory Syndrome of the Coronavirus Study Group Middle East Respiratory Syndrome Coronavirus (MERS-CoV): Announcement of the Coronavirus Study Group Identification of a novel coronavirus as a cause, pp. 14–17, 2013, doi: 10.1128/JVI.01244-13.

[10]  S. Kouhpayeh, L. Shariati, M. Boshtam, I. Rahimmanesh, and M. Mirian, The molecular story of COVID-19; NAD + depletion addresses all questions in this infection, March, 2020, doi: 10.20944/preprints202003.0346.v1.

[11]  C. This et al., Assay Techniques and Test Development for COVID-19 Diagnosis, 2020, doi: 10.1021/acscentsci.0c00501.

[12]  T. Hou et al., Development and Evaluation of A CRISPR-based Diagnostic For 2019-novel Coronavirus, 2020.

[13]  R. Liu, A. Fu, Z. Deng, Y. Li, and T. Liu, Promising methods for detection of novel coronavirus SARS-CoV-2, no. February, pp. 2–5, 2020, doi: 10.1002/viw2.4.

[14]  Detection of SARS-CoV-2 in Different Types of Clinical Specimens, pp. 3–4, 2020, doi: 10.1001/jama.2020.3786.

[15]  J. Ai, H. Zhang, T. Xu, J. Wu, M. Zhu, and Y. Yu, Optimizing diagnostic strategy for novel coronavirus pneumonia, a multi-center study in Eastern China, 2020.

[16]  W. Zhang et al., CRISPR-Based Approaches for Efficient and Accurate Detection of SARS-CoV-2 Visualization and Portable Onsite Detection, pp. 116–121, 2021, doi: 10.1093/labmed/lmaa101.

[17]  Y. Ishino, H. Shinagawa, K. Makino, M. Amemura, and A. Nakatura, Nucleotide sequence of the iap gene, responsible for alkaline phosphatase isoenzyme conversion in Escherichia coli, and identification of the gene product, J. Bacteriol., vol. 169, no. 12, pp. 5429–5433, 1987.

[18]  G. Mojica, F. J. M., Diez-Villasenor, C., Soria, E., & Juez, Biological significance of a family of regularly spaced repeats in the genomes of Archaea, Bacteria and mitochondria, Mol. Microbiol., vol. 36, pp. 244–246, 2000.

[19]  K. S. Makarova, L. Aravind, N. V Grishin, I. B. Rogozin, and E. V Koonin, A DNA repair system specific for thermophilic Archaea and bacteria predicted by genomic context analysis, vol. 30, no. 2, pp. 482–496, 2002.

[20] M. Jinek, K. Chylinski, I. Fonfara, M. Hauer, and J. A. Doudna, A Programmable Dual-RNA – Guided DNA Endonuclease in Adaptive Bacterial Immunity, no. June, 2012.

[21] R. K. Leung et al., CRISPR-Cas12-based nucleic acids detection systems, Methods, no. January 2021, pp. 10–15, 2023.

[22] B. T. Nguyen, L.T, Rananaware, S.R., Pizzano, B.L.M, Stone and P. K. Jain, Clinical validation of engineered CRISPR/Cas12a for rapid SARS-CoV-2 detection, pp. 1–11, 2022, doi: 10.1038/s43856-021-00066-4.

[23] J. P. Broughton et al., CRISPR – Cas12-based detection of SARS-CoV-2, Nat. Biotechnol., vol. 38, pp. 870–874, 2019.

[24] A. Varble and L. A. Marraf, Three New Cs for CRISPR: Collateral, Communicate, Cooperate, Trends Genet., vol. 35, no. 6, pp. 446–456, 2019.

[25] F. Hille, H. Richter, S. P. Wong, M. Bratovič, S. Ressel, and E. Charpentier, The Biology of CRISPR-Cas: Backward and Forward, Cell, vol. 172, no. 6, pp. 1239–1259, 2018.

[26] P. Barrangou, R., Fremaux, C., Deveau, H., Richards, M., Boyaval, P., Moineau, S., … Horvath, CRISPR Provides Acquired Resistance Against Viruses in Prokaryotes, Science (80)., vol. 315, no. March, pp. 1709–1712, 2007.

[27] E. V. Koonin, K. S. Makarova, and F. Zhang, Diversity, classification and evolution of CRISPR-Cas systems, Curr. Opin. Microbiol., vol. 37, pp. 67–78, 2017.

[28] S. Shmakov et al., Diversity and evolution of class 2 CRISPR-Cas systems, Nat. Rev. Microbiol., vol. 15, no. 3, pp. 169–182, 2017.

[29] G. M. Church et al., RNA-Guided Human Genome Engineering via Cas9, Science (80)., vol. 339, no. 823, pp. 823–826, 2013.

[30] M. Jinek, K. Chylinski, I. Fonfara, M. Hauer, J. A. Doudna, and E. Charpentier, A Programmable Dual-RNA – Guided, vol. 337, no. August, pp. 816–822, 2012.

[31] Z. F. Zetsche, Gootenberg J.S., Abudayyeh O.O., Slaymaker I.M., Makarova K.S., Essletzbichler P., Volz S.E., Joung J., van der Oost J., Regev A., Koonin E.V., Cpf1 is a single RNA-guided endonuclease of a Class 2 CRISPR- Cas system Bernd, Cell., vol. 163, no. 3, pp. 759–771, 2015.

[32] J. S. Chen et al., CRISPR-Cas12a target binding unleashes indiscriminate single-stranded DNase activity, vol. 6245, no. February, pp. 1–8, 2018.

[33] S. Shmakov et al., Discovery and Functional Characterization of Diverse Class 2 CRISPR-Cas Systems, Mol. Cell, vol. 60, no. 3, pp. 385–397, 2015.

[34] O. O. Abudayyeh et al., C2c2 is a single-component programmable RNA-guided RNA-targeting CRISPR effector, vol. 5573, no. June, 2016.

[35] C. Detectr, Rapid, Sensitive, and Specific Severe Acute Respiratory Syndrome Coronavirus 2 Detection: A Multicenter Comparison Between

Standard Quantitative Reverse-Transcriptase Polymerase Chain Reaction, vol. 223, 2021, doi: 10.1093/infdis/jiaa641.

[36] R. V Lalla, E. Ballesteros, and M. M. Sfeir, Ultrasensitive and visual detection of SARS-CoV-2 using all-in-one dual CRISPR-Cas12a assay, Nat. Commun., no. 2020, pp. 1–10.

[37] P. Ma et al., MeCas12a, a Highly Sensitive and Specific System for COVID-19 Detection, vol. 2001300, pp. 1–9, 2020, doi: 10.1002/advs.202001300.

[38] L. Guo et al., SARS-CoV-2 detection with CRISPR diagnostics, pp. 4–7, 2020, doi: 10.1038/s41421-020-0174-y.

[39] J. S. Gootenberg, O. O. Abudayyeh, M. J. Kellner, J. Joung, J. J. Collins, and F. Zhang, Multiplexed and portable nucleic acid detection platform with Cas13, Cas12a and Csm6, Science (80)., vol. 360, no. 6387, pp. 439–444, 2018.

[40] F. Zhang, O. O. Abudayyeh, J. S. Gootenberg, and C. Sciences, A protocol for detection of COVID-19 using CRISPR diagnostics, vol. 8, pp. 1–8.

[41] A. Ladha, M. Segel, J. Li, B. D. Walker, A. L. Greninger, and K. R. Jerome, Point-of-care testing for COVID-19 using SHERLOCK diagnostics, 2020.

[42] J. N. Rauch, E. Valois, S. C. Solley, F. Braig, R. S. Lach, and M. Audouard, A Scalable, Easy-to-Deploy Protocol for Cas13-Based Detection, January, pp. 1–8, 2021.

[43] K. H. Ooi, J. Wen, D. Tay, S. Y. Teo, and M. M. Liu, A CRISPR-based SARS-CoV-2 diagnostic assay that is robust against viral evolution and RNA editing, 2020.

[44] C. Myhrvold et al., Field-deployable viral diagnostics using CRISPR-Cas13, vol. 448, no. April, pp. 444–448, 2018.

[45] G. Eraslan, Ž. Avsec, J. Gagneur, and F. J. Theis, Deep learning: new computational modelling techniques for genomics, Nat. Rev. Genet., vol. 20, no. 7, pp. 389–403, 2019.

[46] A. S. Mubarak, S. Serte, F. Al-Turjman, Z. S. id Ameen, and M. Ozsoz, Local binary pattern and deep learning feature extraction fusion for COVID-19 detection on computed tomography images, Expert Syst., vol. 39, no. 3, pp. 1–13, 2022.

[47] C. Liu et al., TX-CNN: Detecting tuberculosis in chest X-ray images using convolutional neural network, Proc. – Int. Conf. Image Process. ICIP, vol. 2017-Septe, pp. 2314–2318, 2018.

[48] A. I. Khan, J. L. Shah, and M. M. Bhat, CoroNet: A deep neural network for detection and diagnosis of COVID-19 from chest x-ray images, Comput. Methods Programs Biomed., vol. 196, p. 105581, 2020.

[49] I. D. Apostolopoulos and T. A. Mpesiana, COVID-19: automatic detection from X-ray images utilizing transfer learning with convolutional neural networks, Phys. Eng. Sci. Med., vol. 43, no. 2, pp. 635–640, 2020.

[50] R. A. A. Mubarak Auwalu Saleh, Sertan Serte Fadi Al-Turjman Zubaida Sa' id Ameen and Mehmet Ozsoz Abdulkadir, Deep learning-based feature extraction coupled with multi class SVM for COVID-19 detection in the IoT era, Int. J. Nanotechnol., vol. 1, no. 1, 2021.

[51] Z. S. Ameen, M. Ozsoz, A. S. Mubarak, F. Al Turjman, and S. Serte, C-SVR Crispr: Prediction of CRISPR/Cas12 guideRNA activity using deep learning models, Alexandria Eng. J., vol. 60, no. 4, pp. 3501–3508, 2021.

[52] J. Luo, W. Chen, L. Xue, and B. Tang, Prediction of activity and specificity of CRISPR-Cpf1 using convolutional deep learning neural networks, BMC Bioinformatics, vol. 20, no. 1, pp. 1–10, 2019.

[53] H. K. Kim et al., In vivo high-throughput profiling of CRISPR-Cpf1 activity, Nat. Methods, vol. 14, no. 2, pp. 153–159, 2017.

[54] H. Zhu and C. Liang, CRISPR-DT: designing gRNAs for the CRISPR-Cpf1 system with improved target efficiency and specificity, Bioinformatics, 2019, doi: 10.1093/bioinformatics/bty1061.

[55] H. C. Metsky and C. A. Freije, CRISPR-based surveillance for COVID-19 using genomically-comprehensive machine learning design, pp. 1–11, 2020.

[56] J. Wei, P. Lotfy, K. Faizi, H. Kitano, P. D. Hsu, and S. Konermann, Deep learning of Cas13 guide activity from high-throughput gene essentiality screening, 2021.

[57] A. U. Ibrahim, F. Al-Turjman, Z. Sa'id, and M. Ozsoz, Futuristic CRISPR-based biosensing in the cloud and internet of things era: an overview, Multimed. Tools Appl., 2020, doi: 10.1007/s11042-020-09010-5.

# Index

**A**

Artificial Intelligence (AI) 7, 9, 49
Attackers 136, 140
Attacks 140, 142
Availability 43, 107

**B**

Big data 68, 104, 109
Biomedical big data 110
Breast cancer 116

**C**

Cloud computing 68, 91, 95, 107
Communication 6, 108
Convolutional Neural Network (CNN) 66, 68, 147
Cost 48, 55, 57
COVID-19 145, 146, 174
Cyber security 134, 142

**D**

Delay 36, 110
Deployment 140
Dose 48, 77
Dynamic 13, 79

**E**

Energy 4, 107, 111
Environmental 4

**F**

False negatives 31, 65, 71
False positives 31, 65, 71, 83

Features 3, 23, 25, 32, 36, 68, 107, 112
Frequency 135

**G**

Genetic 8, 76, 116, 174
Global 134, 160, 164, 174

**H**

HCoV 174
HCoVHKU1 174

**I**

Industrial 105, 107
Internet of Things (IoT) 2, 107, 108, 109, 111, 125, 149
Iterative 165

**K**

Kaggle 27, 39, 79, 82
Keras 37
Key performance indicators (KPIs) 11, 37

**L**

Lifestyle 125, 126
Linear behaviour 38, 43
Long- term monitoring 182

**M**

Machine learning (ML) 12, 22, 65, 95, 114, 147
Malicious 136, 137, 141
Measurements 122, 165
Microaneurysms 43

Microcontroller 5
Micro-hospitals 127
Mobile 3, 12, 149
MobileNetV2 29, 30

**N**

Network architecture 38, 52, 69,
    147
Neural network (NN) 10, 23, 68
Node 12, 23, 29, 78

**O**

Overfitting 30, 32, 69

**P**

Particle swarm optimization (PSO)
    119
Performance 9, 11, 25, 163, 169, 185
Physical models 164

**Q**

Quality 11, 91, 104, 106, 117
Quality of service (QoS) 11, 117

**R**

Radiographs 81
Reinforcement learning 66, 68
Resources 12, 114, 125, 127

**S**

Setup 141, 181
Supervised learning 22, 66, 68
System 11, 91, 94, 141

**T**

Throughput 184
Transmission 12, 184, 185
Trust 22, 121, 127, 139

**U**

Unsupervised learning 22, 66, 68
User 141, 148, 149, 154

**V**

Virtual 11, 12, 109

**W**

Wireless 112, 184, 185
Workflow 6, 178

**Y**

Yield 29, 83

**Z**

Zone 49
Zooming 89